THE
CHANCE OF WAR

THE
CHANCE OF WAR

CANADIAN SOLDIERS
IN THE BALKANS 1992—1995

EDITED BY
JOHN WOOD

BREAKOUT EDUCATIONAL NETWORK
IN ASSOCIATION WITH
DUNDURN PRESS
TORONTO · OXFORD

Publisher: Inta D. Erwin
Copy-editor: Anne Holloway, First Folio Resource Group
Production Editor: Amanda Stewart, First Folio Resource Group
Designer: Bruna Brunelli, Brunelli Designs
Printer:Webcom

National Library of Canada Cataloguing in Publication Data

The chance of war/edited by John Wood.

One of the 16 vols. and 14 hours of video which make up the
    underground royal commission report
Includes bibliographical references and index.
ISBN 1-55002-426-4

    1. Canada—Armed Forces—Former Yugoslav republics. 2. United
Nations—Peacekeeping forces—Former Yugoslav republics.
3. Peacekeeping forces. I. Wood, John. II. Title: underground royal
commission report.

JZ6377.C3C43 2002   355.3'57'09497   C2002-902306-8

1   2   3   4   5   07   06   05   04   03

Printed and bound in Canada.
Printed on recycled paper. ♻
www.dundurn.com

Exclusive Canadian broadcast rights for the *underground royal commission* report

intelligent television

Check your cable or satellite listings for telecast times

Visit the *urc* Web site link at:
www.ichanneltv.com

The *underground royal commission* Report

Since September 11, 2001, there has been an uneasy dialogue among Canadians as we ponder our position in the world, especially vis à vis the United States. Critically and painfully, we are re-examining ourselves and our government. We are even questioning our nation's ability to retain its sovereignty.

The questions we are asking ourselves are not new. Over the last 30 years, and especially in the dreadful period of the early 1990s, leading up to the Quebec referendum of 1995, inquiries and Royal commissions, one after another, studied the state of the country. What *is* new is that eight years ago, a group of citizens looked at this parade of inquiries and commissions and said, "These don't deal with the real issues." They wondered how it was possible for a nation that was so promising and prosperous in the early 60s to end up so confused, divided, and troubled. And they decided that what was needed was a different kind of investigation — driven from the grassroots 'bottom,' and not from the top. Almost as a provocation, this group of people, most of whom were affiliated with the award winning documentary-maker, Stornoway Productions, decided to do it themselves — and so was born the *underground royal commission*!

What began as a television documentary soon evolved into much more. Seven young, novice researchers, hired right out of university, along with a television crew and producer, conducted interviews with people in government, business, the military and in all walks of life, across the country. What they discovered went beyond anything they had expected. The more they learned, the larger the implications grew. The project continued to evolve and has expanded to include a total of 23 researchers over the last several years. The results are the 14 hours of video and 16 books that make up the first interim report of the *underground royal commission*.

So what *are* the issues? The report of the *underground royal commission* clearly shows us that regardless of region, level of government, or political party, we are operating under a wasteful system ubiquitously lacking in accountability. An ever-weakening connection between the electors and the elected means that we are slowly and irrevocably losing our right to know our government. The researchers' experiences demonstrate that it is almost impossible for a member of the public, or in most cases, even for a member of Parliament, to actually trace how our tax dollars are spent. Most disturbing is the fact that our young people have been stuck with a crippling IOU that has effectively hamstrung their future. No wonder, then, that Canada is not poised for reaching its potential in the 21st century.

The *underground royal commission* report, prepared in large part by and for the youth of Canada, provides the hard evidence of the problems you and I may long have suspected. Some of that evidence makes it clear that, as ordinary Canadians, we are every bit as culpable as our politicians — for our failure to demand accountability, for our easy acceptance of government subsidies and services established without proper funding in place, and for the disservice we have done to our young people through the debt we have so blithely passed on to them. But the real purpose of the *underground royal commission* is to ensure that we better understand how government processes work and what role we play in them. Public policy issues must be understandable and accessible to the public if they are ever to be truly addressed and resolved. The *underground royal commission* intends to continue pointing the way for bringing about constructive change in Canada.

— Stornoway Productions

Books in the *underground royal commission* Report

"Just Trust Us"

The Chatter Box
The Chance of War
Talking Heads Talking Arms: (3 volumes)
No Life Jackets
Whistling Past the Graveyard
Playing the Ostrich

Days of Reckoning
Taking or Making Wealth
Guardians on Trial
Goodbye Canada?
Down the Road Never Travelled
Secrets in High Places
On the Money Trail

Does Your Vote Count?
A Call to Account
Reflections on Canadian Character

14 hours of videos also available with the *underground royal commission* report.
Visit Stornoway Productions at www.stornoway.com for a list of titles.

TABLE OF CONTENTS

Now expectation, tickling skittish spirits,
On one and other side, Trojan and Greek,
Sets all on hazard. And hither am I come ...
To tell you, fair beholders, that our play
Leaps o'er the vaunt and firstlings of those broils,
Beginning in the middle, starting thence away
To what may be digested in a play.
Like or find fault; do as your pleasures are;
Now good or bad, 'tis but the chance of war.

from the Prologue to *Troilus and Cressida*
by William Shakespeare, 1602

EDITOR'S NOTE

In 1914, at Sarajevo, a war began. Canada's soldiers distinguished themselves in the eyes of the world and all Canadians were proud of their achievements. In 1992 another war erupted in that same city. Canada's soldiers again distinguished themselves, but this time no one at home seemed to notice. Few Canadians told them how proud we were and how grateful that they had risked their lives to make the world a better place.

I have come to know the 11 soldiers who tell their stories here only through watching the videotapes on which these recorded interviews are based and through editing the words the soldiers used to tell of their experiences, both in the former Yugoslavia and in Canada after their return. These interviews took place in 1999, but I am still surprised by what I've learned from listening to these soldiers — and somewhat embarrassed that I wasn't aware of many of the challenges facing people in our Armed Forces over the past 10 years. But, sadly, I believe that I share that ignorance with most Canadians.

Although only 11 of them appear in this book, every one of our soldiers — whether army, navy or air force — who has served in Canada's missions abroad since the end of the cold war has revealing personal stories to tell. We must listen to these stories and learn what we are doing, both as a country and as a community, when we send our sons and daughters off to dangerous places in the world where the chance of war is an ever-present threat.

I would like to acknowledge several authors whose work has been instrumental in helping me to understand many details of the situations faced by our soldiers in the former Yugoslavia. I am grateful to Jim Davis for his book *The Sharp End: A Canadian Soldier's Story*, about his experiences in the Canadian army; to the invaluable assistance of retired Major-General Lewis MacKenzie, whose autobiography *Peacekeeper: The Road to Sarajevo* vividly describes his time as chief of staff for UNPRO-FOR and commander of Sector Sarajevo; and to Scott Taylor and Brian Nolan for *Tested Mettle: Canada's Peacekeepers at War*, a wide-ranging firsthand look at Canadian peacekeeping during the early 1990s.

I would also like to thank Mr. Taylor, in his role as editor and publisher of *Esprit de Corps* magazine, for his introduction to some of the soldiers whose stories are told in *The Chance of War*.

John Wood
Stratford, Ontario
May 2002

The soldiers in this book were all interviewed for the television series *A Question of Honour*, now in production by the Stornoway Productions.

FOREWORD

My colleagues and I first became interested in the debate about the future of the Canadian military during the discussion of the Chrétien government's white paper on defence in 1994. As documentary producers we had covered some of the cold war's hot spots in Angola, Afghanistan and Ethiopia. In the aftermath of the fall of the Soviet Union we had reported on the beginnning of ethnic struggles in the Balkans, the Caucasus and Iraq, and we had watched while peacekeeping ran its course in Cyprus, Nicaragua and the Golan Heights.

It was clear that some of those calling for a new approach to Canadian sovereignty by downgrading the role of Canada's military contribution to international security were misreading the situation on the ground. The end of the cold war had unleashed a vortex of change, smashing the old paradigm of international relations. Instead of providing opportunities for Canada to consider new and innovative non-military choices for its security, the post–cold war world was proving to be a more dangerous place than we had hoped for. Those responsible for directing Canadian foreign and military policies during the cold war had gambled that our commitments could be backed with token capabilities. Now their successors proposed to gamble that the same approach would not have unfortunate consequences in this new era. UN peacekeeping missions in Bosnia and Croatia gave Canadian soldiers a taste of those consequences and an understanding of the impact government defence policies have at the soldier level.

The conversations in this book were originally recorded for a documentary television series entitled *A Question of Honour*. Our interest in reflecting the national character of the Canadian military was a guiding principle behind the series. The soldiers who spoke to us showed us their collective character and proved that they held up their end of the "soldiers contract" to risk their lives for our country. The question is, have we held up our end of the deal?

I hope that by publishing their conversations and making them available to all Canadians we will in some way repay those soldiers who gave us their time so freely and bring readers to a better understanding of life in the Canadian Armed Forces at the end of the 20th century.

Robert Roy
Producer, *A Question of Honour*
June 2002

BACKGROUND ON YUGOSLAVIA AND THE CIVIL WAR

Originally "Balkan" was just the name of a mountain range halfway between Belgrade and Istanbul. The word was stretched in the 19th century beyond its geographical origins to include the region bounded by the Adriatic, the Aegean and the Black seas. The Balkan States are generally agreed to be Albania, Greece, Bulgaria, European Turkey and the lands of the former Yugoslavia.

The Turks were expelled from southeastern Europe during the Balkan Wars of 1912 and 1913. The Ottoman Empire had finally disintegrated, but there were large pockets of Muslims throughout Albania, Macedonia, Kosovo, Bosnia and other areas of the Balkan Peninsula. Croatia, Slovenia and Bosnia were part of the Austro–Hungarian Empire, ruled by Austria's Hapsburg monarchy. Serbia, which along with Greece and Bulgaria had been instrumental in defeating the Turks, was intent on maintaining its independence and expanding its borders, especially to the west. As this southern Slavic separatist movement gained momentum it promised to undermine the Austro–Hungarian Empire.

June 28, 1914: Gavrilo Princip, a Bosnian Serb student and member of a group called the Young Bosnians, assassinated Archduke Franz Ferdinand, heir to the throne of the Austro–Hungarian Empire, and his wife in Sarajevo. Princip was backed by a secret Serbian terrorist organization, Union or Death, commonly known as the Black Hand. He was arrested and spared the death penalty because of his young age. He died in prison in 1918.

The Austrian government was determined to crush the growing threat presented by Serbia, the nucleus of the independence movement, and presented the country with an ultimatum. Serbia agreed to all of the conditions except one which infringed on Serbian sovereignty by demanding the presence on its soil of Austro–Hungarian officials to find and destroy the organization responsible for the murders. As a result of this refusal Austria declared war on Serbia exactly one month after the assassination. Over the next week the dominoes fell as countries throughout Europe lined themselves up on one side or the other, and World War I began.

November 1918: The armistice ending World War I brought the downfall of the Austro–Hungarian Empire. The Kingdom of Serbs, Croats and Slovenes was created after the armistice and was put under the rule of the Serbian *Karadjordjevic* dynasty.

1929: King Alexander of Serbia dissolved parliament in the kingdom, abolished the constitution and established a right-wing personal dictatorship, conferring upon the country the new name of Yugoslavia.

1934: Alexander was assassinated by a member of the Croatian terrorist group the Ustashi during a visit to France. He was succeeded by his 11-year-old son, who became Peter II under the regency of his cousin Prince Paul.

Late 1930s: Increasing internal and ethnic unrest, accompanied by demands for independence by the various ethnic groups, was resulting in civil conflicts within Yugoslavia, and there was a developing resistance to Serbian dominance as World War II began.

April 1941: When Prince Paul began negotiating with the Axis Powers, his regency was overturned and Peter led the army against the German invasion. After 11 days the Yugoslav Royal Army surrendered and Yugoslavia was occupied. Peter fled to England.

Croatia gained independence as a puppet state of the Axis and leaders of the Fascist Ustashi government vowed to destroy Serbs and Jews. They lived up to their promise.

Yugoslavia's resistance movement was dominated by the Communists, led by Josip Broz. In World War I Broz, who was born in Croatia, had been inducted into the Austro–Hungarian Army, taken prisoner by the Russians and released in 1917, at the beginning of the Russian Revolution. In World War II he emerged as a strong military leader in the partisan movement during the German occupation of Yugoslavia. His forces, along with those of the Soviet Union, were instrumental in driving the Germans from Yugoslavia in 1944.

Serb soldiers throughout the republics had set up anti-Communist *chete* (bands) of resistance fighters under the direction of Colonel Mihailovic, but they were overly cautious and advocated waiting for an Allied invasion before acting to liberate the country.

1945: Josip Broz, now known as Marshal Tito, overpowered opposing factions like the Serbian Chetniks and gained the leadership of the country through his military predominance. Under Tito's provisional government, the political elites of pre-war Yugoslavia were swept away and the monarchy was abolished.

1948: Tito lost favour with his Soviet bosses over disagreements about his deviance from strict Communist doctrine, his apparent support of nationalism within Yugoslavia's borders and Yugoslavia's relationship with the West. He refused to comply with Soviet ultimatums and was excommunicated from the party. In the 1950s, after Stalin's death, the Soviet Union became more accepting of Yugoslavia's differences and tried to make peace with Tito.

1950–1980: Despite the fact that a number of economic crises eroded the power of the federal government in Belgrade and opened the way for nationalist struggles to gain momentum in the republics, the unity of Yugoslavia was preserved by popular support for Tito's more relaxed and independent brand of Communism.

1980: With the death of Marshal Tito in May, an annual rotation of the chair of both the Communist Party and the state presidencies took effect. The Yugoslav Federation, centred in Belgrade and Zagreb, began to fracture.

Mid-1980s: Strong nationalist sentiments already evident in Bosnia began to appear more forcefully throughout the republics. The rise of Serb nationalism weakened federal leadership further and long, drawn-out economic crises throughout Yugoslavia continued. Unrest was on the increase as the system of governing continued to break down.

1986: Ivan Stambolic became president of the Serbian Republic.

1987: Slobodan Milosevic, a former company executive and bank president, and protégé of Stambolic, became the leader of the Serbian Communist Party. He gave a speech in Kosovo promising support for the minority Serbs in the southern province. (Kosovo was among the spoils of the Balkan Wars of 1912–1913, given to Serbia after the breakup of the Ottoman Empire.)

1989: Turning on his friend and supporter Ivan Stambolic, Milosevic became the president of the Serbian Republic. Demands for independence in Croatia, Slovenia and Bosnia continued to grow. The increasing disintegration of the Soviet Union, caused by the growth of ethnic nationalist movements within its 15 states, helped to feed Yugoslavian unrest.

1990: The Serbian Communist Party renamed itself the Serbian Socialist Party. At first Milosevic's policies appeared to be attempts to consolidate Serb influence within Yugoslavia, but it quickly became clear that his real goal was expansion to establish a greater Serbia. As the republics started preparing for elections, he warned that if they opted for independence, he would redraw Serbia's boundaries to include the areas in other republics where Serbs were living. This threat was backed by Milosevic's full control of the Yugoslav National Army (JNA), and the various republics took it seriously. However, their desire for self-determination was stronger than their fear and clashes between the Serb and Croatian police forces began during the summer.

1991: Slovenia and Croatia declared their independence from the Federation of Yugoslav Republics. The JNA was forced to leave its bases in Slovenia and move south into Croatia. As it dug in to fulfill Milosevic's promises to protect the Serb populations outside of Serbia and began taking over territory by force, civil war finally erupted between the ethnic communities in Croatia, led by the JNA on the Serb side and an emerging national Croatian military on the other. The JNA forces were reinforced and Milosevic dispersed his troops throughout southern Croatia.

The European Community began looking for solutions to the crisis.

November 1991: Cyrus Vance, the UN secretary-general's special representative, worked out a deal with Croatian president Franjo Tudjman and Serbian president Slobodan Milosevic. Under its terms, 14,000 UN soldiers in three (later four) UN Protected Areas (UNPAs) in southern Croatia would be responsible for the civilian population, composed mostly of Serbs, within these areas. The JNA would withdraw to Bosnia-Herzegovina or Serbia. The fighting continued.

January 15, 1992: The European Community recognized the two new states, despite pleas from President Alija Izetbegovic of Bosnia and others to delay the announcement. He knew Serbia would react unfavourably, and he was right. This move by the EC was the spark that ignited Milosevic's determination to act.

January 16, 1992: Fifty United Nations military liaison officers were deployed to Zagreb and Belgrade.

February 1992: The UN Security Council approved the resolution for UNPROFOR, the United Nations Protection Force. But the boundaries drawn up in the Vance plan had shifted as the JNA extended its sphere of influence and continued to take more territory by force.

Bosnia held a referendum on the republic's future. The vote was boycotted by the Serbs, who wanted to establish a Bosnian Serb state, but the Muslim and Croat populations, who formed the majority, opted for independence. The Bosnian government at that time was made up of people from all of the region's ethnic groups.

March 1992: The UN swung into action with the following people in charge of UNPROFOR.

Commander	Lieutenant-General Satish Nambiar (India)
Deputy Commander	Major-General Phillippe Morillon (France)
Chief of Staff	Major-General Lewis MacKenzie (Canada)

The plan was for 12 battalions to be dispersed throughout four UNPAs. (See map on page 25)

Commanders:

Sector East	Colonel Alex Khomchenkov (Russia)
Sector North	Brigadier-General Musa Bamaiyi (Nigeria)
Sector West	Brigadier-General Carlos Zabala (Argentina)
Sector South	Brigadier-General Arap Rob Kipngetich (Kenya)

The Bosnian capital of Sarajevo was chosen by the UN as UNPROFOR headquarters. It was 350 kilometres away from where the troops would be based.

March 8, 1992: The leadership of UNPROFOR arrived in Belgrade, where they were briefed by Serb authorities and the JNA.

March 10 1992: The leaders flew to Graz, Austria, and drove south into Croatia because the Serb authorities still controlled the airspace over Yugoslavia and refused permission to land at Zagreb's airport.

March 13, 1992: After consulting with Croatian leaders in Zagreb the party drove south into Bosnia. It became evident that the war between the JNA and the Croatian Army had not stopped at the Croatian border. They were met by the JNA and flown by the army from Banja Luka to Sarajevo, where tensions among the three ethnic groups living in the region were simmering but had not yet exploded into civil war. The Bosnian vote for independence had not yet been recognized by the European Community or the UN. President Alija Izetbegovic of Bosnia and Dr. Radovan Karadzic, the leader of the Bosnian Serbs, were both in Sarajevo anticipating the arrival of UNPROFOR.

March 15, 1992: Advance parties of battalions from the participating nations of Argentina, Belgium, Canada, Czechoslovakia, Denmark, France, Jordan, Kenya, Nepal, Nigeria, Poland and Russia arrived in Belgrade.

End of March 1992: Canadian soldiers stationed in Germany had been preparing since February and were ready to deploy into Croatia.

The boundaries established by the Vance plan had altered further. As the war continued, the municipal boundaries and the cease-fire lines moved, generally increasing Serb territory held by the JNA. These disputed Serbian enclaves were called pink zones.

April 1, 1992: Tensions in Sarajevo were escalating and there were growing signs of preparations for fighting among the three ethnic groups.

April 3, 1992: The Serbs confirmed that they would not abandon the pink zones and declared their determination to include more areas within the UNPA borders.

April 4, 1992: Rumours began about impending recognition by the European Community of an independent Bosnia. Again there were *strong* suggestions that the EC should delay its announcement.

April 5, 1992: Bosnian peace demonstrators were met with sniper fire as they paraded in downtown Sarajevo. Roadblocks were put up between different ethnic areas of the city, as mortar attacks began to occur. The JNA took over the Sarajevo airport.

April 6, 1992: The Bosnian government collapsed and the prime minister resigned just before the European Community recognized the new independent country of Bosnia.

Most Serbs in the Bosnian government moved to Pale, a short distance to the east of Sarajevo, where Radovan Karadzic was establishing the new headquarters of the Bosnian Serbs. There were now two categories of Bosnian Serbs: those loyal to the Bosnian government, who constituted a minority, and those loyal to Karadzic, who wanted to establish their own state within the borders of Bosnia and to have close ties to Belgrade.

Large crowds gathered in the centre of the city despite increasing violence. Many demonstrators were trying to defuse the situation and establish order, while others were hoping to convince the JNA (many of whose members had been born in Bosnia) to become the Bosnian army. Much of the violence was perpetrated by criminals who were not interested in politics, but who were happy to exploit the opportunities for looting and personal gain that the increasingly uncontrollable situation presented.

April 7, 1992: On the verge of anarchy, Sarajevo was shelled by the JNA under the command of General Kukanjac. The Bosnian presidency forces tried to counter the attack, but their military equipment was greatly inferior to that of the Yugoslav army. The Serbs who had joined Karadzic had taken most of the guns and armoured cars with them. Violence was now widespread in Sarajevo, and over the next few days it spread throughout Bosnia.

April 13, 1992: A cease-fire brokered by the European Community one day earlier was broken.

The Canadian troops arrived in Sector West from their base in Germany. Under the command of Lieutenant-Colonel Michel Jones, the unit included members of the 1st Battalion of the Royal 22nd Regiment (Van Doos) and a large company from the 3rd Battalion of the Royal Canadian Regiment. Members of the Canadian Combat Engineer Regiment, who would oversee the dangerous job of mine removal in all four UN sectors, had already arrived and were based in Daruvar. The Canadian contribution to UNPROFOR was called Operation Harmony.

Mid-April 1992: The presidency forces were now called the Bosnian Territorial Defence Forces (TDF). The Serb forces continued their aggression and were emerging as a leading power in Croatia and Bosnia. The TDF intensified its attack on the JNA in Sarajevo and the JNA retaliated by bombing the capital. The non-Serbs in the UNPAs were being driven out and the Croatian army was invading Bosnian territory.

June 12, 1992: Sector Sarajevo was created, commanded by Major-General MacKenzie.

Sector West had become relatively quiet and preparations were under way to move the Canadians south into Bosnia. Bosnia had become a major war zone, where UN troops were badly needed, but a lack of decision by the UN delayed their departure. President Mitterand of France visited Bosnia and three days later the green light was given.

July 1, 1992: Canadian soldiers in Sector West began the drive to Sarajevo.

Mid-July 1992: Canada decided to contribute a second full-size battle group to UNPROFOR. This would bring the total of Canadian soldiers serving in the former Yugoslavia to 2,400.

Mid-November 1992: Twelve hundred soldiers of the 2nd Royal Canadian Regiment (2 RCR) were based in Sector West.

February 1993: 2 RCR moved from Lipik into Bosnia in the region of Sarajevo.

Late March 1993: The 2nd Battalion of the Princess Patricia's Canadian Light Infantry (2 PPCLI) commanded by Colonel Jim Calvin arrived in Sector West. The unit included large numbers of militia, as the Canadian Forces were being stretched by the increased demand for soldiers.

General Morillon declared six Muslim enclaves, among them Gorazde and Srebrenica, as UN protected zones.

Late April 1993: The Serbs cut off all access to the eastern Bosnia city during the siege of Srebrenica. One hundred and seventy-five Canadian peacekeepers, the only UN contingent in the area, were trapped until an agreement was brokered between now retired General Lewis MacKenzie and Radovan Karadzic. After the agreement was reached they were relieved by the Van Doos.

Mid-July 1993: 2 PPCLI began a move into Sector South in the Krajina area of Croatia to try to establish a UN presence between Croatian and Serb forces. This had been attempted by other UN detachments in the area without success. The headquarters for the Canadians was in the Serb-dominated area of Gracac.

Early September 1993: Colonel Calvin tried to establish observation posts close to the Croatian frontline. A platoon of C Company led by Lieutenant Tyrone Green moved into the village of Medak to take over duties from a French army platoon. Medak was on the main road between Gracac in the south and Gospic, a Croatian stronghold to the north. It was also the headquarters of the Serb military in the area. From that point on Medak was controlled by the Canadians, although they were often under fire from the Croats. The events that followed became known as the Medak Pocket operation, the pocket being the area of the Medak valley to the northwest of the town. It was in the villages in the pocket that the Croats wreaked the most havoc; they failed to reach the village of Medak after they were beaten back from its northern fringes.

September 9, 1993: The Croatian army began to attack the area around Medak and move into Serb-held territory.

September 14, 1993: A cease-fire agreement was reached after Serbs fired missiles on the outskirts of Zagreb. French reinforcements began to arrive.

September 15, 1993: This was the date set for the implementation of a cease-fire whereby the Serbs would maintain their trench line and the Croats would move back to the positions they held on September 9. The UN would occupy the buffer zone. The Croats went back on their word and began to attack the Canadians, who were trying to move into the buffer zone. After 15 hours of fighting another cease-fire was established.

March 1994: The Van Doos in Srebrenica were relieved by 500 Dutch troops.

July 1995: Srebrenica fell to Serbian forces.

December 14, 1995: The General Agreement for Peace was signed in Paris after the successful negotiation of the Dayton peace accord.

December 20, 1995: The Implementation Force, IFOR, a NATO operation sanctioned by the UN, replaced UNPROFOR.

Editor's Note:
The dates after 1991 recorded here relate to the stories in *The Chance of War*. I've omitted many other dates and events important to the

Canadian Forces in Yugoslavia, either because they didn't bear directly on the experiences the soldiers related to us or because I was unable to track down enough specific information to be of value. In some cases I felt that more information would be unnecessarily burdensome or confusing.

Southeastern Europe (including the Balkans)

Bosnia and Croatia in the Early 1990s

The Chance of War

The individual Canadian soldier has got a weapon you can't buy. He's got a weapon that most other armies don't have, and that's brains. That'll take you a long way in a place like Bosnia.

Peter Vallée

PROLOGUE

While we were in Sector West we found out we were the caretakers of the area where one of the two national Lipizzaner stallions stud farms was located. And during the war the one in Lipik had been razed to the ground. It had been widely thought that all the stallions and all of the brood mares for these very rare horses had been slaughtered by the Serbs.

During one of our negotiations we found out from the mayor of the town of Lipik, who was a Serb, that this was not the case. He said that most of the horses, about 50 of them, had been walked out of the country and were now at a stud farm in Serbia being cared for by a family there. But, he said, they were in desperate need of veterinary supplies because the embargo was cutting off all material going into Serbia. They needed worming medicine and inoculations against infections and all the normal things you need to take care of a horse.

I had a friend back in Winnipeg, Dr. Patricia Haugh, who specialized in cat medicine. I phoned her, told her the circumstances and asked, "Can you gather donations from all of your suppliers? It has to be a very quiet operation. They can't go public with it because we are in very sensitive times between the Croats and the Serbs, and if they thought we were helping horses, it would turn into a political football. If you can collect anything, we'll ship it over and we'll try to get it to the Serbs in Serbia so they can care for these horses."

She talked to her suppliers and I guess they just went crazy with the idea. She raised between $5000 and $10,000 worth of veterinary supplies in a matter of weeks. Air Canada shipped the medicine, free, over to Vienna, and we sent Captain Steve Murray, a reserve officer who was with us, to pick up the supplies in two of our four-wheel drive UN vehicles. He brought them back to Sector West and then, in the middle of the night, he and another officer headed off into the darkness and winkled their way into Serbia.

They got to our attaché's office in Belgrade and found out where the farm was. They drove up the road, and the poor farmer who had all of these horses broke down and wept when the United Nations arrived.

It was nice to see everyone coming together and doing something like that.

Jim Calvin

JIM DAVIS

Sergeant

Barrie, Ontario. Two brothers, good friends now but fought a lot as youngsters. High school? Bored silly. Within a week of graduating I was on a transport truck headed to the West Coast to work in the ski hills. I bumped around for a couple of years. I think I ended up joining the military because I was sitting in a gas station and opened up a newspaper and saw the big sign that said, "No life like it. Join up." I'd been thinking about joining the French Foreign Legion but, of course, I was gonna have to fork over money for a ticket to France, so how 'bout I sign on for the Canadian military, get some money in my pocket and then I'll join the Legion later on.

I had no dreams of a great military career going in. My grandfather was in World War I. He was a big hero figure for me growing up and I always wanted adventure. I wanted to go off and see a bit of the world, and what better way to do it for a young, broke, Canadian male, 23 years old, than to join the military? I thought I'd do a couple of years, but once I actually signed on, I realized that it was the life for me and I fell right into it. I loved being a soldier.

When you sign on the military gives you an aptitude test to find out whether you're good for intelligence, or you should be flying jets, or you should be flipping eggs in the mess hall. At the bottom of the scale, for those with an IQ just a bit above a disability, are cooks and infantry. And when I walked in, I did the test and, without bragging, I aced the test. I could have been anything in the military I wanted. The recruiter said that they had openings for all these fancy jobs and I said, "No, I want the infantry. In fact, I want to jump out of airplanes. I want to be a paratrooper." He thought I was insane and tried to talk me out of it, but I held my ground. So it was the infantry for me.

There are two regiments that Anglo-Canadians can usually join: the Royal Canadian Regiment and the Princess Patricia's Canadian Light Infantry. And when the recruiter asked me where I wanted to go, he named the regiments and I couldn't remember the Princess ... what? Royal, yeah, I can remember the Royals, and then he whispered, "You know, the Royals are going to Germany soon," and I said, "OK, I'm in. I want to be a Royal."

When I walked into the military I was 23 years old. The vast majority of people joining at that time were 17, 18, 19 years old. Almost all the kids were Newfoundlanders and East Coast people, a few ex-cowboys from the West, but primarily from the East Coast. So I was the old man. I was far older than everyone else and a little bit more mature. I'd got some of that rowdiness out of me by that time.

You walk in and all the guys have long hair, jeans, sweatshirts, running shoes. In your first couple of hours your hair is shaved off. I was standing talking to a couple of Newfoundlanders, getting to know them before we went in for the haircuts and coveralls, and when we came out I couldn't even recognize them. It was dehumanizing. They don't do that now but they did back then. You're given black coveralls, most of which don't fit and stink, and running shoes with no laces so you can't hang yourself.

A lot of these people just were not prepared for it. You start off in a big room. It's just bunks and lockers and everybody is equal. And as you go through training gaps start to form. The "man-eating truck" would show up, and they would call someone's name. He would get on the man-eating truck, and when we would get back to quarters that night, there would just be an empty bed space. Every sign that person ever existed was gone. He just ceased to exist. His name was never mentioned. To be honest, I don't remember any of the people that failed training. They just ceased to exist for me and probably for everyone else. It was a little disconcerting because you thought, I'm working pretty hard at this and I could just disappear and cease to exist.

Essentially that's the recruiting process. You can take people from any walk of life, hard-core trouble makers, quiet types, some Walter Mittys, and you put them through a process that strips their personality away, takes them down to the bare bones of who and what they are, and then rebuilds them in the military mould. You eventually get your personality back, but you also get what the military is selling at the same time. A lot of people cracked. I think we started with about 150 and we graduated with 40. Those were about the average odds in those days. But at the end of the day those 40 were the people who were psychologically strong enough to do the job, the ones you'd end up having to count on later.

You feel you've accomplished so much, you feel like you're untouchable, you've got all the armour in world and you can do anything, accomplish anything. And, of course, that's exactly what the military wants. All my friends and family warned me, "Don't let them change you. Make sure you stay who you are. Hang on to that." And when I came out a lot of them really saw the change. My mother commented that I was so cocky, so confident, that she thought I was going to run into some disaster in life because I just didn't recognize the fact that I was mortal.

Germany

We were told when we joined that we were the best paid army in the world. Sometimes the Australians got a bit above us, but we tended to always match whatever their pay increases were and we were convinced that we were the most respected army in the world. We were told we had the best kit and we believed it. We were the best paid, we were the best looked after, we ate great food. In Canada you had nothing to compare that against. You just had to accept it at face value.

But when we arrived in Germany as part of NATO, we were mixing with German troops and French troops and American troops and British troops and — wait a minute, there's something we're missing here. All of our equipment was designed for extreme cold weather, and of course Europe is very wet. A lot of the time it hovers around slushy zero temperatures and our kit was entirely wrong. Our rain gear, as soon as it got wet, was soaking wet through. So we all ended up having to take our own money and buy proper equipment. We set up our own little shop on base to serve our unit, to get us equipment that the Canadian government wouldn't provide for us.

We would go train with the Americans, and whenever we got together quietly on the side we'd all start trading equipment. They liked our green berets, 'cause to an American a green beret is a sign of Special Forces. We all had them, and for a green beret we could get real rain gear, we could get gloves, we could get good long underwear, we could get fancy Gore-Tex boots. So every time we went in the field we always took a pocket full of green berets that we could get at our clothing stores for a couple of bucks.

Man for man, I would say that Canadians are about the best soldiers there are in NATO, if you're talking a soldier-to-soldier basis. I've worked with the SAS and the French Foreign Legion and the Gurkhas and the U.S. Special Forces and the Rangers and, man for man, we stack up with all of them.

For example, if there was a hill and it had an enemy on it, say a platoon enemy with so many weapons and equipment, and the Americans were going to attack that hill, they would stand off and let their technology do the work for them and blast it into oblivion before the troops climbed up on top. Well, the Canadians, since they don't have all that equipment, would use their heads. They would connive a way to take that hill with the least number of casualties possible and, as a last resort, just storm the thing. And so we always accomplished whatever any other army could accomplish just through guts and determination — and a little bit of ingenuity. When you create soldiers in that mould, what you create is the ultimate soldier as far as regular infantry goes.

One of the things we used to do every year in Germany, for the four and a half years I was there, was a practice for a war in Europe. The Americans would bring over two million troops, Canadians would ship over extra troops and we'd go ranging across Europe and Austria conducting big exercises.

I remember one occasion: we had a Canadian company, which is a pretty small organization in the grand scheme of NATO warfare, and we sat ourselves in a village on a main route called an MSR, main supply route, a road used to get troops from the rear areas to the combat areas. We held that town and wiped out the equivalent of four or five battalions of American troops. We brought down dozens of attack helicopters, and we basically held up the American army — in fact, an entire corps — for about 24 hours, one company of Canadian troops. We had umpires on the ground, and the Americans just could not believe that this stubborn little group of Canadians could hold up their entire corps. I could tell you story after story of Canadians just using their ingenuity and defeating the odds.

Back in World War II General Patton used to say to give him Canadian troops, German officers and American equipment, and he'd take anything. It's still the same. We still have top-of-the-line soldiers, it's just that they've got no equipment or they've got to buy their own equipment. We've got top-of-the-line-people. I was proud to be one of them.

The Gulf War

Canada, at the end of the cold war, had only two combat-ready units at its disposal, the Canadian Airborne Regiment as part of the Special Service Force (but that's a very light assault-type unit) and the Fourth Canadian Mechanized Brigade Group in Europe, 4 CMBG they called it. It was supposed to be combat ready, manned up to strength, ready to go. For the type of conflict we were going to be fighting in the Gulf, that's all we had to offer.

As the situation developed in Kuwait, we were told that we would be going. So we started preparing our kit, we started organizing ourselves. We were convinced that we'd be getting on the planes and the trains with the Americans within a few weeks and heading off to the Gulf. Weeks went by, orders came and went. We had briefings from senior officers that had just returned from NDHQ and, yeah, the plans were in the pipeline, we'd be going any time now. There was just fighting over whether it would be a division or a brigade. And we thought we were going to go. Of course, that didn't happen.

This information for the deployment to the Gulf comes from a friend of mine, a captain up at NDHQ. Essentially the word from the Americans was to plan for 90 days of combat operations with an estimated casualty rate of about 20 percent, so the Canadians sat down and started going through the numbers.

The numbers that came up indicated that were we to send a brigade with the estimated combat casualties over a 90-day period of fighting, we would have to mobilize the entire militia to provide replacements. If we sent a division, we would have to go to selected conscription in the Canadian populace to support predicted numbers. Now we all know the Gulf War turned out to be a bit of a dud in terms of fighting, but at that time we didn't know.

Evidently the Americans told us, "Listen, we want you there. The more coalition members we can get, the better it is for our case — the world against Saddam Hussein — but we don't want you to bring any of your equipment." They didn't want our tanks. They didn't want our armoured personnel carriers because we would be the only ones in theatre with those particular pieces of equipment and because they were so old. Finding spare parts and shipping spare parts just for the Canadians would have been a huge logistic nightmare. So they said, "Tell you what. We'll give you brand-new M1A1 Abrams tanks. We'll give you brand-new Bradley M2 armoured personnel carriers for your infantry. We'll equip you, get you on-line, provide trainers to make sure your guys know what they're doing. You'll leap into the 21st century of armoured warfare."

But the Canadian government decided that just really wasn't a plan that they could go for, and all we ended up sending was a company from my unit in Germany, designated to go over and guard a hospital about 1,000 kilometres behind our lines. We sent another company over to Bahrain to guard a headquarters unit there. A third company from 1 RCR, Charlie Company, went over to look after prisoners of war, once again behind the lines. The only combat element we ended up sending was the CF-18s from my base in Europe, and they were given orders that they couldn't cross the line into Iraqi airspace. They had to stay on the friendly side so they couldn't get shot at.

Parliament said, "Yes, we're on side with the coalition; we'll commit troops." But then, "We'll only commit troops if they're not going to get involved in any fighting."

Up to that point we'd been told that we were good soldiers, we had great equipment and we were paid well. We'd seen that there were some problems, having worked at NATO, but we believed that we were on the team. We were part of the program. And the moment that happened, it was like a slap. Those of us who made a life of learning to be combat soldiers thought, why are we doing this? Why are we here? Why are we giving our all if the Canadian government doesn't have the confidence to send us out to do our job? I mean, we're soldiers. That's what we get paid to do.

Croatia

If you're going to go to a war zone on a peacekeeping mission, plan for the worst scenario. If everything turns out fine, so much the better. What we did was plan for the best scenario and end up in the worst possible situation. We just weren't prepared for it.

The Gulf War happened in 1991. Late 1991 was when Croatia and Slovenia tried to separate from Serbia. We were told in January 1992 that we were going to be going to Croatia. Now, that was a shock. No one believed it after the Gulf War fiasco. We thought, "Oh, yeah? Sure we'll be going! No problem." We didn't take it seriously. Then it occurred to us, the way momentum was building, that we were actually going to be deployed and, frankly, that scared a lot of people.

In the Gulf War there were outstanding numbers on the allied side, tanks, aircraft, huge amounts of firepower. We were being sent into a far more dangerous situation with almost no backup. You have to remember, the Canadian government told us there was peace. "Both sides want to talk. You're going in the middle. You're doing the traditional peace-keeping thing. Chapter VI, no shooting, except in self-defence. This will be another Cyprus. No worries, boys." [See Appendix: Chapter VI of the Charter of the United Nations.]

Most of our operations at that point had been in Cyprus. Cyprus is a dead issue. It's not a war zone. We realized that we're going where people are going to be shooting at us, and we've got nothing. We've got no backup. It was a sobering shock to realize, when we got on the trains in late March, that we were actually on our way to Croatia.

But I was as excited as I've ever been in my life on that train. I could not wait to go. I never believed I was going to go. But when we got on those trains we all looked at each other and said, "All right, we're on our way. For better or worse, we're on our way and this is what we get paid to do." I had no idea what I was getting into. The guys were playing poker on the train, losing all their money. Some guys were getting drunk, other guys were writing letters to their wives that they'd only left a couple of hours before, and I was standing by the window watching the countryside go by 'cause I couldn't wait to get there.

As far as Zagreb we didn't see any signs of warfare. But after Zagreb we took a two-hour train ride down to a little town called Daruvar, about 15 kilometres north of the frontline, and the whole town was levelled. Bullet holes everywhere. You could smell rotting flesh. The train stopped and we started backing our vehicles off, looking around, wondering, "When's the shooting going to start?" But we were in a reasonably safe area because Daruvar turned out to be a rest area for Croatian troops coming back from the frontline.

Things weren't exactly how Ottawa told us they were, and you could see signs of fighting everywhere around us. But the Green Line in Cyprus was pretty beat up as well, so everybody sort of got in that Cyprus frame of mind and went out to the various camps. We had three main camps at that point. They set up and lined their vehicles up like they're on a parade square back in Canada. They lined up their little pup tents that the troops were sleeping in, the kitchen was set up and there was a little mess tent where the guys could have some pop and chips. No machine guns sighted, no trenches dug, no defensive work whatsoever. The vehicles were locked up, the weapons were put away, nobody had any ammunition. We thought, "OK, we're on another normal peacekeeping tour."

But, of course, within hours we were under fire. In the first 24 hours we were attacked in two of our camps. And there was chaos. Absolute chaos.

At Sirac, where November Company and 3 RCR were, they were all standing around, eating their chips, the sun was going down, and all of a sudden in comes a pile of mortars. Mortars are pretty dangerous pieces of equipment and they're the bane of the infantry: we hate those things. Four mortar bombs about a kilometre away. And then four more mortar bombs about 800 metres away. And then four more about 500 metres away. The guys are starting to think, "Those things get dangerous inside 100 metres." Next group lands about 100 metres away, and everybody looks at each other, wondering who's going to panic first, and then of course a whole series of mortar bombs falls right on the camp and it's pandemonium. There's no place to hide, no trenches to dive into.

The guys were all running around, but the only hard shelter there was the vehicles, the big armoured personnel carriers, and they were locked up. All the guys ran to them, but they couldn't get the doors open because our normal Canadian standing operating procedure says you lock them up when you're not in them. A couple of guys climbed up on the vehicles to unlock the driver's hatch to get in and drop the ramp so the guys could get in. The bombs are going off and the guys are getting blown off the carriers. Guys started moving the vehicles and they're all banging into each other 'cause they're too close together. One vehicle drove over the generator and another one nearly ran over the company quartermaster's truck. By this time it was dark. No one knew where any-one was. Vehicles were all over the place. The 8 Van Doos Company, about three kilometres away, were getting hit by 122mm howitzer fire, and they were trying to find a basement or something to get into.

I was sitting in the headquarters camp 'cause we were in Recce platoon. We could hear the bombs going off on one side and mortars going off on the other side. Nobody really knew what was happening 'cause our radios aren't good enough to reach those distances. I was standing around my area of the headquarters camp, and all of a sudden some shots came ringing in over top of our head. Well, where are we gonna hide? We're in canvas tents! We thought, "Oh, yeah, here it goes. They dropped us in the middle of Croatia, no backup, no medical support, no firepower, 30 rounds per man, and we're under attack by the Croatians." I mean, where are you going to go?

The Canadian government or the military — depends on who you want to point a finger at — sent us to Croatia, into a combat zone, into a war, with no medical support. We had our unit MO (medical officer) but he's not a surgeon. So if anyone got shot and required more than a Band-Aid and some Aspirin, there was no place to go. We would have had to count on the Croatians to take care of our wounded. Right after the fighting broke out I asked, "If we take any wounded what do we do with them, sir?" "Well, hope for the best because there's no place to go."

I got laughed at because shortly after I joined up, I bought this big 13-inch Gurkha Kukri knife and I took it with me everywhere I went. It was my good luck charm. Within the first 24 hours I realized that these people, the Serbians and the Croatians, take war seriously. There's no taking prisoners. If I was forced to fire my 30 rounds and I'm out of bullets, there's no surrendering at that point, so I figured that I'd just pull that big knife and I'd charge whoever was pointing a weapon at me and go down fighting because I wouldn't want to be taken prisoner. The knife came out of its sheath a few times and it scared the bejesus out of anybody that I pulled it on.

At that time, in the Cyprus frame of mind, you got one magazine, 30 rounds, and that's all you got. Now, within about 48 hours of our first attack on day one in Croatia, they started handing out grenades and M72s, and some more ammunition. I think at the height I had two frag grenades, two smoke grenades, five mags of ammunition and our vehicle had one M72. Now, that's enough to put up a good fight for about 10 minutes and then we'd all be out. There was no reserve. So it was either (a) the moment the Serbs or the Croats looked at us funny, surrender and hope for the best, or (b) fight like mad for 10 minutes and hope you've done enough to win and then deal with the consequences.

Today every soldier, before he gets on the airplane to fly over to a mission, gets a little booklet containing the rules of engagement, and he has to sign that he's accepted the booklet. That way, if he makes a mistake six months down the road during his tour and he shoots somebody and he's outside of his rules of engagement, he is now legally liable — because he had his rules of engagement and his signature's there saying it. Now, when we first went to Croatia, there was no such thing. No one had even thought, in Canada, that we were going into anything but another Cyprus, so there was no initiative along those lines.

General MacKenzie, down in Sarajevo, quite rightly assessed that this was not going to be a Cyprus mission and he drafted the first tentative rules of engagement which we were issued. However, we were also told that they hadn't been approved by NDHQ, which meant that they really didn't mean anything. So throughout that tour, and I think to this day, the real rule of engagement the Canadian troops work by is that "It's better to be tried by 12 than buried by six."

We had our tentative rules, which said we could only respond to a direct threat "while it is a threat." There's no retribution allowed after the threat has ceased to exist, and we knew that those rules weren't even authorized by NDHQ yet. We thought that whatever we do we'll get hung out to dry for because we could sense that back in Canada they still didn't believe that it wasn't another Cyprus. We on the ground knew it was different.

We thought, "If I hose down a bunch of villagers by accident or by design, it will be our My Lai back in Canada. We'll all get put up on charges and thrown in jail. As long as they're not killing anybody yet, we'll just have to put up with it 'cause that's the UN." We knew we couldn't finish any fight, so why start one? We just had to duck down and soldier on because that's all we had. If we had gone in with the NATO force that's in Bosnia now and has jets, attack helicopters, full-blown tanks and artillery, then we would have had the backup to start a fight and know that we had the capability to finish it. At that time we had nothing. So the commonsense soldier says, "Don't start a fight you can't finish."

Sector West

There was a village on the route down into Sector South, and we had to drive it every day. In that village there was a Serbian who had an AK-47, and every day he would take a couple of shots at one of the Canadian vehicles that drove by. He'd never attack the armoured carriers, but he'd shoot at a supply truck or a jeep that he knew couldn't fight back. He'd fire his couple of rounds and then put his rifle down beside him and stand there and smile. We knew where he was, we knew who he was, we knew what he did, but unless we could shoot him at the moment he fired at us, we couldn't get him. We couldn't stop him because if he put his rifle down, he's no longer a threat — end of story. We can't shoot back.

Because I worked in reconnaissance and intelligence, I knew the big picture. Early on in Croatia we were responsible for an area where there was a little pocket of Serbians inside what was now Croatia. They were well armed — tanks, artillery weapons and everything. The Croats were sitting around that pocket, eyeing them, but they didn't have all the equipment the Serbs had, and our orders were to go into the Serb area and disarm them, take all of their weapons away. We knew that the moment we did that the Croatians would attack and wipe them out. So when we got our orders, my question to my platoon commander was, "Well, sir, once we disarm them, are our orders to protect those Serbs?" And we were told, "Yeah, that's your orders." So Recce went in, snuck around, found all the sites where the Serbs were hiding the equipment, and we got it out of there.

Then I went back and I asked my platoon commander, "OK, now, when the Croats attack, what are our orders? What's our defensive position? How are we going to protect these Serbs?" I was told that the orders from on high were that if the Croats want to attack, just step aside and let them have at it because we had no ability to stop them.

So essentially we managed to defeat the Serbs for the Croats by putting in place UN rules and policy that made no sense on the ground. It may have made sense back in New York, but definitely not on the ground. You have to believe you're there to do a good job, to have some idea that you're helping, somehow. I suddenly realized at that point, "Wait a minute, we're not helping here. We're part of the problem. All I've done is disarm a bunch of people who are going to get killed." And sure enough, in 1993 the Croats rolled in and wiped that whole area out.

One of the towns inside the Serb area of Sector West was called Okucani, and we would go into Okucani each day at the beginning of our patrol, about 8:00 in the morning. Okucani tried to maintain a semblance of normalcy — everybody's walking to market, lots of Serb families and kids going to school. At the end of our patrol day we would stop for a little while, gather our patrols together and head back to Croatian territory where we had our camps. We had little Canada pins and we would buy tons of bubble gum and when we were stopped the kids would all gather around the vehicles. There was always this big crowd of boys, but one day there was a little girl, she was maybe eight or 10 years old, standing in the back. I'd handed out almost all of my Canada pins and I could see she couldn't get through. So I told the boys to get back, and I waved her forward and gave her this pin. And she immediately ran away. And I thought, OK, whatever.

Just as we were about to pull out of town, she came running down the street, yelling at us. Our vehicle was starting to pull away, and I told my driver, "Listen, hold on a sec." She ran up and she gave me a white rose.

I was floored. There were tears in my eyes. It still breaks me up. But what kills me now is that I know she died when the Croats attacked.

The world likes to say that the Serbs are evil and they've done all these horrible things, and I'm not going to defend them. But many Serbs lived in a portion of Croatia that was under the control of the Croatian army where I've seen ethnic cleansing. The Croatians did it, in village after village. It was like there was a line drawn in the ground about 25 kilometres long and it was a dead zone.

At first the Croats didn't want us going in there, but, of course, we were Recce platoon and we weren't going to listen to them. We just stormed our way in. That was our job. We had to find what was going on in the dead zone. Every village you came into just smelled of rotting flesh. It was scary. It was like a ghost town. But that was our job, so we just had to suck it up and do what we got paid for. I try not to think about it. I try not to. Sometimes, though, you just can't help it.

We got sent on a patrol. It was about midnight, we were driving around the Serb pocket and a report came in from the Serbs that the Croats were marshalling tanks in this wood line. We didn't believe it. We were told to drive to this tree line and find out if there were tanks in there, which of course is an idiotic order but we thought, "OK, here we go."

My APC happened to be first. It's about quarter after twelve at night and we're driving along, nice and slow. We figured we'd run across land mines because they laid them everywhere, but they'd usually lay them on the surface so you could see them. All of sudden my driver pulls on his binders and the whole vehicle rocks. "What's going on?" I asked. "I think I saw a mine," the driver said. We climbed up and looked over the front of the APC. "No, just a rock, a round rock." So we started driving again. About two minutes later, *bang*, the whole world disappears in a big white light. Next thing I know, I'm flying through the air and there's dust everywhere. We'd hit a stack of land mines. I landed on top of the vehicle and my driver was thrown around. The guys in the vehicle behind us saw us disappear in this bright flash. They thought we were all dead.

It took a little while till we figured out we were all right. But we're in a minefield, we can't move. Our vehicle was destroyed so we just

41

gathered together our ammunition. We could hear troops moving in the woods so we thought, "Here we go. Full ambush." We're lining up all our magazines, and we're priming our grenades, taking the safety clips off, lining them up on the top of the carrier. We figured this is it, the big battle to end all battles for us. The night wore on and we kept shining the light on the UN flag and yelling "United Nations" in Serbo-Croatian.

Dawn came and we were still there in one piece. Some engineers came in to clear us out. They swept in with their minesweepers and found another mine right behind our vehicle, so we couldn't have backed out. Sergeant Mike Ralph was one of the engineers that came to rescue us. Brave, brave man. Shortly after he got us out, he had to go back and find out where the rest of the mines were. And sure enough, I heard it, *whompf*! A couple of his soldiers were walking along in front with their minesweepers, and they went right over a stack of plastic mines. Big anti-tank mines. Mike was driving a five-quarter pickup truck and he drove over a stack and just disappeared. He was blown to bits. We ran up and we could see he was dead, but we called for an Airevac. But having no medical coverage, the only helicopter we could call on to get him out was a civilian-hired helicopter that refused to fly after 5:00 p.m. They wouldn't come and get him. The nearest hospital was an hour away, so that was it.

I was in the Canadian War Museum for the first time this summer and I was showing my son around. We were looking at the vehicles and I walked into this place called, I think, the Hall of Heroes. I walked into the room and as I turned the corner, the first thing I saw was Mike Ralph's flak vest and his beret. That brought it home. It really brought it home.

There's two kinds of fear.

There's immediate fear when something is happening and your adrenaline and your brain are going a million miles a minute and you're responding. As a commander I was more worried about what my troops were doing, what the plan was and what the next step was than about my own personal safety. So although I was involved in some exceptionally hairy circumstances, I was never conscious of any fear at the moment. It was there, definitely, like a feeling in your stomach. I could feel it bubbling up sometimes but I'd just have to choke it back down, almost physically push it back down, get it out of the way and then I was good to go.

But the other kind of fear is a constant nagging fear in the back of your brain.

I wasn't sure what to expect when I went to Croatia, but within a week I wrote a letter to my wife and said, "Listen, there's a fair chance I'm not coming back." I sent a letter to my cousin telling him to keep an eye on my younger brothers if I didn't make it back. I really thought I wasn't coming home. And I could deal with the fact that I was going to die there. That's my job. That's what I get paid to do. I accept the Queen's paycheque. I'm willing to do the job.

There's a constant level of fear, all the time, and as you go through more stressful situations it gets higher and higher. And the times I was truly afraid were not when I was out getting shot at or under machine-gun fire. It was when I was laying in my cot at night. It's dark and everyone else is sleeping and that's when it catches up to you. You kind of get the sweats and you get the shakes and you can't sleep and your mind starts turning the incidents over and over. And you're wondering, "What am I facing tomorrow?" That's the hardest kind of fear to defeat. I never understood it till I was there.

Soldiers say that as long as you're busy and you can focus on what you're doing at that moment, you're OK. So I would get up in the morning and start putting on my equipment. I'd shave. I'd check my weapons, I'd clean my rifle, I'd polish my Kukri and sharpen it every morning 'cause I'd never know when I was going to have to use it. But the thing that saved me and probably saved all of us, and has probably been saving soldiers for centuries now, is this: I would look at my soldiers, my guys and my detachment, and my peers, the other sergeants that I worked with, and I'd say, "Well, I can't let those guys down." So I would just choke that fear back down, put on my equipment. The platoon commander would come in and say, "OK, we've got three missions. One of them's really hairy, the other two aren't too bad," and I'd always volunteer for the hairy one 'cause I figured, "If I'm going to be out there I might as well have a bit of adventure."

THE CHANCE OF WAR

Sarajevo

Let's say you took the City of Toronto, took away all the police, then gave every 16-year-old an AK-47 and an unlimited supply of ammunition and turned him loose. That's what you've got in Sarajevo. It was a beautiful city, gorgeous. Looked like Vancouver. Modern buildings, boulevards, the Olympic stadium, surrounded by hills, nice river. An old town like the old part of Quebec City. And it looked like gangs had been turned loose on it. All the windows were busted, buildings were burnt out. It was a surreal place to work 'cause every time you got up in the morning you never knew what your day was going to hold for you.

In Sarajevo we were shot at every single day.

I was standing on top of this five-storey building, sort of an office building, and behind me was an elevator structure. It didn't cover the whole roof and I was standing away from it, so there was open sky behind me. I was looking out over the city of Sarajevo, thinking about life in general, the mission, and just catching some air really, taking a breather. All of a sudden I hear this little wasp go zinging past my ear. And I thought, hmm, that's the fastest moving insect I've ever heard. I walked a little further. And then I heard it zing past my other ear. It was only maybe half an inch from my ear 'cause I could feel the air as it went by. Then a third went by and it just touched my hair, but this time the "bug" hit the building behind me and I suddenly realized I was being shot at. There was a sniper out there who just missed me with three rounds within two inches of my head. I felt so stupid at that moment. I just dropped to the ground and I started going, "stupid, stupid, stupid." After that, every time I went out, I was always looking around wondering when those insects were coming back.

We were staying in this office tower and there used to be a group of teenaged girls that would come up, very well-dressed, nice-looking young ladies, Muslim, Croat and Serb — in this area they all lived together peacefully. And you know our guys can't resist young ladies, so they'd lean out of the windows, talk to them and throw them chocolate bars. And I came along and I said, "Boys, you gotta stop that," and they're going, "But why, Sarge? You know, we were just talking to them." And I said, "Something bad's gonna come of it." Sure enough, in come some mortar rounds. The guys see the bombs fall past the window, right into the middle of all these kids and they're just blown to bits. The guys are in shock. I'm grabbing them and we're running down to our bunker, the bombs coming in. Then they stop, and it's all quiet. We find out we're missing one guy. He had been one of the guys hanging out the window; he saw the bomb come by and ran out into the middle of a mortar barrage trying to save these kids. When we got out there he was finding a leg here and an arm there and a torso here, and he was trying to match them up.

One day we got a mission to rescue some hostages. The people we were rescuing were Serbs. They were inside the Muslim area. We had to go through Serb areas to get into the Muslim areas and then back out through the Serb areas without anyone knowing why we were there. So we had come up with this cover plan. We made our way into that part of town and we were about 100 metres from the frontline, and we're moving along. At every cross street, coming our way, was machine-gun fire and rocket-propelled grenades, and we had to go through them. Every intersection was a deathtrap 'cause bullets were flying everywhere.

We got to the building where we thought these hostages were being held. They weren't there, but we did find an old Serbian couple who had been starving in this little apartment. We figured, no sense wasting a trip, so we hustled them into the back of the vehicle and went racing out of town, ducking down because bullets were pinging off the vehicles and you could see tracer fire over our heads. We got them back up into the Serb lines and dropped them off.

I had to go down to the headquarters building and get a mission out of Operations. Now Ops is right in the busiest part of the headquarters. Officers are running back and forth, and here's me, this big six-foot sergeant, strapped with equipment, big Kukri hanging off me, weapons and everything, and I was just out of place. I'm covered in dust and these staff officers are running around in pressed uniforms. I was being bumped around in the middle of this hall, wondering where I was supposed to be and who I was supposed to be meeting and what my job was. All of a sudden, this door opens behind me, and I get bowled over to the other side of the hallway. I turn around and right there is General MacKenzie.

He's surrounded by a hive of young officers shouting at him and waving sheets of paper. It was like something out of a movie. And he just looks at me and recognizes that I'm all kitted up, ready for patrol and he knows he doesn't know me. He just sticks out his hand and says, "Hey. Lew MacKenzie. Damn glad to meet you." "Sergeant Davis, sir. Recce platoon." And he starts chatting away with me. I could see in the background all these staff officers wondering, "Why is General MacKenzie worried about this sergeant? He's nobody, he's nothing. He's just a peon in the grand scheme of things." But that's just who MacKenzie was, and I saw right in his eyes that he was interested in who I was and what I was doing. And, frankly, I think he was taking a moment's respite so he could put off all the hangers-on.

"Recce platoon is the best job to have." That's what he said to me that day anyway, and he was a former Recce platoon himself, so we were coming from the same place. There were a few occasions when I saw him under pressure or in a situation where a lot of Canadian soldiers probably would have choked or done the wrong thing, but he always was composed. He always seemed to have a sense of what it was he was doing and what he wanted to achieve — and damn the odds. And he did damn the odds. He broke a lot of laws and a lot of UN regulations.

There was always a sense that we weren't getting any support out of Canada. We knew that the UN headquarters didn't understand what was going on, not at the ground level — maybe at the strategic level, but definitely not at the ground, tactical level. But we got the sense early on that MacKenzie was someone we could trust, who wouldn't sell us down the river. We knew his hands were as tied as ours, but we could see him make commonsense decisions. And common sense is the operating fundamental of an army. If you have common sense you can accomplish anything. MacKenzie, unlike most senior officers, seemed to be abundantly full of common sense. He would look at a situation and find a soldier's solution rather than a political solution or a textbook solution. And we respected him for it. I felt safer knowing that MacKenzie was around. And sure enough, he put his life on the line to save my neck one day, and you know, there's nothing more you could ask of your fellow soldiers.

We were trying to push a new aid route through the city. There was a patrol of about 25 of us and I was in charge of security, and we were taken hostage. We pulled into this neighbourhood. We're surrounded by big office buildings, it's a narrow street, no way to turn around — when we realize that the Bosnian Muslims have blocked the front with big concrete blocks. As soon as we were in there, they came wheeling in behind us with a couple of tractor trailers filled with cement, so we couldn't get out. They had us pegged.

They surrounded us with about 100 troops. The local commander was drunk and he was convinced that we were shipping arms to the Serbs. Well, we had access to the Serb line, so why the heck would we come through his zone to ship arms to the Serbs? He wanted to inspect our vehicle and it got very hairy. Everyone in my patrol was grabbed and we refused to surrender our weapons, something that didn't happen with Canadians in later tours. They grabbed our officers and took them away, so they thought they'd taken away the command structure of the patrol. Fortunately Canadian troops are all taught from the junior level to think on their own feet.

We were sitting in an area right in the middle of no man's land, and up the hill was the Serb line. We knew that the Serbs had snipers and machine guns trained on us all the time and hiding around us were Bosnian Muslims, the guys that were holding us hostage. They were threatening to kill us. I had an AK jammed in my chest and the soldier holding the AK was told to shoot me. Fortunately he didn't.

We had a quick-reaction force about a kilometre away, ready to come in, guns blazing, to rescue us and we all would have died. None of us would have made it out of there. But I told my guys, "OK, when the first round is fired, give it all you've got, and we'll see where the pieces lie when it's all over." None of us had any hope of coming out of that. But most of us had already made up our minds that if we were going to go, we'd go down fighting, so we had a little bit of a Mexican standoff.

MacKenzie heard this was going on. At that time he wasn't allowed to travel 'cause both the Serbs and the Muslims said they were going to kill him if they got hold of him. He immediately jumps in his jeep against all common sense and orders, and drives to the place where they're most likely to get him — right to the office of the president. MacKenzie goes in and tells the president of the Bosnian Muslims that five minutes after we all get killed, he'll have it all over CNN. And of course the president has to say, "Well, maybe it's not such a good idea after all." They had to get into a vehicle and drive down and order the local Bosnian Muslim commander to surrender. MacKenzie was just asking to be killed, but he stuck his neck out for us, saved my neck and saved the necks of all the guys in my patrol. What more do you want in a commanding officer?

We were actively being targeted by Serb and Bosnian Muslim snipers. General MacKenzie deployed our snipers, part of my platoon, to respond to that threat and, although the numbers are classified, I would say that a lot of Serbs and Muslims never survived to the end of our time in Sarajevo. That's countersniper work, which was totally against the rules of engagement, totally against the United Nations Chapter VI role. But it was a matter of the needs of the moment. It solved the problem. The Serbs and the Bosnian Muslims and the Croats expected certain behaviour from us. The moment they realized we were playing for keeps and were going to break the rules if we had to, they backed off.

The Serbs and the Bosnian Muslims had some very good shooters and they had some very bad snipers. The good ones got a 7.62mm thank-you note for their efforts; the bad snipers we tended to let alone because we didn't want them being replaced by people who could shoot. They could shoot at us all day and couldn't hit anything, so we didn't mind that so much. We went out with our countersnipers, killed a bunch of their guys, so at night after dark they would sneak mortars in beside our UN positions, fire off some rounds at the opposing side. And of course the opposing side would figure out where the mortar was and mortar us back.

When the UN camps were getting hit, MacKenzie's response was to authorize black-kit patrols: UN berets off, camouflage on. We would go out into the dark and find the various groups with these mortars and run them off. Totally illegal, against the rules, but that's what we had to do. Then they moved on to some other trick. As long as we were prepared to show them that we wouldn't tolerate a certain behaviour, they were quite willing to move on to something else, and it was our game to guess what their next scam would be.

We had a few guys hauled away to the medics to get tidied up. Guy shot in the knee, a couple guys got rounds in the head. Driver in the vehicle in front of me had a 7.62 round come in right in front of his nose. Fortunately for him it just grazed the front of the vehicle, shattered, went up and just creased his hair. But he got a couple of pieces of splintered bullet in his forehead so it was bleeding. We got on the radio and said, "Our driver's been shot in the head. We don't have time to take him to the hospital. We'll take him in later." Of course, that caused havoc around the battle group because we were using an open frequency: everyone thought our driver had been shot and what the heck was he doing still driving? But he was a Newfoundlander, you know, thick skull.

The PR machines in those countries were so well tuned that within minutes of shooting a UN soldier — say a Serb sniper shoots at a UN soldier — it would be on the media, the Serb media, that a Muslim had just shot a UN soldier. Then the Muslims would retaliate, saying, "No, it was a Serb," and then it would become a PR battle. So we became tools in the PR battle between the two sides for world opinion.

On many occasions it was thought that the Muslims mortared their own kids so that they could come in and say the Serbs had done it. And they would do it right beside a UN position, so that they could show that we were there where it had happened — 'cause there were blue berets on site. The ability to manipulate information was phenomenal on both sides. Shooting a UN guy had nothing to do with the fact they disliked us; it was a means to an end for them.

I was up on top of a mountain one time, walking along this trail with this brick wall beside me. There's a hole in the wall and I'm just about to walk past it, and all of a sudden a Bosnian Muslim throws himself on top of me and knocks me to the ground. The Serbs had a machine gun set up to cover that gap and anytime anybody walked by they just opened up. He risked his life to save me. It was such a strange, strange place — you just never knew.

We would get news clippings faxed to us over there. Most of them were military articles, and they'd be distributed amongst the units. One day one of them was from the desk of the minister of national defence, Marcel Masse, the famous Quebec politician. His memorandum to the entire Canadian Forces while we were in Sarajevo getting shot at every day was: "All bases in the province of New Brunswick will buy their maple syrup from Quebec producers, not from local New Brunswick producers."

I realized then that the Canadian public had no idea what was going on. We're in Sarajevo getting shot at, people are having their feet blown off, we've lost Mike Ralph, we're losing equipment all the time, the locals are getting killed left, right and centre, and the most important and pressing issue on the minister of national defence's desk was where New Brunswick bases were getting their maple syrup. It was, like, bang! You couldn't have hit me any harder. I realized: they just don't get it back there.

I flew out of Sarajevo on leave, landed in Germany and met my wife. At that time there were so many stories in the media in Europe about the fighting and how horrible it was. All my friends wanted to know, "What was it like?" So I'd start to tell them, but in the first two minutes you could see their eyes kind of glaze over, and then they'd stop paying any attention at all. After five minutes they'd start asking what the hockey scores were. There really wasn't any frame of reference for them to put what I'd been through into perspective. I tried to talk to my wife, but she had no idea. I found that at the end of my two weeks' leave I wanted to go back. As dangerous as it was, I felt more at home there than I did back in my home in Germany with my wife and family and my friends.

There was a Canadian soldier when I was there — just got fed up and one day took a grenade, stuffed it down his flak vest and blew himself to bits. The story that came back to us a week later, after it had made the rounds through Canada, was that there'd been an accident in theatre and a soldier had been killed.

There was a case where a Van Doos patrol went into an area that they weren't supposed to be in. It was blocked off on our maps, but I assume that maybe their maps weren't marked correctly and they got attacked. They hit a land mine, there was machine-gun fire. The report for the week didn't even mention that it had happened, and when we asked the officers that we were working for, they said, "Oh, it was just a mistake." It seemed to me that there was almost a planned campaign of downplaying any sign that we were in deep trouble. The attack in the first 24 hours hitting Croatia, as far as we knew, never made it to the press back in Canada. We never got any response saying, "Oh, yeah, it is dangerous there. We're sending reinforcements," which is what we expected. What we got was, "Just keep doing what you're doing. No worries."

When we were overseas we'd get letters from whole classrooms of kids, an entire school would take it on as a project for all their kids to write to peacekeepers. We would have letters from average citizens addressed to "Any UN Peacekeeper." It was like gold when you got these letters. And from that we thought, "OK, the average Canadian's probably on side here."

But when I came back from Yugoslavia, there seemed to be a huge gap where we thought everything was *this* way, when everything was really *that* way. What's the truth here? The Canadian public just doesn't seem to know what's going on in these places, what's going on with this military. So am I dedicating my life to the Canadian people? At least the government has the decency to abuse you in the open. The Canadian public just doesn't seem to care and that's even harder to take.

There's a real reluctance on the part of the Canadian government to let the Canadian people know how dangerous it is out there because they might start asking some tough questions. Reports that Canadians were involved in combat action were being rewritten, playing down the danger, because people would start saying, "I thought these guys were peacekeepers." That's not what we were. We were cannon fodder in a lot of cases. Especially in Sarajevo. Told to do a mission that was almost impossible to complete with the resources we had, and only because MacKenzie broke all the UN's rules did we get anything accomplished.

In New Zealand every Friday their prime minister is expected to make a comment on the state of rugby in the country: it's just part and parcel of being a Kiwi. Rugby is part of your life. I've never understood why, with Canadian troops deployed all over the world, our prime minister, once a week for 10 minutes, couldn't make a comment on what Canadian troops are doing this week. You know, "Our boys in Bosnia are doing this," and, "Our troops in Haiti have just signed this agreement." Something that would show the Canadian people what their troops are doing 'cause it's so easy to send them away and forget all about them. We get all caught up in where we're putting our investments and what's the new plot on *Ally McBeal*. We forget that out there, in the real world, there are real Canadian troops who are doing a damn fine job for Canada. But no one seems to know that.

I love being a soldier. I love the action. I was never happier than when I was in Sarajevo or Rwanda or jumping out of the plane with the commandos. But if you're a soldier, you've gone to your country and said, "I'm willing to offer my life for the country. In exchange for a paycheque and a bit of adventure, I'll offer up my life for you." But there's also a sort of unwritten clause that says you believe the government will not throw your life away.

The Canadian government's been handed the lives of 70,000 Canadians to do with what they will, but at some point in my career I stopped believing that the government had the best interest of their soldiers at heart. And if you don't believe in the program anymore, why do you go to work? You go to work to get a paycheque. Well, then I'm just a mercenary and the only reason I show up everyday is 'cause I get paid to be there. There's no belief in the system anymore and I didn't want to be a mercenary. So I left.

RUSS BEATON

Sergeant

We like to say in the military that you're hard core. If you're hard core that means you buy into everything. You're Sergeant Rock, you're G.I. Joe, you always want to do the keenest jobs and look good and be super fit. And that was Russ. Russ is the epitome of the combat soldier. Super fit, super determined. It didn't matter how much he got hurt, whatever the mission was, he would achieve the mission. You could break Russ's legs and he'd still be out there on patrol. He just was a soldier. You could look at Russ and say, "I want to be that guy. That's Sergeant Rock. That's who I want to be."

Jim Davis

My mother, father, brother and sister were all in the military and I was what they call a base brat. They were all air force and we moved around, not staying more than a couple of years in each place. We were pretty well everywhere. When your parents are doing it, you almost expect that's where you're going to go next. I really didn't think about it that much. It just happened. My dad was stationed in

Greenwood, Nova Scotia, and we, myself and a bunch of my friends, joined the militia as soon as we turned 17. It was an infantry unit. I much prefer the more physical field-type of job than the air force.

I can remember when I went to the recruiting centre to join the regular force they asked, "What would you like to do?" and I said, "Oh, definitely infantry." I'd qualified on the entrance test to do any job I wanted. They gave me a call the next day, saying, "There's an opening as a clerk if you'd like to go tomorrow." I laughed at the guy and said, "I don't think so. I want to go infantry 'cause that's the only trade there is."

My dad was pretty upset and he still bugs me about that today, thinking I went the wrong route. I got a little bit of razzing at home like, "What do you want to do that for? You're better than that." And I thought, "What are you talking about? That's where it's at." I mean, no one hopes for war but soldiers used to, years ago, join the army expecting that at some time they would be in battle. It's what they trained for, it's what they wanted to do.

In the infantry you were the guy on the frontline where all the excitement was. You were the guy firing the weapon, having the rounds fired at you. You weren't back in the rear echelon supporting. In the infantry we always felt everyone else was supporting us 'cause we were on the frontline. We always felt that we were some of the most fit, well-trained people in the world. You're one of a kind. There *was* no life like it, it was true. There was no one else like you anywhere in the world. You wanted to serve your country. You wanted all that camaraderie and to go off to other countries and travel around the world and fight battles. All the exciting stuff.

With my family being in the military and myself coming from the reserves, I already knew how to march, I knew the rank structure. I knew all of that stuff so it wasn't a culture shock to me. But it was a shock that the regular force was a lot more stern in the way they'd try to break you down and build you up again.

They try to break everyone down to a basic level where you don't think about anything except what they want you to think about. Every waking moment, when thoughts are going through your head, it's what they're putting in. "You're gonna do this now. You're gonna do that. It's time to go to bed." You're fed when the military tells you to eat. They structured you and they disciplined you and tried to get everyone on the same line.

In 1983 when I joined, the first introduction you got to the military was much like everyone sees on TV. You get off the bus and you're being screamed at — "Line up in three ranks!" — but no one knows what three ranks is. The first morning PT [physical training] period was a run from hell. They run you till everybody's dropping just to show you that you were not at the standard, to show you that it's going to be tough.

The harder the sergeants were on you the more you respected them. When you graduated they were like your father, you had all the time in the world for them. You'd do anything they told you to do, you wanted to emulate them and be like them when you were a sergeant. There's so many things that the bonding did for you, going through basic training. They'd break you down again and again, and they'd teach you that you'd have to rely on each other and have to watch each other's backs.

I was on the American Rangers course in 1995. The Rangers is an organization of soldiers that are highly trained in a certain aspect of the infantry. The Americans use it as a leadership course as well. It's one of the more difficult courses in the world, the equivalent of the Canadian Pathfinder course. The Ranger course would have anywhere from 200 to 400 people on it and last three months. We'd send between two and eight people on it, and they would always be in the top few positions. The Ranger course not only improved the skills and abilities of the person that went there, but that person was able to come back and run courses and teach different ways of doing things. Better ways. That's kind of the Canadian way, to take the best from different countries. We've done it with our equipment, our uniforms, our training.

Germany

While I was stationed in Germany we competed in numerous competitions and the Canadians came back with all the awards, all the trophies. Back then you could take the average Canadian corporal and put him up against any other soldier from any country and he would, hands down, be more rounded, more highly trained than any other soldier in the world. And the other countries knew that. They knew that the Canadians were the ones to be dealt with.

I don't know if we just had more heart or if we trained more. Canadian soldiers can drive the vehicle, shoot, strip the weapons, work around the communications gear, fix it if need be. They can utilize almost every piece of equipment that we have, as opposed to just knowing how to fire their own personal weapon or drive a jeep. Compared to the average American soldier, they're really well trained. No one likes to be too high on themselves, but it appeared to us after competing against the other countries that we're pretty good. And it was good for Canadians to be participating with other countries; it showed them our abilities and was good for public relations when you shared a couple of beers afterwards. It was a lot of fun, and there were no disadvantages to it.

I was part of a team — six soldiers with a sergeant in charge and a master corporal second in command — that went to Püttlach, Germany, for a competition called the Northern European Command Infantry Competition.

It was a competition in navigation, obstacle courses, shooting — every infantry skill you can think of — and we did really well. We surprised them. They look at Canadians as the nice guys, not as a major force in the world. It was a five-day competition and one of the phases was an individual phase, and everybody would compete. I was the master corporal and my personal goal was to beat all the guys on the Canadian team. When the competition was over someone ran up and said, "Hey, Russ, you won! You beat everyone." It really didn't hit me until a British soldier, the top guy on their team — the British were very impressive and usually won — came running over and wanted to shake my hand. That was in 1986. I'm not sure if we still enter a team. I don't think we do.

I spent five years in Recce platoon in Germany. We were a close-knit bunch of guys in Recce platoon, some of the more physically fit, better-trained people within the battalion. It was a gung-ho type of thing. If you wanted to get out front where the action was, then Recce platoon was the place you wanted to go. The elite of the battalion. We thought so, anyway. I was looking forward to going to Yugoslavia, but at that point we didn't know that Recce platoon was going for sure. I was asked to go with a section of Pioneers, as the engineers were short, and they gave me the option of leaving the next day or waiting and possibly not going with Recce platoon. So I jumped at the chance because I wasn't going to miss Yugoslavia. We were finally going to get to use the skills that we'd been trained in all these years. That's all soldiers ever want to do.

Yugoslavia

Being the first Canadian contingent into Yugoslavia, we didn't know exactly what we would be confronting. We had been briefed quite extensively. We were told that it would be peacekeeping and that our arrival in the country would calm most things down. We started getting introduced on the train ride. We all had our weapons and our UN paraphernalia, our hats and armbands, with our armoured vehicles on the back of the train. My section was doing security, and we were on a flatbed rolling through Slovenia and into Croatia. It was exhilarating, it was different. We were seeing all the devastation, the buildings that were still burning and smouldering, complete towns that were flattened by artillery rounds, things we'd never seen before. It's hard to explain. We were taking it all in and looking forward to what our mission would be.

When we got there, to the town of Daruvar, the Croatians and Serbs were battling between the areas that we were first sent to. Each side thought that we were there for them, to sort out the other side. We were treated really well by the Croatians when we arrived. A few Canadians had been on an advance party setting things up, and the Croatians met us and had pamphlets and maps for us. They were greeting us with handshakes and were really happy to see us, but they were under the wrong impression. We were greeted the same way when we went to the Serbian side. They were so happy to see us, but they thought that we were there to save them from the other side. We had a hard time explaining, "No, we're not here for one side. We're here to mediate, to become peacekeepers and stop the fighting." But it didn't happen like that. I would call it a war. Probably everyone who was in the theatre would call it war, especially during the first couple of tours, where everyone was subject to shelling. If that's not war, what is? Canadians aren't exactly familiar with war. What's that fine-line difference between a confrontation, a battle and a war? At what point do you start labelling it a war? If you asked the Yugoslavians, they were at war and we were in the middle of it!

We were in Daruvar when the Royal Canadian Regiment was about 10 Ks out, and the first night they were shelled. To be shelled is something you can't really train for and it happened every day. A lot of the guys still remember every minute of it. We figured that there'd still be shelling going on, but it would be from one side to the other. We didn't think that we'd be the recipients. We were the UN. I think they took advantage of us being there and used us as cover. I was pretty lucky not to be under fire much over there. But I was with the engineers and we weren't like the rest of the soldiers out on the frontline, watching all the rounds getting fired.

It was a day-to-day experience and whatever popped up, you dealt with it. You'd have a woman come crying to the soldiers guarding the front gate, saying, "My husband wants to kill my kids. He's from one side and I'm from the other." And they'd expect you to go in and take him away. We'd say, "No, we can't. But we can show up and stop him from committing any of these crimes and ask him to leave." It was a daily occurrence to have people coming up, asking questions like, "What do they look like over on the other side? Do they have gas? Do they have cigarettes over there?" And it was just months ago that they were married to someone on the other side. It kind of blew your mind. It was an eye opener.

At no time were peacekeepers ever supposed to clear minefields. Our mission was to organize and oversee the clearance of minefields that was done by the Croatians and the Serbians. So we weren't supposed to clear mines, we were supposed to just observe. But a lot of times because of the politics, there wasn't anyone from either side that was claiming the mines, so we had to clear them ourselves. The mine clearing that we did was unauthorized. It was done by our soldiers because it needed to be done, and we were qualified to do it.

If we were clearing minefields, we had drills and we had routes that were clear and we'd be able to get people out. Our minefield reports are really detailed, right down to inches. But the Yugoslavians clearing minefields had no drills and no plans. We were showing up at minefields to supervise and we'd ask to see their minefield reports, and there were a couple of X's scribbled on a piece of paper or a little drawing on the back of a cigarette package.

There were periods where we worked with the same Yugoslavians for several days in the minefields, and one day they just wouldn't be there. Or you'd watch one of them stepping on a mine. There were multiple incidents where people got their feet blown off, guys getting hands blown off or part of their foot. Sometimes it's even more devastating watching someone who's injured, screaming in pain as opposed to dying, because you're standing there and you can't do anything about it. You can't run out there and help. You can't do anything. I watched a guy clearing mines with a rake, walking backwards. He stepped on a mine. You couldn't run out there 'cause the area was riddled with mines. We had to stand there and watch him screaming in pain, his blood spurting all over the place. You couldn't help him at all. Thankfully I wasn't there when any of the Canadian soldiers were injured.

There was a bunch of Belgians setting up some OPs and they had located some antipersonnel mines located in and around where their camp was to be built. Trying to figure out who put them there was almost impossible and waiting for someone to come pick them up was even more impossible. We had people that were trained to do it, knew how to clear it. It took 10 minutes.

If you can't challenge yourself as a leader, you shouldn't be challenging anyone else. Don't ever tell a soldier to do something that you wouldn't be prepared to do yourself. The officers that I worked for in Yugoslavia were really good. The majority of them were out there, on the job, accepting the NCOs' knowledge and taking it into consideration in their planning. It's good for the officers to listen to the more knowledgeable people.

The Canadian infantry — and everyone will have a different view on this — but we weren't that badly off for equipment. Our equipment's old, our tanks are old, our APCs are old. We have one of the best rifles in the world. We use some of the best night-vision equipment. We are now getting one of the newest armoured vehicles in the world. We got by. But as a small country, or a small force, we rely on other countries to support us in food, water, transport, stuff like that. And in Yugoslavia we were lacking in this kind of support.

Being the first tour and not knowing what to expect, it would have been difficult to give a black-and-white statement for a rule of engagement. We were told, as we are for all conflicts that we arrive at, that you can fire your weapon in self-defence. If someone's firing at you, you can fire back. But through the tour the rules of engagement changed. They changed to meet the requirements of what we were confronted with.

Being with the engineers, we weren't on the frontlines, we didn't have to worry too much about rules of engagement like the infantry soldiers had to. I had a very exciting tour, but I never had to fire my weapon while I was there.

Home

I don't think that the word got out back in Canada on what we were doing. When I came back from my tour I talked to my family members, who had no idea what our UN mission was. Six months is a long tour away from home, and we all were kind of expecting a huge reception from the general Canadian populace: to greet us and cheer us on, not for being heroes, but for doing our job. We got it from the base and from our family and friends — they were more than happy to have us back safe and alive — but it wasn't publicized much in Canada and the majority, even my aunts, uncles, knew nothing of what I did, where I was or why I was there. Sure, we were off doing something we were paid to do and we were just doing our jobs, but we were representing our country. But when you come back and people aren't greeting you in the way that you had hoped, you say, "Oh, well," and you just take it as another day.

The Airborne Regiment

I got to the Airborne Regiment after the disbandment. I got there when it was the Airborne Holding platoon. We had taken off the Airborne cap badge, but we still wore the maroon beret. We became a jump company and I went with Pioneer Platoon, holding a jump position as a section commander. I wasn't there for any of the scandals and I wasn't in Somalia. Most of my friends were, and like every Canadian soldier, we all have an opinion. Most of us never saw any of the things that people talked about. Some of the things were blown out of proportion and introduced to the Canadian civilian in a wrong way.

The Canadian government thinks that they know what the general populace wants to hear, but I think they were wrong in getting rid of the Airborne Regiment. No civilian I ever talked to thought that it was a good idea, yet the government thought that the general populace thought it was a good idea to get rid of it. We received letters from around the world asking, "How can you have a military without an airborne regiment?" And we said, "We don't know."

I think that every bad incident or difficulty that the Canadian military has had, the media have had no problem throwing it out on the table and letting every single Canadian know about it. Why let every Canadian know about every difficulty that we have, but not tell them about the proud things, about the accomplishments, about the heroism? Everyone in the military's marked for it, because it's really hard on individuals in the military and their families to come back and not be recognized for the service that they've done, just because of a blemish that was caused by a few people.

In the past 17 years there've been huge changes in attitude and training. Today to pass an entrance test you only have to do something like 17 pushups. Now when a soldier shows up for basic training on an infantry base, the first day he's given a tour of the base, he's explained his human rights, and he's given SHARP training. They spend about a week on all of this introduction stuff, and it's not the big scarer at the beginning. It's a kinder, gentler type of introduction.

When I became a sergeant we used a lot of what the sergeants that taught us did, or we'd try to do the same things, but we couldn't. You couldn't use a lot of the terminology anymore. You had to watch everything you said. You had to watch your back all the time. There always seemed to be someone overseeing everything you did. Because the soldiers aren't being broken down like they used to be, they're a lot more free-spirited, like a lot of children nowadays. They lack discipline. They're not toeing the line. "I don't want to do that. You can't make me do that. I can show up late for parade, what are you gonna do to me?" Stuff like that. Nowadays the courses are shorter and getting more slack and the instructors are not allowed to discipline or put soldiers through more difficult training.

Where it was all right years ago to break people down mentally, physically, to order a group of people to drop and give 50 pushups, nowadays — and I'm not knocking human rights — you can't yell at a soldier and tell him to do something because he might feel humiliated. You can't discipline someone by giving them pushups because he's already at the standard required for the job. He passed the entrance test, so why should he have to do pushups when you tell him to?

Back when my father joined, the average person had a Grade 6 or Grade 8 education. When you had a section full of guys with that education and you told them to run across the field, they ran across the field. Stay in line, they stayed in line. Nowadays a huge majority of the recruits have degrees; you tell a bunch of guys to run across the field, they're going, "But there are rounds comin' back at us" or "There's a big puddle there." If you ask pretty well anyone, you'll see that the training has dropped and the physical standards to get in have dropped. And we're lacking in the area of esprit de corps. I don't think a soldier nowadays would throw his life on the line for another soldier anywhere near the way he used to.

I think that something definitely has to be done. They have to decide very quickly what direction they plan to go with the military. We seem to be in this quasi-grey area where they don't know if they want to drop us down to under 50,000 personnel in the Canadian military and just do border patrol or have an effective force that can defend us if need be. The Canadian military is not losing anything in having a large force present and ready at all times. It not only creates employment, it does wonders for the people who are in it.

It also gives that sense of security to the general populace, having troops that can be deployed for problems within the country, like the floods in Winnipeg, the ice storm in eastern Ontario, the Oka crisis. They're needed constantly and we're having a hard time sending troops to these things because we're off on UN tours — which are great and which are needed — but we just haven't enough troops. We need more. I think that everyone wants Canadians to be the peacekeepers in everything we do in the world. They want us to be the mediators, but that's not the soldier's job.

You could send over a bunch of civilians to do peacekeeping. OK, soldiers can do it because they multitask, they can do everything. But they are much better at peacemaking than peacekeeping in my view. If I was in charge, I would concentrate on getting the soldiers courses and training to be the best that they could ever be, and to again be like we were in the world wars, one of the best militaries in the world.

I don't want to throw blame on anyone. I don't think it's any one person. I don't think it's one institution, I don't think it's one area of the government. We always used to be a model, if you talk to people in a lot of other countries. The government thinks that we *are* a model, but for something different than what we should be. They want us to be a model for the newer age peace. That's great. We all want peace, but I think they're going about it in the wrong way. We once had, if not the best, one of the best military forces in the world, and we're losing a great commodity. It's falling apart and if it's to be saved, it's got to be done now.

There's very little challenge now and it's very frustrating for the majority of highly trained military personnel. They leave and go to a civilian job. They go to a civilian job where the type of leadership is totally different. But the majority seem to find fitting in very easy, and they're highly regarded in whatever they go into. I hear stories from all kinds of guys that got out, and within no time at all they've been picked out as leaders and gone up the chain of command in the civilian job.

I got out because there was no mystery anymore, there was no excitement. We weren't even going out in the field. It was becoming a day-to-day desk job. We have a lot of highly trained soldiers who are not able to do the jobs they are trained to do. Each individual likes to get out and do what they've been trained to do, and that wasn't happening anymore. It's frustrating for someone that was trained in a certain way to see all the changes and have to start training other people in a different way, knowing that the results will not be as good.

The lack of training, esprit de corps and respect from the government and civilian populace combined to lower the standard of training and the attitude of the soldiers. There's no one reason why the attitude has changed, and it will probably take a lot of years to get it back. It took a lot of years for it to go away. That change in attitude is one of the biggest reasons why I got out.

I became an instructor, training the police. It seemed like an interesting kind of paramilitary thing to do because I got to work with all the skills that I had. Every day I was allowed to train people in weapons and repelling and snipers and all that stuff. It was exciting again.

But I miss the guys and the stuff we did, the way we worked together. I talk to a lot of my friends, my peers, and tell them how much I regret getting out of the military, and how much I miss it. The first thing they tell me is, "No, Russ, you did the right thing getting out. Things are falling apart and we're looking to get out, too."

LEWIS MACKENZIE
Major-General

General Lew MacKenzie visited me in the hospital and shot the shit with me. There's a man's general. Lew MacKenzie had a problem when he was in Bosnia-Herzegovina. He pissed the wrong people off. He spoke his mind. Lew MacKenzie spoke the truth. Told it the way it was. He didn't bullshit anybody. Worried about the men, put the officers in their place and told the government exactly what he thought about the organization and how they were running it.

Tom Martineau

I joined the military for a summer to buy a used car. When I got behind the gate I liked it, and six months turned into 33 years. I never intended to stay, but once I was exposed to the military behind the gate, I found an unbelievable comfort in the military family. I always equated it to climbing a tree with a big net under it. I always knew that if I fell, the net would catch me. Providing I wasn't a rapist or a murderer, the organization would give me the best protection it could. I also knew that there'd be a constant interplay with the people you're working with, and that you'd get a tremendous amount of satisfaction.

There was never any illusion that I was going to reach general. I hoped very much to retire as a major when I was commissioned, or a captain. That's where most of my heroes retired because small inconveniences — called World War II and Korea — interrupted their career progression. Before they retired these vets tended to reach the rank of major in the commissioned ranks. There were those, but a very, very tiny number, that were seen early on to be destined for the highest ranks.

But the criteria tended to change. In 1960 when I was commissioned, the cold war was hot and heavy, and it was assumed that we would be fighting a war pretty darn soon somewhere in Europe or southeast Asia. But the longer we moved into the cold war, the possibility of large, conventional types of operations diminished, and following unification [of the Armed Forces] in the mid-1960s we rewarded the senior officers who did very well within the bureaucracy at National Defence Headquarters in Ottawa by leaving them there. And their performance at NDHQ became the criteria for advancement.

Some of us recoiled from this and wanted to stay where the fun was, soldiering in the field. That was entirely selfish on our part because we probably should have shared some of the agony of what we called "capital punishment" (working in Ottawa).

But then the criteria for advancement changed. It use to be a stigma to go on a lot of UN work. You were deemed to be avoiding *real* work, and people like us only went there to have fun. When UN peacekeeping became high profile in the early 1990s, it became the flavour of the month as it started to hit big-time television coverage and people starting getting international exposure. Then all the senior officers were tripping over themselves to get on UN duty.

Yugoslavia

When Yugoslavia started to self-destruct, that was a new type of peacekeeping: in the conversion from cold war to post–cold war, Yugoslavia represented the change. All of a sudden we were not dealing with cross-border types of conflicts, Israel versus Syria, for example. We were dealing with factions.

I'd already commanded an entire UN mission in Central America, and, historically, once you've done that, no matter what nation you were from, that was it for your UN peacekeeping career. So when I volunteered to go to Yugoslavia some eight months later I was told, "No, you've done your time in the UN." But the UN said they'd like someone with recent UN experience and none of the other generals who were selected from six other countries to be the force commanders had been on UN duty before.

Talk about luck! Right place, right time! My background got me the job of my career.

To clarify an often mistaken recollection of that mission, there was never any intention whatsoever of the UN having any responsibility in Bosnia, other than the location of its headquarters in Sarajevo. Our responsibility was in the occupied areas of Croatia. It was nothing to do with a humanitarian operation, which it subsequently became. It had nothing to do with the forceless separation of parties. It merely had to do with protecting an area that was under occupation and giving a pause for the politicians to do their work.

The original concept of Cyrus Vance, who was representing the secretary-general of the United Nations when he went to Croatia in November of 1991, was to set up what we think of today as a conventional cold war–type of peacekeeping operation. Fourteen thousand international UN troops would go into the occupied areas of Croatia. They would protect primarily the Serbian minorities in those areas that had already been occupied by the Yugoslavia National Army. During that pause — not peace but a cease-fire — diplomats and politicians would try to find a solution. As usual it didn't work out that way, but that was the original concept.

Sarajevo

As we described to the Security Council representatives, it wasn't the dumbest decision of the 20th century to put the United Nations Protection Force (UNPROFOR) headquarters in Sarajevo, but it was probably in the top 10. It just made no sense whatsoever. Everything went against it: communications, roads, single airfield, snow. Communication was going to be very difficult on the ground. There was a good chance that Bosnia was going to seek international recognition of its independence, and then we would be in a country where we had no mandate to be there, which is exactly what happened on April 6, 1992.

Diplomats and politicians ignored our sort of simplistic warnings and the red flags we put up in Sarajevo when we said, "Hey, don't recognize this country on April 6. We're going to be in serious trouble here." We were ignored, so we did what soldiers do pretty well: we started a pool — throw in 10 bucks and guess when the war starts. And one of my guys won $1,200 picking 2:30 on the afternoon of April 6.

It didn't take a degree in political science or 20 years in the diplomatic corps to see it coming. But the institution, the United Nations institution, is not capable of adjusting to that sort of short fuse. It's a failing within the international community, but the institution of the UN is the one that failed to see what was coming.

While there was a war on and people were being killed by the score every day, we had lightly armed peacekeepers on the ground risking their lives. Over 100 were killed, over 1,000 seriously injured in UNPROFOR, doing that work. The war-fighting machine capable of imposing a solution only came in after the cease-fire. I was hoisted on my own petard because I was the guy who appeared in front of the United States House of Representatives and Congress *twice,* saying to America, "Don't get involved in Bosnia until there's an enforceable cease-fire." Because I think, in the words of Wellington, "big countries don't fight small wars." They risk their credibility. I don't think America should be involved in these situations in a peacekeeping role.

The military agrees with me, but the executive branch in the United States tends to deploy them anyway. And so NATO followed on after an American company employing a number of retired general officers outside the Beltway in Washington had reorganized and trained the Croatian army, which enabled the Croatians to conduct the operation to cleanse Krajina of Serbs. *That's* what changed the situation on the ground. *That's* what brought about NATO involvement.[1]

When it was directed that we were going on a UN conventional peace-keeping mission, the last thing we wanted was too much kit. As the situation unfolded and it was no longer conventional peacekeeping — it was actually using such force as was necessary to ensure the safe delivery of humanitarian aid — that's when more equipment was needed. And that's, paradoxically, when the UN in New York refused to let us have more equipment. And that's when I began to cheat.

I began to authorize, to the Canadian contingent in particular, high-explosive ammunition for the mortars and missiles for the anti-tank weapons, etc. In the very early days of the operation, Canada and France both cheated by bringing in more than 80 armoured vehicles. The UN declared we could only send in 15, period. Full stop. We were actually paying the fuel and maintenance costs of those extra vehicles just at the time the Sarajevo operation was created, and I needed those vehicles, so I borrowed them from the Canadian contingent.

My Canadian seniority was very much subordinated to my UN responsibility. At the time I had other nations under my command, some of which were having difficulty coping with the challenge. Some of their soldiers were sent there with very little preparation, and unfortunately some of them were killed early on in their deployment. So they required a lot more care and attention. I didn't have to worry about the Canadians; they looked after themselves.

April 13, 1992

A lot of folks were on the ground when the Canadians arrived. Other nations had contingents there in small numbers fairly early on. When the Van Doos arrived, I wanted to be there in Sector West to welcome them as a United Nations officer and also as the senior Canadian on the ground. So I got them together, explained to them that we had been invited here by the Croatian and Serbian authorities. We were separating their forces, we were protecting people on the ground and there was no rhyme or reason why they should be targeted. "So get a good night's sleep. Delighted to have you well-trained Canadians here. God bless you." And off to the next meeting.

I think it was about 12 minutes later that they were shelled.

The artillery started to land around the area and tents do not provide very good protection against artillery shrapnel. It used to be that one of the worst things that could happen was that you had to ask a soldier to dig a hole in the ground and live in it. But this was the only time in my life when I had to tell people to stop digging. The sky was blanked out with the dirt that was flying because they were all digging holes to get underground.

I said, "OK, you know, everybody makes a mistake." Their morale was good. Probably because I made a fool of myself, one of life's more humorous-slash-embarrassing moments. There weren't any casualties, fortunately.

I enjoyed briefing the Van Doos again when they came down to Sarajevo to spend a month with us in July, guarding the airport. I'd never had a chance to look a bunch of Canadian soldiers in the eye and say, "I want you to ignore every stop sign, every traffic light. I want you to drive as fast as possible, and if you're shot at, fire back." Well, you've never seen a happier bunch of guys in your life.

UNPROFOR

In the beginning there was a unique sort of setup in Sarajevo because it was merely a headquarters with 250 staff officers, with me as chief of staff, and 50 Swedish conscript soldiers. Mind you, we had the war all around us while it was relatively calm where our soldiers were deployed in Croatia. This could be the first time in history where our troops were actually feeling sorry for their headquarters because we were the ones at the centre of the civil war in Bosnia.

So not only were you the commander of the headquarters and a modest number of troops, you were also the senior international representative in town. We were hated by the local people because we stupidly called the group that we brought into Sarajevo and set up there UNPROFOR — United Nations Protection Force.

Now, if you were a citizen of Sarajevo and you'd been bombed for the last two and a half months, and 20 or 30 people were being killed in town every day, and then, riding into town on their white vehicles comes this organization called the United Nations Protection Force, and a week later the war is still going on and the bombing's still going on, and you're still having your citizens killed every day, then you could say that doesn't meet the expectations of the citizens of Sarajevo. But the Security Council had decided that all we were going to do was run a modest humanitarian operation: the airfield's protected and you're bringing in food and medicine. That was it. Full stop. And use your good offices to maintain contacts between the belligerents.

So not only is this international representative not stopping the war, every day he is going and meeting with, as far as the Bosnian government is concerned, the enemy, the Bosnian Serbs. He's seen Dr. Karadzic, leader of the Bosnian Serbs, every day, he's seen General Kukanjac, zone commander of the JNA, every week and he's meeting with the Bosnian leadership on the same regular basis, so we're being treated as equals. And the Bosnians couldn't understand that. They said, "*We* have a flag flying in front of the United Nations. *We* have a delegation there. *We* are a country. Why do you treat the Serbian aggressors like a country?" I was certainly the most unpopular guy in town, riding around in a military vehicle that's sort of a bullet magnet. It's a nice French armoured car, a VBL, which is tremendous, goes about 60 miles an hour, and it makes a more interesting target. The locals would say, "There are no video games around, so let's fire at the UN vehicles floating around town, and MacKenzie's is a little faster than everybody else's."

There was sniping going on and certainly our people reacted properly. We weren't supposed to talk about that in public back then, but we all know that our sharpshooters over there — we weren't allowed to call them snipers, that was a pejorative term — engaged those who were shooting at them and killed them because that's what had to be done. These people were trying to kill our people and they were trying to interrupt the mission.

There were always wackos within these factions, on all three sides. And factions tend to drink a lot. When you have to deal with factions, you try to move in the morning because people are really hung-over then, but by mid-afternoon they're pissed. That's not a good time to move around in your patrol group. Soldiers get to know these things after a while.

THE CHANCE OF WAR

May 3, 1992

The infamous convoy incident was certainly the darkest day. Bosnian President Izetbegovic had been kidnapped by the Bosnian Serb forces at the airport on his return from a European Community meeting in Lisbon. Most of the EC representatives had left town by then, and it was now the UN's responsibility to take over negotiations. At the same time the Yugoslavian army commander, General Kukanjac, was being besieged by the Territorial Defence Forces [TDF] at his headquarters in downtown Sarajevo. So we worked out a deal with the Bosnian Serb side and the Bosnian government whereby I would take the general to the JNA's headquarters outside of town and exchange him for President Izetbegovic. It would be as simple as that until the Yugoslavian army commander decided to bring his entire headquarters, about 300 people, with him. We agreed that we would accompany the convoy to the exchange, along with television cameras to get the international community's eyes on this particular event.

The TDF decided to ambush the convoy. They executed a number of the senior Serb officers and kidnapped about half the convoy. If I was unpopular on the Bosnian side, I was now even more unpopular on the Bosnian Serb side. There were a number of attempts to take me and my staff hostage. At the end of the day the whole affair had resulted in the death of a number of people.

At the time there were more media people crowded together in Sarajevo than there had been at any other time in any other conflict in the world. Some of the well-known media outlets were very supportive of us and the quickest way to bring pressure on the two sides was to use them because all of these factions had satellite dishes back in their rest areas, and they were watching media reports from Sarajevo. We got the prisoners released and we were released the next day, primarily by threatening to use the international media.

When you're under fire, I find you very quickly have tunnel vision. You lose your peripheral vision and you become very conscious of a few people on each side of you. That's why I say soldiers rarely die for God, Queen, country, or even, in some cases, regiment — which is sacrilegious. They put themselves at risk, they die for their buddies a few feet on either side of them. That's the group that is really cohesive.

The other thing is that it's almost an out-of-body experience. You're almost watching "yourself" 'cause there's screw-all you can do about it. By that I mean you can't change the situation. It's not like being in the kind of war where you're going to have a whole whack of people with weapons trying to defend you. In a lot of these cases you're going to have to negotiate your way out of a particular problem, and therefore it's no good being scared. So you're sort of sitting back and watching yourself as you're conducting these operations. It took a little while to get used to.

I got very used to it in April when the war started because we eased into it. Then we were pulled out and sent to Belgrade. Three weeks later we were brought back in again. When I came back with a small contingent, we were ambushed outside of Lukavica. It was night, there was a fire-fight going on and we didn't know what was really happening. We were held up for a couple of hours and I was scared. It really bugged me because I thought I was losing my nerve. Twenty-four hours later I was OK. It was like jumping into a swimming pool: you have to adjust to the temperature. I had gone back into a war situation thinking I would feel like the day I left. It wasn't like that at all. It must have been bloody horrific for guys going ashore in Normandy because they were going from training for a year and a half and, all of a sudden, they're right there and everyone's trying to kill them.

July 20, 1992

The Bosnian army had taken an advance party of the Royal Canadian Regiment hostage, Jim Davis among them, on the south side of the main river which runs east and west through Sarajevo. We were trying to get some food through to that particular area and the RCR were checking out the route. They were threatened with being killed because supposedly they were "smuggling ammunition to the Serb side." In fact, all of the ammunition in the back of their vehicle was Canadian ammunition, except for the anti-tank ammunition, which was American. Nevertheless, that's what they were being accused of.

So I phoned the UN in New York because I wanted to get a hold of the Bosnian ambassador to see if he could sort this out with President Izetbegovic. That's when the infamous conversation took place with an official within the peacekeeping department. It was late in New York. He answered the phone, and I said, "I'm General MacKenzie."

"Which mission are you with?"

(Now, I've been told by the BBC reporter Martin Bell that I was interviewed more than anybody else in the history of television in a 30-day period because of the smallness of the area and the number of journalists we had there.)

"I'm with UNPROFOR."

"What country's that in?"

"Sarajevo, Bosnia."

"Uh, what do you do?"

I hung up.

So I was left with the challenge of trying to resolve the situation by myself. I whipped down to the presidency and confronted the minister of defence for the Bosnian army and said the Canadians didn't have Serbian ammunition. I grabbed him and tried to take him over to show him, and he refused to go. He was scared to death.

The BBC helped us more than anything because Martin Bell had a tape of the incident which clearly showed that Canadians were involved in humanitarian activity. I confronted the president and the minister of defence and told them that I had this tape, and that I would release it to the international media within an hour if they didn't release our soldiers. They sent an individual over with a Canadian representative, a young major, and the people were released. It was as simple as that. Without that tape, I would have had to launch a rescue mission.

Now, this is a tale I told many times during the political campaign, about the French and English and how they work together better in the military than anywhere else in this country.[2] The people back at headquarters were mostly Van Doos, francophones, and this was an anglophone group of the Royal Canadian Regiment which was being held hostage. When I got back to headquarters, the Van Doos were all loaded up ready to go. They knew exactly what they were doing; they were ready to take the risk and rescue these RCR soldiers.

Now, soldiers would say — 'cause we tend to be cavalier about this — that no francophone wanted to be shown up by an anglophone and no anglophone wanted to be shown up by a francophone, and that the Van Doos were going to go in so they could say, "We rescued the anglophones." Bullshit! They were all part of the team there in Sarajevo, in the middle of this horrific situation. All I would have had to say was, "Go." Fortunately that wasn't necessary. I was just blessed.

Equipment

Our personal equipment is good. In some cases it's very good. Our personal weapons are very good, but our fighting vehicle fleet is pathetic. I know people talk about all the new equipment we're buying, but it's nowhere near the numbers that are required for serious operations. But it's better than nothing and the military's always happy with "better than nothing." We're delighted to receive a few scraps.

In the case of the vehicles, I was the only person born before the vehicles we used in Bosnia were made. I would watch the Jordanians and Nepalese and Brits and Argentines and Czechs and Slovaks and Poles all drive by in vehicles that were adequate for the task. Then the Canadian armoured personnel carrier would come by, built in the 1960s. We tried everything, including putting sandbags around the cupola to protect the driver and the commander from sniper fire, which makes it look like you're scared to death and hiding from everybody. We needed protection, armoured protection. We didn't have that.

I mean, they're not a bunch of dumb people making dumb decisions on purpose when it comes to equipment purchase. It's a matter of assigning priorities within a limited budget and it didn't look, at the end of the cold war, like the army was going to be very important.

Let's face it: navy and air force equipment, as modest as they might be within the Canadian context, generates a lot of employment in the local economies when there's shipbuilding on the coast or airplanes being built in Montreal or Winnipeg. The army doesn't generate that type of employment and profit.

All of a sudden this new type of peacekeeping came along and we were busier than we'd ever been before. It takes 10 years to get from the drawing board to actually having the equipment. A lot of army equipment had been dropped down on the priority list, one of which was the armoured vehicle. So we were using some pretty antiquated equipment.

Later we sent in the Cougar, which is a six-wheeled vehicle with a small 76mm gun on it. I had, along with a lot of other senior officers, stood in front of our troops in the late 1970s and said, "This is a training vehicle. Do not worry. This will never be deployed to an operational theatre!"

I was told that by my leadership. The leadership was told that by the political leadership, that this was strictly a training vehicle, because "Trudeau doesn't like tanks and this will give you the ability to maintain your tank skills. Maybe you'll get tanks after Trudeau leaves." Nevertheless, we deployed that vehicle into Croatia and Bosnia in 1993. So there goes my credibility!

Helmets! We were short of helmets, for heaven's sake. We could buy helmets off the shelf tomorrow but we don't do that because, naturally, we want to produce them in some member of Parliament's riding, where the jobs and the profits go. I'm not saying that's a bad thing. I'm just saying it's a bad thing for the military because it takes so long for that process to unfold.

The Canadian soldier ranks certainly in the top 10. As far as individual skills go, we're probably in the top three or four. That's because we don't have large organizations, we don't have the proper amount of equipment for divisions, maybe 10,000 to 12,000, to train together regularly. We focus a lot on individual and small-group training. By small group I mean sections of 10, platoons of 30, companies of 100, that type of thing. Occasionally battalions of 600 or 700, but those are expensive to put in the field and to train. So the individual skills are absolutely outstanding.

But I still argue that it's our national characteristics that create the synergy within a well-trained soldier that makes for a very valuable product on the peacekeeping side of the house. We have no territorial ambitions. We can't look after what we have, so we don't need any more territory in this country. We have a very evenhanded foreign policy, evenhanded foreign aid program, looked at from outside this country. We will pick ourselves to death internally, but from the outside we are seen as a very generous, compassionate, evenhanded sort of nation, multiethnic, probably the most multiethnic in the world, and therefore it's very acceptable for us to go over people's borders at their request and give them a hand at solving their problems. Let me give you an example.

When I went to Somalia in 1992, General Johnson, who was the overall force commander, an American, three-star, told me that the Canadian troops were the best in his 14,000-person force. He said:

> You know, it's not because they're better soldiers. I'd like to think my American soldiers are just as good as your Canadian soldiers, but it's all the extra things the Canadians do. I send Germans, Bangladeshis, Americans into an arena, I tell them, "Here are your operational responsibilities," and they go and do it brilliantly. But at the end of the day, that's it.

> Your guys, at the end of the day, go out and build schools, find an orphanage, fix it up, purify the water in the town, organize the police force, provide guards for them because the police force isn't allowed to carry weapons. They put bridges across; the locals steal the bridges and steal chains from them, and the guys go back and replace them. It's the extra things. Their wives and spouses and kids send chalkboards over and crayons and paper. The government doesn't do that. The spouses of your soldiers do that and then these guys set up the school. So that's what makes them sort of extra, and that's why I like putting other contingents with your guys, so they can see what else can be done.

And they're doing the same thing in Bosnia. They'll do the same thing in Kosovo. As soon as a Canadian contingent arrives in Kosovo, the second thing they'll do after they dig in is find an orphanage somewhere so they can fix it up and adopt it and start making life a little bit better. That is not something that's ordered by the commanding officer, by the colonel. It's not something the regimental sergeant major orders. It's just something that Canadian soldiers tend to do.

Before I left Sarajevo I asked the United Nations to give me a few days so I could visit our combat engineers. My dad was a sergeant major in the engineers, so I've got a warm spot for engineers. I was visiting a de-mining operation in Croatia and I went up to a Canadian armoured personnel carrier, opened the combat door in the back and looked in. A young master corporal was in there and I said, "What are you doing?" And he said, "Well, I'm not in the de-mining operation, sir. I've got Croats and Serbs on both sides working parallel, and I'm co-ordinating."

"Who are you talking to on the other end of the phone?"

"There's a Croatian colonel running this one, and there's a Serb colonel running this one, and I'm running the two colonels."

So here's a Canadian sapper, an engineer, running a couple of colonels who are running de-mining operations on the ground. And he's not impressed that he's doing that. It's just another thing for a Canadian master corporal to do.

Early on in the Cyprus mission there was a clearly defined Green Line, a demilitarized zone between the Turkish Cypriots and the Greek Cypriots. And because of the weather and the cheap goods, particularly around Christmas time, a lot of MPs and bureaucrats would show up to visit the United Nations contingents. Every other contingent along the line would have the officers showing the visitors around. In the case of the Canadians, every unit always had our privates, corporals, sergeants and warrant officers give those briefings. They would do it every bit as well or better than the young officers or the CO because they knew what they were talking about. They were living there.

Being intimidated by rank doesn't happen in the Canadian Forces. You ask a question of a young private or corporal and you'll get an honest answer. In fact, you'd better be careful what kind of question you ask because you'll get a *very* honest answer.

There's a higher percentage of Maritimers and Newfoundlanders in the military than the population would indicate. It's very much a tradition, down home. Clyde Wells, when he was premier of Newfoundland, asked to see me when I was visiting St. John's after the Bosnian mission. "Why were so many of the casualties in the first group from Newfoundland?" he asked. I said, "It's fairly simple. Every recruiting centre in Canada has a quota and when the quota's filled in St. John's, Newfoundlanders hitchhike to somewhere else, as far as Toronto or Regina or somewhere else, until they find a slot."

I ran the combat training centre in Gagetown for a couple of years, 1988–1990, where we trained NCOs and young officers in leadership. Three years later, after about four months into Bosnia, the head of the Canadian battalion, which was also in Gagetown, asked me to send them a message. My message was, "Whatever you change in the training package back there, be really careful because what you're doing now is working. I have seen the Canadians compared to all the other contingents here, and the young NCOs, the warrant officers and the young officers are outstanding. So don't screw around with the training too much because it's working."

I would like to think that this will not change. Once soldiers leave the field and go into the hierarchy, don't leave them there too long. We've got to drag them back to the field to maintain that credibility with other soldiers. And it's harder in Canada than anywhere else because of the size of our organization. Nevertheless, those that are going to be at the top can't reach the top by spending most of the time at the head shed in Ottawa.

The soldiers will support you providing they know that when the chips are down you will support them as much as they support you. It's hard to remember that when you spend most of your career working at headquarters level. You had to have your nose rubbed in that frequently.

Sometimes you don't feel like being the leader. But you've got to act your way through those bad days and be like you are on your good days.

I appeared before the Somalia inquiry, so let me use that as an example of leadership. A number of witnesses at the Somalia inquiry, commissioned officers, thought their audience were the three commissioners of the Somalia inquiry. That wasn't their audience. Their audience was the 60,000 members of the Canadian Forces sitting in canteens and messes across this country watching CPAC, watching the vice-chiefs, watching the colonel, watching me, watching the senior leadership of the Canadian Forces — and listening to them. Those witnesses that forgot that the soldiers were their audience and thought it was the three commissioners missed an opportunity, big time, to communicate with the soldiers. You've got to remember who your audience is.

I get invited to do interviews, and it gives me a chance to put a shot in for an institution that has in many ways defined our international reputation more than any other activity that this nation undertakes. Our military, under the public eye, reflects our values to the rest of the world. Yet within our borders, as soon as we see a wart, we want to turn it into cancer.

Peacekeeping, Perceptions, PR and the Public

I get asked one question more than any other from American audiences, particularly military audiences: "Hey, General, doesn't all this peace-keeping destroy the warrior ethic?" And my answer for years, from 1992 to 1997, was, "No, it doesn't. Well-trained soldiers will always respond to what they are told to do at the moment of crisis. They'll do it well if they're well disciplined and well trained." Lately I've answered, "Yes, it does destroy the warrior ethic, or erode it, but not in the minds of the soldiers — in the mind of the population."

If one thing really upsets me — you'd think it shouldn't — it's hearing Canada described as a "peacekeeping nation." We are *not* a peacekeeping nation. World War I, World War II, Korea — we have gone off and done the right thing and there're tens of thousands of crosses around the world to prove that we've done that.

There are politicians who naively believe that a bunch of constabulary-type Canadians, just 'cause they're Canadians with pistols on their hips, running around the world, will be a popular source for the international community to use for peacekeeping work. That is B.S. We will not be invited. You have to have well-trained soldiers to do this work. And sailors and airmen. Airpersons. Whatever.

The government, which presumably represents the will of the people, has to know that the people of Canada support this type of operation, and it is misleading in the extreme to try and convince the Canadian population that this is some sort of, as the prime minister has said, "boy scout" operation. It's not a boy scout operation. That's an insult to the Boy Scouts; it's an insult to soldiers. We have well-trained military personnel carrying out the foreign policy of our nation, and we're normally subordinate to an international alliance like the UN or NATO. We have to be honest with the Canadian people about the activities of our Armed Forces.

When I tell large Canadian audiences that we've had 17 killed in the former Yugoslavia and over 100 seriously injured, the vast majority think I'm misleading them. They don't believe it because we don't have the president meeting the body at Andrews Air Force Base when it comes back. We don't have the parents — and I'm not being facetious — on *Larry King Live* the next week.

We don't have national television coverage. The bodies are laid to rest with dignity and respect in Regina, Kelowna — wherever the deceased was from. Don't get me wrong. It's done properly, but it's not a high-profile event. And as a result, the public misreads what peacekeeping is all about. It's not peacekeeping anymore anyway: there's rarely a peace to keep.

The Canadian Forces have no public affairs department. People say, "Oh, come on. I see people wandering around with captain's and major's rank and they're public affairs officers." Yes, they are but they're in the public affairs department of the Department of National Defence. Their number one priority — it's not their fault — is the minister of national defence and the political process. It doesn't mean they're bad guys. It doesn't mean the process is totally corrupt. But it is different from the requirements of the Canadian Forces. The Canadian Forces would put a different spin or emphasis on a story than the minister would because the minister has other priorities.

Look at the Medak Pocket battle. The fact is that the Medak Pocket battle was kept quiet for over two years just because they thought, "Gee, we shouldn't be telling the Canadian public we're actually killing people for peace." Somebody's raping and murdering and nailing babies to boards and Canadian soldiers stop that, and while they're stopping that they have to kill a few people. I think probably the Canadian people can live with that, providing that it was for a just cause. And it would have been easy to explain that just cause.

They didn't because of what went on in Somalia. But one despicable act of torture and murder in over 60 years is not a trend for heaven's sake. Any PR firm in the world would have turned that around and created a positive story out of Somalia, with all the good work that was done. But the military took it over the head, big time, and a unit disappeared.

It's not only government public relations. There is within the public itself a warm and comfortable feeling with our reputation as peace-keepers. Any poll that has been done in the last five or six years on what defines us as a nation, if it's multiple choice and peacekeeping is put down as one of the choices, peacekeeping will always appear in the top three, and frequently as number one. But if you then went out and grabbed people who responded to the poll and asked them, "What is peacekeeping?" they'd normally talk touchy-feely. They'd normally talk humanitarian operation — to exaggerate, helping little old ladies across the street in Bangladesh. They wouldn't talk about stopping people from raping and murdering while they're in the act. What do you do when someone is slaughtering or massacring somebody? They would not see that as peacekeeping. Regrettably that's become more and more the norm.

I don't think, though, it's going to be the norm in the future because governments are becoming more conscious of the limitations of peace-keeping in these inter-ethnic conflicts, and quite frankly you're not about to sacrifice your sons and daughters for something that's not measurably in the national self-interest. So we'll be doing less of that.

Certainly the current UN secretary-general is doing a lot less of it because he's turning to the Security Council and saying, "If you guys aren't going to give me the resources — America, France, Britain, China and Russia — I can't do the job." Whereas secretaries-general before him have said, "I'll try and do the job with fewer resources."

There has never been, in my lifetime, a higher degree of public support for the military and enhancement of its resources and numbers, some-thing between 65 and 70 percent, depending on what poll you read. That being the case, the time has come when the military, in the public opinion world, should be on the offensive. It's trying very hard to con-vince people that if we're going to continue with this type of work inter-nationally, then we need the resources.

Vets of Korea and World War II have frequently said to me, "You keep talking about overworking the soldiers, or working too hard. We went off, went to World War II or Korea, did our thing, won it and came home. Staying abroad for six months to a year, what's the problem with that?" To which my reaction is, World War II lasted six years. We went into UNTSO on the border between Israel and Syria in 1948. We're still there. We went into Cyprus in 1964. We left in 1992. We are talking about missions that are 20, 30, 40 years in length. You just can't go there and stay until the end of them. You have to rotate people through as we did in the Korean War; we rotated every year.

The fact is that these missions, because the diplomats and politicians are incapable of resolving the underlying issue, like in Cyprus, go on for decades. To ask people to go back on repetitive tours, six months a tour, you might as well just give them free divorce papers on their way out because marriages can't survive that type of tension. Not to mention the fact that they've seen a lot of innocent people being killed.

I'm told by real vets that one of the great characteristics of war is that you can get rid of some of your fear by fighting back. We frequently put our people into situations where they have to take fire but, in the case of artillery fire or mortar fire, you don't know where it's coming from, and you can't fire back. There's nothing more frightening than being in a bunker waiting for the one that's going to penetrate and come in and explode.

Combine that with seeing women and children targeted — not collateral damage, being targeted. In Bosnia children and elderly people were high on the priority target list because that's the greatest way to insult the other side, to show your contempt for the other side. And all sides were doing it.

When you see that, month after month after month, there's the tremendous daily grind of just dealing with it. Even the good news day, when you take food and medicine and deliver it to people, or you take someone to a hospital or you stitch somebody back up, doesn't take away that level of horror, which we in Canada, thank God, are not exposed to.

The Siege of Srebrenica

In April 1993, as a civilian and a journalist, I was on my way back from a visit to our troops in Somalia. I was in Nairobi when I was watching CNN and saw that Canadians were blockaded in Srebrenica, Bosnia, and relief aid was not allowed to come in to the displaced persons. I saw Dr. Karadzic and I recognized the hotel, Hotel Yugoslavia in Belgrade. You always have to play the media game with Dr. Karadzic, so I pick up the phone, what the hell. I phone the hotel and I ask for Karadzic's room and 10 seconds later I'm talking to him. I couldn't believe it. I said, "What are you blockading Canadians for? Drop the blockade, let the Canadians be re-supplied, and reinforced, and let some of that food come into Srebrenica." And he said, "Why don't you come to Belgrade and talk about it?"

The news agency that I was representing at the time was more than happy to pay the ticket, along with the TV crew, because they were going to get an interview with Karadzic. So we flew to London and on to Budapest.

In every airport I phoned back to Canada, External Affairs and the military, just to make sure they wanted me to carry on with this because I didn't want to step on anybody's toes and get in over my head. Each time the government said, "Carry on, carry on." Even in the hotel, 15 minutes before I'm meeting with Karadzic, back to Ottawa I asked, "Do you guys want me to continue with this?" Their answer was yes. So I went and had a meeting with Karadzic (in the presence of Tom Clark of CTV) and asked — told — him to allow the Canadian soldiers there to be reinforced, to allow humanitarian aid into Srebrenica. But you always had to give him something, an idea. So I said, "Ask the UN to put observers with your artillery positions around Srebrenica. You say you're not firing at Srebrenica, then prove it by putting some UN observers there."

He asked for those observers. Twenty-four hours later they lifted the blockade, temporarily anyway, for a week or two. Canadians were reinforced, food came in and I was hammered in the press.

Karadzic had told the press of our meeting and what he had promised me. The next day the editorials in Canadian newspapers, *The Globe and Mail*, etc., condemned me for freelancing (in spite of the fact that External Affairs had privately blessed the meeting) and getting involved where I had no experience. They also said Karadzic would never live up to his promises. Within 24 hours Karadzic had implemented all three of my requests, but not one Canadian newspaper acknowledged the fact.

But I didn't really care about that. The guys were reinforced and the people got some food and medicine.

Unification, Civilianization and Centralization

Ever since the civilian and military staff were integrated in Ottawa and made co-equals in the decision-making process, military decision making has been pretty well emasculated. The senior military guys and gals move around every one and a half years, but the civilian bureaucrats — not bad people — will stay years in the same job. The authority has shifted in this co-equal relationship to the civilian side of the house. As a result, we rewarded those senior officers, colonels and generals, who were good at maintaining some influence within that structure by leaving them at National Defence Headquarters for long periods. But when the soldiers look up, what they want to see are those people returning to the field to touch the "stations of the cross," so they know that they can trust them.

The perception is that these guys are wedded to that process in Ottawa to enhance their careers, which in the vast majority of situations is not the case. But that's the perception. Other militaries have recognized that and they insist on these people coming back to the field. Well, guess what? We don't have a lot of field left in Canada. We don't have generals commanding brigades, we have colonels. We don't have divisions in the field, so we don't have jobs for majors-general. We have senior ranks competing with their civilian co-equals at the executive level in Ottawa. This perception drives a wedge even deeper between the senior ranks and the junior ranks, and between the headquarters and the field.

You can't go to every unit in Canada and sit down in the junior ranks club and explain all of this with a straight face to 500 corporals. I mean, they'll turn you off and they'll say, "Change it. Why the hell don't you change it?" And my reaction is, "Why the hell don't we change it?" I agree with them.

At unification we had to decide how we were going to support the Canadian Forces, army, navy and air force. It was decided to adopt the air force system of base support. It would be a centralized system. That works for the air force because they have operational squadrons and they're looked after by the base where they're parked. For the army, the responsibility to look after our soldiers used to be taken by the individual's regimental family, the Van Doos or the Royal Canadian Dragoons, or whatever. They looked after their own. If one of them went to the hospital, there was an officer or an NCO assigned, and every day an individual would visit that casualty in hospital. They would maintain contact with his wife, with his kids. They would look after getting the garbage out or getting the car repaired. That family looked after that individual.

With unification that disappeared. A centralized system, no matter how good it is, can't be as good as the regimental system. It doesn't have the personal touch to it. So some of these people who suffered long and hard in post-operational theatre, with medical problems or whatever, haven't had that personal touch. The soldiers say — and I would echo them — "Change it." Because we've had this operational burst of activity in the 1990s, all the peacetime things we did to keep the bean counters happy are being seen not to fit terribly well with an operational army, and now they have to be changed.

Social Experiments — Women in Combat

The military's very good at doing what they're told. Without mentioning other government departments by name, when they're told to be bilingual in 10 years, they won't necessarily do it, and they'll get away with it. But the military, we're always can-do, always do it, and we do it better than anybody else. As a result we've had a problem.

I mean, I'm the guy, I'm the general, who on the first day I was promoted was put in charge of introducing women into the combat trades of the Canadian Forces. I never thought there should be any restrictions, I thought we should just maintain the standard. Anybody who can make the standard, that's fine. But it was deemed that we would run trials. The trials were taken out of our hands because the human rights commission said, "Thou shall not discriminate by sex, except in submarines," which I find bizarre because a slit trench is a hell of a lot smaller than a submarine, but that was the decision.

Then we talked about targets. Maybe 25 percent of the combat arms would be women. Now, a target's fine because if only one percent of women who actually want to join the infantry meet the standard, then you've missed your target. But very quickly that target appears to have become a quota, and once you have a quota, "Thou shalt fill the quota," and the only way to fill the quota is to lower the standard, both for women and for men if you're going to have a non–gender-specific standard, which seemed to be the case. Well, any time you change the make-up of the military organization it should be done for one reason and one reason only: to enhance the operational capability of that organization.

Now, I don't think the Russians sat up in their beds with the hair standing up on the back of their heads when Canada made this decision, saying, "Oh, shit, we don't ever want to get involved in a conflict with Canada or the Canadian Forces because they now have 25 percent of their infantry made up of females." If the operational capability has not been enhanced, we shouldn't be experimenting with that type of thing. We can experiment with the NHL. We can experiment with the CFL.

The introduction of women into the combat trades, as far as I'm concerned, enhances the level of bravery because bravery is acting and neither sex wants to be shown up in front of the other sex. The behaviour of women under fire in Sarajevo, and I had 25 Dutch NCOs, was absolutely outstanding.

However, I want everybody to meet the standard. We in Canada are lowering the standard, and the people that are the most pissed off about that are the female soldiers. They don't want people looking at them and saying, "The only reason you got in here is because you're a woman and the standard's lower." They don't want that. They will compete on a level playing field as long as they're accepted and trained properly. But we must not lower the standards. And that's what's happening today.

Not only that, but it's hard enough to find enough guys masochistic enough to run around digging holes in the ground and letting people sneak around at night trying to beat you over the head. In the case of women in combat arms, very few want to join, so finding sufficient numbers of females will certainly be difficult.

There is a lot of pressure within the department, on both sides, to make this thing work because not everyone in the department and within the military is operationally oriented. They're not thinking about the operation. They're thinking that if they do a really good job on this, there's a chance they can get that particular equipment purchase through more easily than if they dig their heels in and get into a pissing contest with Cabinet. There are those that understand the system up there who would argue that in the overall context of things, it's probably better to play the game, but I'm not one of them.

In Ottawa on the day I came back, I had to do a conference at the National Press Centre. I was used to dealing with the media in the field, but all of a sudden there was this sterile environment in North America. Someone said, "How do you like being a Canadian hero?" And I still remember my immediate reaction was, "Don't do that to me. Don't do that to me." It's a tape I've kept, in fact. This country doesn't like heroes, and I've often been told the higher the pillar, the harder the fall. Sure enough, it didn't take long. Within a couple of weeks there were lots of folks sniping.

We are the only nation in the world, when we are voted number one, apologize for it. It's a national characteristic. Japan was number one five years ago, we were number two. The next year we became number one, Japan was number two. A fellow said to me, "You'd better watch those Japanese, they stole our second place."

Our neighbours south of the border elevate people to heroic status, but they don't stay there very long. In Canada it's exactly the opposite. We don't want the responsibility of being good at something or being heroic. You don't want to get too much exposure, Wayne Gretzky notwithstanding. And that's where the military misses the boat.

The best spokesmen for the Canadian Forces, bar none, are not the generals, not the minister, not the commanding officers. The way for the Canadian military to enhance its image nationally is to get a whole bunch of junior NCOs and junior officers and soldiers together. They have the real, hands-on experience. They'll be a little bit nervous and they won't be slick, which gives them credibility. Forget about the public affairs department of National Defence. Hire a PR firm. Make heroes out of these guys and gals. It's not something we have to hide.

In the presentations that I give, where I talk about the Canadian Forces and international disorder, the vast majority of the audiences say, "I had no idea our soldiers did this kind of work. I had no idea whatsoever. Why don't we know about this? Why don't people tell us about this?" To which my reaction is, "I don't know. That's why I'm here telling you about this."

But the most rewarding thing since my retirement happens when spouses of soldiers come up to me and say, "Thanks for supporting our guys."

There's not an award, there's not a cheque that can equate to that.

NOTES

1. It should be remembered that the United States was not, officially, a part of UNPROFOR. When IFOR, a NATO operation, took over from UNPROFOR in 1995, the American forces were involved. General MacKenzie is referring here to MPRI — Military Professional Resources Inc. — an American company, with ties to the U.S. State Department, established in 1988 to engage in defence-related contracting in the U.S. and international markets. It is located in Alexandria, Virginia, and operated primarily by former military personnel. It is believed that this private security service was supplying weapons to and training the Croatian Army for Operation Storm, which in 1995 led to the expulsion of the Serb population from Karjina. The following mission statement of MPRI was taken from the Internet:

   > MPRI's mission is to provide the highest quality education, training, organizational expertise and leader development around the world. We serve the needs of the U.S. government, of foreign governments and of the private sector with the highest standards and cost-effective solutions. Our focus areas are defence, public security and leadership development. Our primary resource is the talent, expertise and dedication of the thousands of professionals we call upon to serve our customers.

   Also from MPRI Web site:

   > MPRI can perform any task or accomplish any mission requiring defence-related expertise, military skills short of combat operations (or generalized skills acquired through military service), law enforcement expertise and leadership

development … MPRI maintains and draws its workforce from a database (carefully managed to maintain currency) of more than 8,000 former defence and other professionals, among whom we find a wide range of skilled, experienced and motivated personnel to provide expertise in these and many other areas.

2. MacKenzie: "I ran in the 1997 federal election as a response to the results of the 1995 Quebec referendum. I spent a good deal of the campaign on the road, from Victoria to Cape Breton, talking about national unity. Nowhere is the synergy of francophones and anglophones working together better demonstrated than in our military. I spent the entire campaign carrying that message across Canada, a mission a good deal more important than trying to win my riding. Fortunately I paid the price for my convictions on election day. I had no desire to go to Ottawa."

SANDRA PERRON

Captain

M y father was a fire marshal in the Canadian Forces. I joined the
Royal Canadian Army Cadets in Chilliwack when I was 13 years
old, and spent five years in the cadet program, first as an engineering
cadet and then an airborne cadet and really enjoyed it. It's the best
introduction I could have had to the Armed Forces. When I joined, of
course, there weren't as many girls as there are now.

I took my basic parachutist training through the cadet program, which
is the same course that they offer the regular force. In fact, there were
regular members on our course that graduated with us. You do seven
jumps and you graduate with parachutist's wings. It's tough. It's three
weeks of very challenging, long, exhaustive days. But probably one of
the best experiences I've ever had in the military. On our course we
started off with 54 and we graduated, I think, 24.

The year I graduated from my parachutist course I joined the regular
force, went to Chilliwack for my basic training for seven weeks and then
continued with university for four years through the Regular Officer

Training program. When I graduated I went to Valcartier as transport officer because at that time they didn't allow women to serve in combat classifications. I requested for six years to be transferred to the infantry and finally, in 1990, they allowed me to transfer. I had to start from scratch. Right after basic training, you would start infantry training and I had none of that. So I went to Gagetown and did phase two, phase three, phase four of infantry training graduated and went on to the Royal 22nd Regiment.

I have a lot of respect for the instructors in Gagetown. They were excellent in getting our attention, in putting us through challenges that you never thought you could go through. When you move on to the infantry, it's hard-core army training where you learn to do defensive manoeuvres as a section, attacks as a section, patrols, all at the section level. When you move on to phase three, you start doing manoeuvres as a platoon. You start commanding a platoon, and phase four is commanding a platoon, but mechanized. You have the armoured personnel carriers and you learn to mount, dismount and attack from mechanized vehicles. My advantage lay in the experience I'd had in transport, in regards to administrative details: how to prepare your platoon administratively, logistically, make sure that they have everything — water, ammo, rations. But nothing really prepares you for the infantry part of the training, apart from good physical fitness and health.

When I joined the Van Doos there were no women in the infantry, so it was a new challenge for the battalion. There's a period where you have to prove yourself and you're put thorough several challenges, physically, but once you've broken that barrier, you've proven yourself and they will recognize the competence. I quickly realized that soldiers don't really care what gender or colour or culture their platoon commander is as long as their platoon commander is competent.

Because it wasn't within their paradigms to see a female as a platoon commander, the first thing they had to confirm was that I was fit enough to do the job. We did 10-kilometre races, we did military patrols, we did warrior testing. Warrior testing comprises a 13-kilometre rucksack march, shooting, first aid, navigation, different soldier skills. Once they saw I not only could do it, I could excel, then it didn't seem to be a problem.

Yugoslavia

We got our first indication that we'd be going to Bosnia shortly after I arrived at the battalion. I commanded an infantry platoon for six months and then I was asked to be the assistant operations officer to deploy to Bosnia. We completed all the training and then headed for Visoko, which is about an hour away from Sarajevo.

At that point no women had been in the combat arms in operations in a theatre of war, so it was a dilemma for commanders. Would this female platoon commander be able to deal with the belligerents in theatre? They thought it would be best for my first tour to be in a support role, so I was relieved of commanding the infantry platoon and put in an operations cell. I think the commanders made the decision based on the information and their paradigms at that time. I was very disappointed, but I learned so much in the operations centre. I did the situation reports that went to the minister of national defence, so I was aware of everything that was going on. When we got in theatre I think it was realized that I could have done OK as a platoon commander. And on my second tour they put me, not only in charge of a platoon, but in charge of the senior platoon of a battalion, which was the anti-tank platoon.

The Second Tour

We had to deal with two belligerents that had very little respect for the peacekeeping forces there. So here we were, not *at* war, but we were *in* a war. It was frustrating. In Canada when we do our infantry training, we're trained to "close with and destroy." We got to Bosnia and we were dealing with taking care of abandoned children at a mental facility and escorting convoys and going through barricades. We were trained to do that, too, but the mental aspects of closing with and destroying the enemy, where you actually get rid of the rage, were so different from peacekeeping, where you're between the factions.

On the other hand, we weren't as prepared emotionally for what we saw in theatre as we could have been. I'm not sure what kind of training can give you that. One day you're in between two belligerent forces fighting one another and you're receiving fire in between these factions, and another day you're building a playground for kids in a village that was completely destroyed. Another day you're doing prisoner exchanges with bodies. Emotionally it's a roller coaster and it's hard to understand.

As a woman I don't think I faced any particular challenge. I had a platoon of 42 men, outstanding soldiers. We developed a bond. I think it may have taken a little bit longer because I, as a female officer, was always thinking, how would a man do this? How would my father do this? How would my company commander deal with the situation? This is what my second-in-command, my warrant, said to me at one point. He said, "You've proved yourself. You've proved yourself, just be you. Just deal with situations like you would deal with them." And I did. In a short amount of time I developed a bond with my soldiers.

When we would do patrols and hit checkpoints I would get out, and it was very difficult for Serbs to acknowledge that a woman was commanding. They'd say, "You can't possibly be commanding" and they'd speak to my driver. But because of the lack of respect that they have toward women, they would allow me into their platoon houses, onto their defensive positions, and they would show me their minefields, thinking she can do no harm, she's just a woman, and I would bring back intelligence to the battalion.

If there's one thing you want with your platoon, it's group cohesion. And we think group cohesion comes from all wearing the same uniform and all having the same body parts, which I don't think is the case. I think group cohesion comes from having a mission and having discipline, and it's very rewarding when you do develop that group cohesion. Out of 42 soldiers, I had five soldiers who came from the reserves. To this day I wouldn't be able to tell you which were reservists. They were well trained, they were disciplined and they contributed enormously to my platoon.

We all have our image of a perfect soldier, the Arnold Schwarzenegger or Jean-Claude Van Damme, but I don't think there is a perfect soldier. In a platoon you want different strengths and weaknesses. You want the brawn, you want a sprinter; you want a good communicator, a good negotiator, a good navigator. You want all these talents in a platoon, not 30 six-foot-four square-jawed soldiers. You want different abilities.

I had a soldier in my platoon who was borderline porky. He was not in shape. He was struggling with the physical training and, as a matter of fact, I didn't even want to bring him in theatre because I felt that he was not a soldier, because I'm working so hard myself to keep fit and here I have a soldier who can't keep up after a few kilometres. And I thought, there's no way I'm bringing him to Yugoslavia. I brought him because I was left with little choice. I realized when I got in theatre that this was one of the most valuable members of the platoon. He didn't fit my image of the perfect soldier, but he was so important in my platoon that at one point I made him my driver, and I would not leave camp without him. He spoke Serbo-Croat. I had totally undervalued this individual because he didn't fit my image of a perfect soldier, and here I was in theatre and I couldn't have done half the things over there without the corporal who spoke Serbo-Croat.

We have the best soldiers in the world, and I said this to a NATO committee on women in the military. We may not have the best equipment, we may not have the biggest budgets, and we may not have the best training because of budgets, but we have the best soldiers in the world. And I think my soldiers would have done anything for their country.

A TOW missile is a missile that could pierce any armour in former Yugoslavia. There was nothing there that we could not engage. It's a wire-guided missile that can engage in direct fire, so you have to see the target and there can't be any obstruction between the vehicle and the target. It's wire-guided, with a joystick. You can use it either with optics or thermal imagery. You can use it in the rain, you can use it at night within four kilometres.

The mandate of a TOW platoon would be to engage and destroy any tanks of the enemy. So in a peacekeeping role we were tasked, because of the night-vision equipment that we have and the thermal imagery, to do three patrols a day, to ensure our area in the zone of separation was kept clear of both belligerent forces. We were also engaged in prisoner exchanges. The long-distance protection was very useful for prisoner exchanges, which were done in between the two factions. We used to brag in my platoon that we were the most powerful platoon in the former Yugoslavia because we could engage anything in almost four kilometres.

We did more patrols than any other platoon, even the battalion that had been there before. Unfortunately we hit more anti-tank mines than any other and had some wounded when we were there. The engine on an armoured personnel carrier with the TOW could not support add-on armour, extra protection. So my soldiers were driving around with less protection than a basic infantry platoon.

When I pushed this up the chain, people bent over backwards to provide ceramic plating and eventually saved the lives of my last crew, who hit an anti-tank mine on August 3, 1995, right before the Croatian offensive. Because of this added-on protection, we burned, I think, four or five engines. But we saved the lives of four soldiers, so efforts were being made.

We were engaged in effective fire quite a few times. As far as I'm concerned, section commanders who brought back all their personnel alive made the right decision, whether they returned the effective fire, or didn't and decided to negotiate. There were times when there was no negotiation to be had because the belligerent forces were drunk. You had to just leave. At other times there was a place for a return of effective fire, and every time soldiers engaged in the return of effective fire, they knew that they would be evaluated by people in Ottawa who perhaps had never been in peacekeeping. There are certain decisions that we have to make in theatre, based on the information that we have, that in hindsight might not be the best decisions. But after every situation our platoon, our sections, would get together and brainstorm to see what could go better next time. Our infantry training gave us the confidence to be good peacekeepers. It gave us the ability to know that in any type of situation we could defend ourselves.

I think it's important to differentiate between our going to war and defending our country, and helping nations deal with their difficulties. In a situation where we're peacekeeping, the warring factions have decided to make an effort to resolve their differences. So we're in a position to try and help them. Whereas in peacemaking we're part of the process. We're not isolationists in Canada. We are contributing to world peace. So it's looking beyond the scope of our neighbourhood, our city, our province, our country and knowing that we are contributing to countries that don't have the advantages that we have here. I consider peacekeeping to be as important as the International Red Cross, helping countries that are in distress because of floods or earthquakes.

Home

I think there was significant frustration for peacekeepers who came back, and all they read about in the paper were the mistakes that we'd made in situations that were totally new. I don't think that soldiers do what they do in peacekeeping so that they can come home to receive awards and shake hands with the prime minister. They do it out of a deep-seated desire to do what's best for their country and they really enjoy what they do. On the other hand, when they do come home to face article after article of negative media attention about mistakes made during their tour, it's difficult and it takes its toll on morale.

Most people coming back from peacekeeping eventually have scars, but that's what they are: scars, healed wounds. I think most of us would agree we have scars from our six-month tours because of some of the atrocities that you see, some of the situations that you have to deal with.

A five-year-old little girl brings you a grenade in exchange for candy, or a dog eating the insides of a dead body, or abandoned children in a mental institute that are barely surviving are experiences that will live with you forever. We now know that when soldiers come back from peacekeeping, they will have lived through experiences that need to get out, that need to heal.

In the year of my tours I grew 10 years.

Women in Combat

I'm probably more adamant about quotas than anybody in Canada. Women don't want quotas. Nobody wants quotas. Setting targets means that you're going to make a special effort to catch up to that target number. Then, if you don't meet that, examine why. Is it because you've cut the support services and that's where all the women were? If we can explain it, then that's OK. If we can't explain it, then we have some work to do.

I think there has to be an important distinction between how the military will be operational despite having women, and how we will be more operational because we have diversity. There's a big difference there. It's not, "I'm going to trade in bullets for gender-awareness training" but rather "I'm going to make my army more operational by picking the best people from the whole pool of our population, not just half."

In the last years standards have been readjusted for the population and the generation that we have. Youths are not as fit as they used to be. But I don't think standards have been lowered for women. I have to disagree when I hear that standards have been lowered to allow women in.

I think the way you train has been readjusted. Before we would get young men and women coming in, young recruits being able to, say, run a kilometre in five minutes. Now maybe they're taking more time to arrive at that standard. So our training has been adapted to compensate for this generation, the Nintendo generation, coming in.

We need to tap into that generation that's coming in with more technology than we ever dreamt of. I think we need to leverage those qualities that this generation has that my generation and the generation before didn't have. Technology will be the great equalizer. When it comes to physical fitness, you still need the basic standard, but let's get other qualities in there. This is not a football team. It's not just physical. There are other aspects.

The military's looking at different ways to be attractive to women. The advertising or the marketing template was always to attract a certain area of the population. Now they're looking to readjust that to be attractive to visible minorities, women, Aboriginal people. There's definitely an increase since I was in. We have female officers at the captain level that have already commanded infantry platoons and have acted as second-in-commands in companies. There's progress being made. Still a ways to go, definitely. And the attrition rate is really outrageous.

But we're years ahead of most countries when it comes to the integration of women. We've made mistakes. We'll probably make a few more, but the important issue here is that we're learning from those mistakes. That almost sounds political, but I do believe it.

I left the Forces because I had adapted to the military for 12 years. I was different. I was at the point where battle fatigue sets in. After adapting to a certain group I wanted them to do a little bit of adapting to me, and this was too slow coming. I felt that one of the most important qualities of an officer, for any soldier, is loyalty and I was at the point where my loyalty to the system was being challenged. It was time for me to leave.

The military will always be close to my heart. It will always be a part of me, a part of who I am, and I'm very, very proud of that. I haven't lost touch. I still work with cadets whenever I can. I think that's an outstanding program for youth which focuses on physical fitness, adventure training, confidence building and citizenship. I work with the minister's advisory board on gender integration and employment equity, advising the minister on how to make the military a gender-friendly environment, and I wouldn't do that unless I believed that they can change. The one thing the military needs to be better at is change. Officers and members of the forces in general need to be better at dealing with change.

All my life people told me that women could not be in the infantry. Not only did I achieve a career in the infantry, but I think I did it well. It gave me the self-confidence to know that there's nothing I can't take on.

It's important for young women, young girls out there, to believe in themselves, to know that they can be in the combat arms. To know that they have the ability, if they have the desire, to find the drive to get in shape, to get physically fit and prepare themselves for a career in the infantry. It's not inaccessible. On the contrary, it's very, very accessible. Young women don't have very many female role models. You look at Nintendo games and cartoons and superheroes and most of these characters are males. It's important, whenever we have the chance, to show young women they can do anything they want to do.

JIM CALVIN
Colonel

I'm the eldest son of five children and when it came time to go to university we didn't have a lot of money to go around. My uncle told me that the military paid your way through if you signed up for a hitch, and I thought that was a pretty good deal, so I put my application in. No more thought than that. I had no idea about military life beyond a five-week stint in the militia that I had done one summer and I knew we had to dig holes in the ground and wear a uniform and polish our boots.

Next thing I knew I was heading off to Royal Roads Military College in Victoria. I applied for the air force. I thought it would be more fun to punch holes in the sky than it would be to dig holes in the ground. But because I'd had some previous experience within the militia, they guided me into something I was more familiar with.

I went over to Cyprus in 1981 with the 2nd Battalion Princess Patricia's Canadian Light Infantry, commanded by Colonel Ashton. It was traditional peacekeeping, where there was an actual agreement on a peace that both sides had signed. By and large we were observers in a reasonably stable environment. It was a wildly different tour than what we experienced in Yugoslavia.

Croatia — Sector West

In Yugoslavia, before we actually rotated with the 900-man battalion group, we had the benefit of a reconnaissance. My command team and I had gone over two months before and we had a very good reconnaissance within Sector West. It gave us a pretty good appreciation of the kind of dangers that we would face. I have to tell you that we had not appreciated the level of danger by the time we went on that reconnaissance. So in January 1993, when we got back, we immediately changed our entire training plan to focus far more on low-level combat skills, as opposed to the checkpoints and vehicle inspection that we had experienced back in Cyprus.

The first three months of our tour was exactly as we'd imagined it based on our reconnaissance, and we went into a sector which was reasonably stable. There was a peace of sorts between the two sides. There certainly was tension and the occasional shooting across the sides and grenades being tossed. One city was divided, with only 100 yards between the two sides, but by and large it was a stable environment where we actively disarmed the population because the UN had control. Anytime we saw anyone with a weapon we had the legal right to take it and to put it into our confiscated weapons lockup, a dangerous task in itself, to take away weapons from anyone who was keen on shooting either the Croats or the Serbs in the area. Nonetheless, we were clearly in charge of that sector.

The geography of the region in Sector West, where we began our tour, I would liken to Ontario farmland — agricultural, rich soil, rolling hills. Go 100 miles north of Toronto into the Muskokas, and that's what you'd have in Sector West.

I think we still hold the record for the number of reservists that formed part of our contingent. Three hundred and eighty-five out of a total strength of 875. And I think the most significant thing that people have to understand about that is that when you actually put close to 400 reserves in a contingent of 875, they gravitate to the frontline rifle companies because they don't come with the technical skills to be vehicle maintainers or to man your highly technical weapons systems. And of course it's the frontline soldiers and the rifle companies that bear the brunt of the actual close combat situations or the mine strikes and the shelling.

In terms of their abilities to see the mandate through, they were every bit as good as our regular soldiers. There were some things that they were lacking in. In two and a half months of preparatory training you can't give the range of skills that you can give a regular force soldier over three or four years of experience. But at the soldier level, I would say that they were more than adequate. In fact, they did a damn fine job in my contingent.

I think that it's important to understand that we started off with a 2 PPCLI cadre of only 320 soldiers, and we had to grow to 875. The army realized at that time that Yugoslavia was going to go on for a lot longer than they'd originally expected, and we just did not have the number of sergeants and warrant officers to fill the slate. So people like Matt Stopford were brevetted to the rank of warrant officer for the tour. We had something like 70 NCOs that were bumped one rank up for the purposes of our tour.

There is no NCO rank that is not important within a battalion and that goes from corporal to master sergeant to warrant officer to master warrant officer. Everyone has a key role. I had one warrant officer who was actually a platoon commander of my anti-tank platoon and handled all of my eight TOW weapons systems. Matt Stopford was a platoon 2IC, which meant he was really second-in-command of 35 soldiers on the line. Anytime his platoon commander put his head down or went on leave, Matt was the guy carrying the weight of those 35 soldiers.

Equipment and Rules of Engagement

I believe General MacKenzie, when he first went into Sarajevo, was offered certain equipment by Ottawa that he didn't think was necessary. There were certain situations in which aggressive outlooks were not thought to be in the role of peacekeeping. But he was the first guy in. He was going on the experience he'd had in his many peacekeeping missions where there was a peace to keep. Times had changed and he changed.

So many people point to a lack of equipment in the early days. When I was there I never felt, until we hit the Medak operation — which was clearly an aberration, even for that theatre — that I was overly constrained by the equipment that I had. Yes, our armoured personnel carriers were 30 years old (older than the drivers driving them), but my personal small arms and machine guns were the equal of any nation's in the world. I had my TOW weapon systems with me, I had some mortars there for the tour. Clearly there was better equipment in the world, but if I measured myself against some of the other nations that were beside me, I had better equipment than most of them, with the exception of perhaps the French and the Danes.

Now, there were better toys out there that, when I went through Medak, I would have dearly loved to have had, and it would have made my soldiers a bit more secure if we had had them. But again, Medak was at the higher end of what people are expected to do, and I'm not sure you can tailor every contingent to the extreme.

When we sent people abroad in 1993 we operated under the UN rules of engagement and they were far less clear than the ones which we have now. We did not have the system that is in place today, where there are purely Canadian rules of engagement that are in accordance with Canadian law, and which are extremely detailed and spell out virtually every action that a soldier is expected to take in whatever situation.

One of the most difficult things that a commanding officer has to do is to get his intent all the way down the chain of command to the individual soldiers who will eventually be manning the checkpoints in the middle of the night, when all hell breaks loose, and make sure they have a clear understanding of his expectations at the moment. Because there is no time for him to come back. They are in charge at the scene and they have to make a decision. We had at least two, perhaps three, incidents where we had OPs fired upon back in Sector West at the start of the tour, and the soldiers did not return fire. On at least two of those occasions I had the expectation that someone should have fired back.

However, there's a natural reluctance by any Canadian soldier to take that first shot: "Am I going to be backed up? Is this the time I'm supposed to do it?" And, of course, if two minutes go by and they aren't still firing at you, the moment has passed and it's now not really the time to open up into the darkness. So until there have been one or two successful returns of fire within the unit and the soldiers' grapevine starts working, it's a difficult hurdle that every unit has to overcome and it's something the command chain has to work at very clearly.

We had a standing policy: if you were shot at, I expected you to fire back because you can't just become a punching bag for somebody when you're in theatre.

So there was a great deal of interpretation and I would imagine if you asked the three or four commanding officers between 1992 and 1993 how they expressed their intent, there would be a common theme. There would be a theme that you would return fire when you were fired upon because the right of self-defence was never denied a soldier. Clearly my interpretation was that I was not about to lose Canadian soldiers, and I would not have a unit that was going to have the reputation that we were just punching bags for any Serb or Croat who wanted to take shots at us. There was a certain level of aggressive action needed in the dangerous theatre, and I wanted to make sure that if someone took a shot at a Canadian soldier, he knew that that Canadian soldier was going to shoot back at him.

Sector South — Medak

In July we rotated into Sector South. This was a sector where open warfare was being fought between the Serbs and the Croats. Disarmament had long since passed. The UN had lost control. The Serbs had taken all of their tanks and artillery out of the containment sites and were firing with abandon at the Croats, and the Croats in turn were using all of the weapons that were being supplied to them by different countries, and they were firing back at the Serbs. The operational tempo rose hugely, and the danger to the peacekeepers went up exponentially as well.

Sector South was closer to the coast, south of the Velebit Mountains. I would say that the climate was more like you'd get in the area in southern Manitoba, scrubby grasses, scrubby brush, not a lot of trees, not a lot of large forests, stony and much drier — more like the Canadian Shield region only without the coniferous trees and rain. There wasn't a lot of material on the ground to fill sandbags. Temperatures rose to 44 degrees Celsius during the day and would drop sharply at night. So in the midpoint of the tour we transferred from a place where the climate was reasonably comfortable into a very, very arid climate.

In Sector South we were strictly observers for a period of time and we weren't taking positive control. But when Medak happened, we clearly crossed the line and we began a peace-enforcement mission where we did things that certainly were not indicative of a normal peacekeeping mission.

Our role there was never clearly enunciated and communicated to us. Clearly the mandate that the UN was operating under had been overtaken by events in Sector South. And whereas we were supposed to have the right to seize and confiscate weapons, it's bloody hard to seize a tank. So the contingents were by and large left to determine their own role in Sector South.

We weren't the law of the land, we were just the peacekeepers and the enforcers of the mandate. I believe it was a fair rule that we had to have some concrete knowledge that there were weapons in there. Many times it frustrated the soldiers. They wanted to do things on a more proactive basis, but if you're going to set the example to a country that really had degenerated into lawlessness, I don't think you can start breaking the law yourself. I'm not sure that we would have passed the litmus test back here in Canada in terms of just cause, but at least we set up the guidelines over there and we applied them equally to both sides of the conflict.

The attitude of some non-Canadian contingents was, "We will sit well back and let the two sides fight it out," but we took a different approach. If we were going to be there on behalf of the United Nations and Canada, we had to be up where we could report accurately what was actually happening between the two sides because if there was ever going to be a peace process carried on in that sector, the politicians and the UN had to know what was going on. We took a very aggressive stance. We moved well forward to the frontlines of the Serbs, and we reported all incidents of shelling, all incidents of tank fire between the Croats and the Serbs, and the number of casualties to both sides, if we could possibly do that.

Life for the soldier on the frontline at all times in Sector South was extremely dangerous and extremely stressful. The Croats and the Serbs were spread apart by some two to three kilometres, sometimes as little as a kilometre. But when the Croats pulled the lanyard on an artillery piece, they weren't exactly sure where that shell was going to fall, and we were equally in the beaten zone of all those artillery rounds, as were the

Serbs that they were aiming at. In fact, in some cases the Serbs saddled up pretty close to our positions to try to get the UN to shelter them, which it was our job to make sure we did not do.

There were several incidents on our tour where some of our platoon houses were physically attacked by one side or another in the middle of the night, and they had to roll out of their cots, man their defensive positions and return fire at a range of 25 to 50 metres and beat them off.

Toward the end of August, when we had been in theatre for pretty close to five months, the situation in Sector South got very tense. The Croatians started shelling the Serb side very intensively. We had one company, D Company, where Matt Stopford was located, that was shelled for four days. Fires were raging all around the observation posts with all the brush burning. Tank fire was going back and forth between the Croats and the Serbs, and the whole level of danger the soldiers were being exposed to just rose.

On September 9 the Croats attacked into the area around Medak. Now, Medak is not a huge village — maybe 50 houses, one main street 150 to 200 yards long — a typical rural community in Croatia. Clearly they were targeting the Serb brigade headquarters that was located in the village of Medak. The Serbs at the time had a salient that moved into the Croat area and came very close to a town called Gospic, where the Croats had a major headquarters. So we called the whole operation the Medak Pocket operation and it was about a 30-square-kilometre area.

The Croats started their attack with artillery bombardment. This barrage was a prologue to the Croat attack to take the pocket. My entire sector was subjected to artillery: B Company down in the far south, Delta Company in the centre at the Maslenica bridge and my headquarters in Gracac. But they really focused on the village of Medak.

Five hundred and twenty-five shells fell in the first 24 hours. We had 9 Platoon, commanded by reservist Lieutenant Tyrone Green, in a Medak house at that stage of the game. The reason we know how many shells fell is that they actually had a small notebook and recorded all the shells as they fell in their backyard or hit a house across the road. They'd fall 10 shells now, a pause of five minutes, four shells now, and so on over a

24-hour period. None of the soldiers knew when the next round was going to hit their house.

In the lulls in between, Warrant Officer Trentholm would jump into his APC with his driver, cruise the village, find out what house had been hit, pull out the Serb family that had been hit, take them to the Serb bunker and then try to get back to their house before the next rounds fell. In the first 24 hours we suffered four Canadian casualties due to artillery fire. Two of them from that house. A couple of lads were outside trying to service the generator when the shells fell around the house and they picked up some shrapnel. They had to be operated on at the French surgical unit that we still had with us. Three other lads were driving a lorry, maybe 15 kilometres behind the frontlines, and a shell shredded the front of the truck. The two soldiers on the outsides of the cab picked up shrapnel and had to be operated on.

So in the first 24 hours: Canadians, zero; Croats, four.

I describe it as the Stanley Cup finals of our tour. We were very well seasoned. We'd had five straight months of shooting, being shot at, shelled, and all of our soldiers knew what they were all about. I would hate to think what would have happened if we had been thrown into this in the first three weeks of our tour.

So the Croats launched their attack and over two days of intense fighting with the Serbs, they seized the entirety of the pocket. At one stage the fight moved so close to Medak that tank fire was shooting right down the street of Medak and hitting the house across the street from Lieutenant Green's platoon house.

The Serbs reinforced and brought up a railroad train with eight or nine tanks on it, and they had busloads of soldiers coming into the area. After about 48 hours the two sides stabilized the fighting and UN negotiations kicked in. But there was still sporadic shellfire going back and forth. After a couple of days, primarily because the Serbs fired a FROG-7 surface-to-surface missile at Zagreb, the capital of Croatia, and landed it in the suburbs, the two sides reached an agreement that basically said the Serbs would stay where they had been pushed back to, the Croats would move back to the 9 September line, and the Canadians would occupy the buffer zone between the two sides and create a bit of breathing space between them and reduce the tensions between the two factions.

I received my orders on September 13, and over 24 hours we moved the better part of 1,000 soldiers into the village of Medak. I moved my Charlie Company and my Delta Company, my reconnaissance platoon and my anti-armour platoon up from different parts of the sector into the town of Medak. I was given two companies of the French army — the first time that had ever happened, that the French nation had let their troops be commanded by another nation. But General Cot, the force commander, was a Frenchman. He had been impressed by what he saw of us up to that point and he gave up close to 500 French soldiers for the operation. He came to visit me the morning of September 14 — I think he really wanted to check us out, to see if we were really ready — and told me two pieces of information. He said, "The UN truly needs a successful operation here. Up till now, every time we've said we were going to go in to do something and somebody had said no, we backed off. So we have no credibility in Sector South." He said we needed to have a successful conclusion to the operation.

The second piece of information was that he did not believe the Croatian generals had told the soldiers that they had to withdraw. It meant my soldiers were coming from behind the Serb sides, through the Serb frontlines and occupying positions in between the two warring factions, and one side didn't know that they were supposed to stop firing!

At noon on September 15 we gave the orders to move forward. With Charlie Company on the left, the Canadians moved forward past the Serb frontlines and one of the French companies moved forward on the right. As they passed the Serb line, the Serbs stop firing. As they got into what we call no man's land between the two sides, the Croats opened up on the Canadians, initially with just single shots, bouncing them off the APCs. We thought it was a bit of a mistake and they just didn't know that it was the UN, so the soldiers put up their flags a little higher so everyone knew what was going on. Then the Croats opened up with machine guns and we knew we were in the soup.

For 15 hours, particularly Charlie Company on the left, we were engaged in firefights at ranges of about 150 to 200 metres with the Croat forces. We fired everything we had except for our anti-tank weapons. We received fire from all of the small arms, 20mm cannon came down on our positions, rocket grenades came whizzing into our positions. For a soldier on the frontline, no matter how you cut it, this was a warlike situation. He was in close combat with an enemy. A soldier's pretty simple. Somebody's trying to kill me, he's my enemy until he stops, and that was what we were into. Not constant. One minute it would be 7 Platoon having a firefight, and then everything would stop. The Croats would go to ground and suddenly someone would start shooting at us again. That went on until the next morning.

Sergeant Rod Dearing and Scotty Leblanc were in the thick of all the firefights. They were in 7 Platoon and Sergeant Dearing was the section commander. I think their section took part in five separate firefights and two other artillery engagements in the 15 hours that we were actually in close combat with the Croats. At one stage several members of their sections were being pinned down by Croat fire and Scotty and Rod exposed themselves to get to the machine gun, jumped on the C6 machine gun and lay down covering fire while the rest of their section got under cover. It's just truly impressive what soldiers will do to take care of their own.

Now, in the interim the Croatian general, about 6:00 that night, called by the military observer net and said he wanted me to come over to his headquarters in Gospic, which was on the wrong side of where we were trying to go. I had to somehow get across to the Croat side and they were the ones who were firing at us. And it was dark. There was no power generation over there at that time. The whole place had been a war zone for a couple of years.

In the end Major Danny Drew, my regimental sergeant major, Mike McCarthy, one of the Danish military observers and I ended up doing the 1,000-metre walk in the darkness with nothing but a red-filtered flashlight, flashing three times to tell the Croats that this is the party coming over to negotiate, so don't shoot. As we were walking toward the Croats, gunfire went off on the flanks every once in a while. It was unsettling.

We had a meeting with the general in charge of the Croat forces and we hammered out an agreement whereby we would be permitted to go across at noon the next day and they would start to withdraw back to the 9 September line.

That night Major Dan Drew and Matt Stopford set up our crossing point — a couple of armoured personnel carriers, manned by Matt and six men — on the paved road north of Medak on the Croat side of the line. We thought we had secured both sides of the eventual crossing site. We tried to go to ground and hold our position until first light the next morning, but we started to hear massive high-explosive explosions coming from inside the pocket and a lot of small arms fire, and we knew that we had made an error in delaying until noon.

Next morning at daybreak when we looked out over the pocket, everywhere you looked there were smoke rings coming up from all of the villages within the pocket. By this time the battle had finished. There were no more Serb military that we knew of in the pocket. The only thing that we could determine was that the Croats were systematically ethnically cleansing the entire pocket. Now, it's a difficult thing for soldiers to have to wait in a situation like that because they've made an agreement, but that is the nature of the UN. Besides, it's difficult to force a crossing when they have tanks and you don't.

At noon Major Drew, with Delta Company, began the crossing toward the pocket. They found that on a hill just between the pocket and Matt Stopford's position the Croats had dug in a new defensive position. They'd moved up a tank. They'd put mines on both sides of the road and those large metal dragon teeth across the road so that we couldn't pass. And they said, "Stop. We're not going to let you go into the pocket." This created a very tense situation because Dan Drew had 16 or 18 APCs of his own, along with all of my anti-tank armour and TOW weapon systems in his first vehicle convoy, and we were not about to be stopped.

For a period of about 90 minutes at that crossing site, tensions escalated as I moved up and tried to negotiate our way through, saying we had an agreement with the senior commander on the Croat side. We knew that they were ethnically cleansing the pocket all this time, and we were getting into a state of enormous agitation. At one point I said, "I'm going to force my way through," and they cocked their weapons, took all the covers off their Sagger missile systems and moved their tank into position. My TOW weapon systems were trained on all of their positions, and all of my soldiers had cocked their weapons too. It was a situation that, if one person had erroneously fired off a round, it would have been devastating because we're talking at 50 metres, 75 metres, and we were sitting in the beaten zone of a company defensive position. We had to find another way to get through at this stage of the game.

I had only one real alternative. Over the past several days five or six camera crews and 20 print media reporters had been accompanying our first column. This was the world's first view of the Medak Pocket. I went behind one of the APCs and explained to the media that I had to try something other than force to get through. Could I hold a press conference in front of the minefield? And they agreed. I stood with my back to the Croat general on the other side of those dragon teeth and I started explaining how I believed that the Croats were ethically cleansing everybody in there and the whole international community should be aware of what we were dealing with.

I knew this man spoke English because he had been speaking it the night before, so I started attacking their reputation on the international stage. He got quite agitated and called his soldiers out. They cleared everything off the road and then he offered up his own impromptu press conference. And we went through the crossing to the other side. At about 13:30 hours we finally rolled D Company through; they started taking up the frontlines of the Croats and moving their tanks back to the 9 September line. I followed at 14:30 with the first French company and my reconnaissance platoon and we moved deeper into the pocket.[1]

At last light we rolled into the town called Licki Citluk, more or less in the heart of the pocket. It's a devastating feeling when you roll through, just at last light, not going very fast because you don't know what you're going to find, and every single building is either burning or has been blown to the ground. Not one is still standing undamaged.

Now, we're talking about a lot more buildings than we had in the village of Medak. I'd say in the first village alone, we saw maybe 60 buildings that had been just levelled or were still in the process of burning. We saw livestock slaughtered all over the roads and in the courtyards, and later that night we started finding our first human bodies. At 8:00 that night, the French company commander called me on the radio and said to come up and see this. And when I arrived, under searchlights, he walked me into this basement room in a house that had been burned out at the top.

Inside of that room were the remains of two young women who had obviously been held captive for the better part of the five days of the operation. And as the Croats went back, they had torched the room. All that was left of these young women, one of them just had the legs up to the torso, the rest having been burned away, and the other had the torso down to the navel, and the rest had been burned away. Those bodies were so hot that when our young soldiers had come to try to treat them with dignity and take them away, they had to pour water on the bodies. They were still so hot they would have melted the body bags.

You can't prepare a young soldier for something like that, that kind of brutality. It's one thing to look at it from afar and think that they're ethnically cleansing. It's another thing to think armed military professionals have slaughtered innocent civilians. That made the soldiers very angry. Much more angry than knowing the Croats were shooting at them. You can somehow at a gut level understand when two soldiers are shooting at each other because it's our job. You just can't understand why soldiers would kill unarmed civilians, old men and young women. We found four or five bodies on that evening. That night we went to ground because the mine threat was extreme and we were moving into territory that the UN had never been into at this stage. There were no guideposts, there were no maps. We were working blind.

It's difficult to build a professional army within a year and a half, and clearly the Croats had no professional army in 1991 when the war started. Between 1991 and 1993 you don't build a professional army. You end up with volunteers and you give them a rudimentary amount of training. Some of those people are responsible, and some people are thugs with guns. I think that in the Medak operation, a large majority were thugs with guns.

The next morning the soldiers were angry as they moved forward. The French were in the lead at this stage of the game, and they started pushing the Croatians back very, very quickly. We were on a timetable, and by the end of September 17 we were supposed to hit the 9 September line. The French were determined that we weren't going to get there one minute after that, and we reached the 9 September line by the end of the day on the 17th and established a buffer zone.

Any time the Croats would stop, with whatever excuse, the French were right on their tail and moving them back smartly. We took no nonsense from them and we took a very aggressive stance now that we knew who they were. We knew what they had done and we wanted to get them out of the pocket and save whatever we could.

In the end we couldn't save anything.

They had a very well-orchestrated program. They had brought in wood from the outside to seed the fires. They had their police integrated with their military, so the police were having roadblocks set up while the military were exploding buildings with anti-tank mines. No buildings were left untouched. This was a systematic case of ethnic cleansing and there's no doubt about that.

Any time a body would be found, the sweep team would get the call on the radio and rush to the scene. Our sweep team consisted of Major Craig King in charge, my two doctors, Kelly Brett and Cam Ross, two RCMP constables who were there as part of the UN Civil Police organization and who had some rudimentary forensic-analysis training, plus some soldiers from my motor platoon. They would try as much as they could to determine type of death, time of death, and write up the report for handing in to the UN and eventually to the war crimes tribunal. Some of the bodies had been there for five or six days and were quite decomposed and maggot-riddled, and there were other ones that were very fresh.

On September 19 the Croats sent in a 16-man fighting patrol, fully armed with sniper rifles, machine guns, claymore mines and a pretty slick-looking organization. Just because we had moved them back didn't mean that they had bought into the fact that they had to stay out of the buffer zone.

One of my officers was driving back from a meeting and he ran into this patrol on one of the trails. He immediately got out of the jeep, put up his hand and said, "Halt. Throw down your weapons. You're under arrest." Here's an officer with a pistol, facing 16 people and he thought nothing of it. Of course they said no, and he got on the radio and called up some reinforcements. My Ops officer, Major Grennan, sent up a French platoon with all the big toys. They surrounded them and the

Croats promptly threw down all of their weapons. We trussed them all up, threw them into the back of a lorry, deposited them at the end of the buffer zone and confiscated their weapons. There were numerous incidents like that.

We heard from people who were in theatre after us that the Croat general was relieved of his command. I know of no other punitive action that was taken against him. War crimes tribunal people from The Hague have been over twice to interview people from my battalion about the ethnic cleansing. But at this stage I know of no definitive action that has been taken other than the investigation.

At this point the Croats were feeling pretty full of themselves. Their tails were up and they thought they were the big guys in town. I started anticipating that within a matter of days, at the beginning of October, we were going to hand over to the 1st Battalion of the Van Doos Regiment. I remembered back to how nervous my unit was when we first got in, back in April, and I knew that every unit that comes in is just a little hesitant when it first gets on the ground. They take a certain amount of seasoning before they understand the rules, the unwritten rules, between the two sides. I wanted to give them a little bit of breathing space before they were suddenly under this onslaught of a whole bunch of arrogant Croat thugs with guns. Now, I don't know whether they needed that breather or not, but I was just going on my own experience when we first got to Sector West, which was a lot tamer than the situation that the good old Van Doos were going to be thrown into. I just wanted to do whatever I could to make sure they got off on the right foot.

I thought we were in the best position to make sure we taught the Croats who the new boys in town were, and I told all of my checkpoints to move the Croat checkpoints back 100 yards. This was a clear show that we were not going to be pushed around. It was a little dangerous, but it was going to be dangerous either to my unit or to the unit that came in, and I thought that my unit was in a better state of seasoning to take that. By doing that, I wanted the Croats all to know that they're now dealing with Canadians. They're not dealing with some of the other nations that they could push around.

I think Canadian soldiers make the best peacekeepers. They have an inordinate sense of fair play, even when they're under extreme stress and extreme danger. It's hard to take the Canadian out of the peacekeeper just because you put him into a war-torn country. Some of the value systems we get just by being Canadian make us pretty fair peacekeepers.

You're expected to do the right thing at the right time. That's the one thing I think that all of our military training embeds in us. When there's a decision to be made and something to be done we expect you to do the right thing. You don't have to brag about it. You don't have to be patted on the back. We just expect you to do the right thing at the time, whatever that is. I certainly believe that even if you're just doing your job, if it turns out that that is an extraordinary job, people should be acknowledged for what they've done, whether they've had physical or mental sacrifices or not. If they've done something well, they deserve to be told that they've done something well. I don't think that we've been all that good at telling people they've done something well, and I'm not certain that people appreciated that what we had achieved in Medak was perhaps at the higher end of the scale.

Home

We had a great homecoming. Our families welcomed us home into Winnipeg in royal style. There were ribbons wrapped around every tree from the airport all the way into our garrison. Signs on all of the overpasses. The City of Winnipeg was wonderful to us, but it all happened in a period of days and then it was over.

Those 400 reservists, within three days, were scattered to the winds all the way from Newfoundland to Victoria. For those reservists that we sent back to their armouries, there was no one to talk to. None of their peers knew anything about their experiences. It was such an emotional and significant event in your life that you just didn't feel confident in sharing it with people that didn't have the same attachment to it. A lot of those soldiers never had a chance to bring closure to their tour.

Within the 2nd Battalion we still had that nucleus of 300 people who would carry on for another six months together and we could work it out of our system as a group. It's still a pretty significant tour for most of the people in the regular army who were there. We had a lot of learning to do. We still have a lot of learning to do. I don't know who can actually help us out in that regard. There's a certain onus on the individual to try to bring closure to his own demons. Some never will.

In the years since our tour ended I've found that there's a real difficulty acclimatizing back to what reality is here. You do a lot of living in six months when your life is on the line. There's that heightened sense of anticipation because shells are falling or you're being shot at, but what you're doing is truly a value to the people that are there. You're making a difference.

When you come home, suddenly what is real here in Canada — polish your boots, press your uniforms — those small things seem so inconsequential compared to what you have been doing for six months. And an irritation sets in.

Soldiers don't as a rule brag about what they've achieved. Notwithstanding that, I don't know how the nation is to be kept aware of what the soldiers are doing, but somehow we have to develop some kind of a structure so that when we know that something significant is happening we're able to give credit where credit's due. The soldiers who appeared before the Croatian board of inquiry constantly felt that no one acknowledged what they did.[2]

The majority of the reserve soldiers that were scattered across the country within three days of getting home are probably not even aware to this day that the force commander, General Cot, in charge of all of UNPROFOR, awarded us the very first Force Commander's Unit Commendation for what we did at Medak. One hundred and sixty units served in UNPROFOR over four years and only three of those commendations were handed out — one to the 2nd Patricias, with all those reservists; one to the 1st Van Doos, who followed us into theatre; and one to another contingent from another nation. Yet most of those reservists still don't even know that we got that level of recognition.

When we came home in October of 1993, Somalia was just breaking and the focus was all on what had happened with that particular tour. I think it's fair to say that for the next two years Somalia consumed most of the focus of the public's attention on the military, and all of the other things that had happened, including our tour, were cast into the background. The Department of National Defence was probably reluctant to praise people who were shooting at the side that eventually won the conflict in Croatia at the same time that we were getting severely criticized for the actions that happened in Somalia. So to a degree it's just bad luck.

It's not a story that would have been told if it wasn't for one reporter, David Pugliese from the *Ottawa Citizen*, who was looking around for a good news story to counteract all of the bad press that the military was getting on Somalia. He came down to Kingston to visit me and when he heard the Medak story he broke it to the public. After that it was "Go and ask Calvin about Medak." That's why I was summoned to Parliament Hill and that's why I told the story.

The events that have occurred over the last five or six years, from Somalia through the Croatian board of inquiry, through to how we've dealt with our Canadian soldiers' lack of recognition, you name it, have created a great rift between the ranks and the officer corps. There's a lack of faith and trust between those two groups out there now. Once, the default position was, "We don't understand why the brass are telling us this, but we'll trust that they're looking after our best interests." I feel now that the default lever has fallen the other way. People are not trusting anymore. Most of the officers that I know have got the best interests of the soldiers at heart, and with the operational tempo at an all-time high in these financially difficult times, they take care of them as best they can. So whatever we can do to rebuild the confidence and trust between those two groups will do yeoman service for the Canadian Forces. And when soldiers get injured because they have been doing the right thing, then without question the whole nation has the non-negotiable responsibility to take care of that soldier. It is the nation's business that he's doing when he goes abroad. There just can't be any quibbling about it after they come back.

I'd like the public to be reassured that the military that they have right now is still a very fine institution. I'd like to re-emphasize that the young men and women who go over and try to represent the nation, in my experience, do the very best that they can and genuinely try to be ambassadors for the nation. They all know that the nation's reputation is riding on their shoulders and they keenly feel it every minute that they're out of the country.

A leader has to have a certain number of qualities. A good leader has to be a good tactician. If you don't know tactics and can't adapt even to a peacekeeping scenario, you'll fail. You have to understand soldiers. You have to be able to communicate with soldiers, you have to be able to express what your intent is, and you've got to get them to believe that what you're saying is not just a speech. You have to get them to believe in what you're saying and to buy into the mission. You better be able to anticipate the enemy or the warring factions, have a good appreciation of what they could do, and second-guess them ahead of time, because if you can't second-guess what he's doing, you'll always be on your heels.

And you'd better be lucky. I'd never follow an unlucky commander if I had an option.

NOTES

1. The villages in the Medak Pocket were Donji Selo, Licki Citluk, Brljici, Njegovani, Raicevic, Rogici, Krajinovici, Budici, Jovia, Putkonjaci, Strunici. "The entire area of the Medak Pocket was subjected to a systematic and violent plan of ethnic cleansing by the Croatian military and police forces. This cleansing operation probably began soon after the occupation of the area on September 9, 1993. However, the full implementation plan of cleansing began in earnest on the morning of September 16 and the bulk of the destruction was completed within 12 hours." (From the UN Restricted Report on Medak Pocket Operations, October 31, 1993.)

2. The Croatia board of inquiry — Croatia was called in August 1999 to investigate whether members of the Canadian Forces serving in the Canadian Contingent of UNPROFOR, and assigned to the area commonly known as Sector South during the period 1993 to 1995, were exposed to environmental contaminants in quantities sufficient to pose a health hazard during the course of their duties. The operational name given to this mission by the Canadian military was Operation Harmony. The board of inquiry, presided over by Colonel Joe Sharpe, examined a wide range of subjects that influence the health and welfare of Canadian soldiers. Among other things, the board concluded in its report in 2000 that there was no scientific proof that the soil in Sector South contained contaminants in sufficient quantities to cause the serious health problems

suffered by some members of the Canadian Forces who served there over the three-year period. However, the board was unable to rule out environmental contaminants entirely as a possible cause of at least some of the symptoms reported by veterans of Operation Harmony, including Matt Stopford.

MATT STOPFORD
Warrant Officer

I knew Matt as Bird Dog over there. On the first half of the tour one of our tasks under the mandate was to confiscate weapons, and Matt just had an unerring sense of knowing where the two sides were stashing their illegal weapons within the sector. I don't know if he sniffed them out or what, but he could just look around and have that unerring sense as to where the illegal weapons caches were going to be. So we'd set up some kind of observation post, wait for nightfall and watch with the night observation goggles and, sure enough, we'd watch somebody walking in and out of a house with a weapon. So Bird Dog was the name I gave him. I don't know what everybody else called him, but I was sure glad he was on my side.

Jim Calvin

I was the type of kid that grew up playing Cowboys and Indians, graduating to BB guns and just about anything that had to do with soldiering. At 17 I dropped out of high school to join the army.

I was from a small town and the army's the perfect chance to get to go all over the world and do stuff. The high school's pretty small and we had an English teacher and her name was Miss Macken, we used to call her Moose, and I failed her English class twice. By the third time round she was getting tired of chasing me with a yardstick taking swoops 'cause of a couple of smart-aleck remarks in class, and when I told her that I was going to join the army she said, "Don't do that, you're going to wreck your life. What's more important school or the army?" And I remember that day 'cause I said, "Well, the army is." And that's the day I walked out of school, joined up and off I went on my happy-go-lucky career.

When I wrote the entrance exam I qualified for just about anything, and at the recruiting office the recruiter tried to talk me out of doing the infantry thing, but I wanted to be a soldier with a rifle and pound the ground.

We did boot camp at Cornwallis and then got sent to Wainwright to infantry school. When you first get into the recruit world you're still a civilian and you get off the bus with the long hair. It's just like the movies; they take you straight to the barber and somebody with clippers chops you right down until you're bald and look like an eagle. That's the big thing that happens 'cause when you're 17, your hair was it.

Every two weeks you get to go to a different level of training. In boot camp one of the first things they teach you is to sew. Every other course that's in front of you calls you "Suzy Homemaker" because now you're learning to sew. The next week you get to know how to cook rations and use the stoves and the lanterns; now you're "Sally Homemaker." There's a progression in the 16 weeks of your boot camp as you go from all these different names. Now, this is a long time ago. That's pretty politically incorrect now, but back then it wasn't. And female courses going through got called the same things.

I remember, and it sounds weird, but we had to carry our drawers out on the parade square and our coat rack with all our uniforms hanging off, and it's pouring down with rain and out comes the sergeant to inspect us. Our inspection wasn't good, so he says, "OK. That's it. Be ready for tomorrow morning at 6:00." So you're back in the shacks at 9:00 and all your kit's wet. Everybody has to work as a team now to get everything ready for tomorrow. If it's not ready you're back on the square again that night. That's what it was like in the old days.

After boot camp we all thought we had it made. Then we ended up, just like in the movies, rollin' into a camp that had big cut-in-half garbage cans, and we were looking out the bus windows going, "That must be where they keep the ammunition and the rifles." Lo and behold the door opened on the bus and in came the eight-foot giant infantry sergeant that scared us half to death 'cause he started telling us he was our new mother, father, God, Queen and country, and threw us into one of those shacks to live in. That's exactly what it was. It was a huge garbage can cut in half, with a row of 26 beds straight down, with one little locker. And that was it. That's when we got taught how to be soldiers.

I loved it. They're my fondest memories. You start recruit training and you hate the sergeant and you hate the warrant. The hatred's unbeliev-able, but by the end of the course you'd follow them anywhere and that hate's turned him into some sort of sick godlike figure in front of you, and that's the guy you're going to follow.

And once you're done and you're a soldier, you don't talk to the recruits because they're not even close to being dirt, so you're not going to talk to them, you're going to your battalion now. Of course, you hit the bat-talion, now you're the youngest guy on the totem pole and you're back in the bottom of the pile again. The best advice for hitting the battalion for the first time is to keep your mouth shut. Don't say anything to any-body for six months until you know what's going on.

The NCO Hierarchy

You have private, corporal, master corporal, sergeant, warrant, sergeant major and RSM (regimental sergeant major), so a warrant officer is get-ting to the upper end of the food chain for non-commissioned officers. The sergeants, and especially the warrant, train the lieutenant when he comes into the battalion. Unfortunately with the Yugoslavia tour, we were getting brand-new lieutenants, and once I'm in a theatre that's active and my guys can get hurt, I don't have time to train my lieutenant anymore. You either know your job or you're left behind.

Most senior NCOs that I knew, we've all been incarcerated at one time or another. Now, when I tell you "incarcerated" or "in jail," that's army jail. We're not talking about shoot-'em-up bank robberies; we're talking about maybe a bar fight, or you slept in one morning 'cause you were partying too hard and didn't shave for a parade. A little bit of mischief can be anything that's kind of humorous, like you go downtown, you have too much to drink, you take a nice dolly to her house, and in the morning you wake up and it's 11:00 and you've missed parade.

Your experience is what counts more that anything else, so when you're dealing with a private, as a warrant you know exactly what the private's going through because you've been there. An officer hasn't been where a private's been. With a warrant officer, that guy who's a private knows you've done everything he's done. You need that experience to be able to deal with the soldiers correctly.

"Garrison troopers" or "garrison boys" are stars that are shooting up the chain that have never been in trouble, never been charged, never gone to jail. How do you deal with your soldiers when they're getting into trouble — other than automatically charging them? With my guys I used to say, "If you're AWOL, first of all make sure you phone me because I'll cover you in front of the sergeant major, but I've got to know you're alive." The worst thing is if one of your soldiers turns up in hospital and you've already told the sergeant major at 8:00 in the morning, "I know where he is, don't worry about it." Then you're going down the tubes. I also used to tell them, "If you come up with a story that I've never heard or used, you're off. I'll let you go." I had one guy come in and tell me that two girls took him home and handcuffed him to the bed. I was going to get him into it because I really didn't believe it, but then he lifted up his sleeves and his pant legs to show me the marks where he had been handcuffed, and I let him off.

The old army was a huge family. It was a family like you've never experienced before: "We'll look after you one way or the other." There was a soldier downtown and he went into the wrong bar. He was knifed and almost died. The next day the whole battalion showed up in that bar to talk to the bike gang that had stabbed this 17-year-old soldier.

Back in the old days if you went downtown and got into a fight, you came back, you're on parade and the CO's looking at you, you say something like, "Well, sir, these three guys belittled the regiment. They called us sissies." More than likely you'd get off. He'd go, "Well, good for sticking up for the regiment. Good for sticking up for your buddies. Off you go." It was a different world back then and it was a different army.

Unfortunately we changed the rules: the Puzzle Palace keeps putting more and more stuff in there and we're losing the comradeship and the family that we used to have. The more trust we lose, the less combat-efficient we are.

Yugoslavia

I did three tours in Cyprus and I'd done a five-year stint in Germany before I got over to Bosnia. I'm tempted to say that Cyprus was like a holiday. Now and then somebody got shot or there was a riot, but it wasn't a big deal and you did your job. It was like a picnic. But I was there almost 30 years after this conflict had started and I don't want to take anything from anybody who served in Cyprus when it was bad.

Bosnia was completely different. Right from the get-go it was a war.

Most of my career has been with the 2nd Battalion Princess Patricia's Canadian Light Infantry, but after Germany I was posted to Peterborough as a regular support staff for the militia. When Croatia came up I went back to the battalion for the tour. The battalion gave us three months' work-up training with the platoon commanders, and I got to pick most of my platoon before we went overseas. I only had five, including myself, who were regular force, the rest were reserves, and I'll tell you, those guys did a bang-up job. The militia were involved, and they're still involved in quite a few operations because we don't have enough regular force soldiers to keep doing back-to-back tours. So we had a lot of reserves in my platoon.

Just after Christmas 1992 we went to California for two months because the terrain and the heat were almost the same as in Yugoslavia and in Manitoba it was very cold. In California we went right through what we call the "shoot to live" program. We did live-fire platoon attacks. We did everything we were supposed to do before we went over there and we were ready for what could or couldn't happen. We came back to Winnipeg for three weeks and then went overseas.

At the end of the training program I had enough flexibility to pick the guys I wanted to go. I had one guy that was limping on one of our 2-by-18 marches, back-to-back marches during one day. I was pretty fit back then and I ragged on him the whole march, and when we were done I sent him to the medic. My intention was not to take him with us because he was starting to slack off on the march. When he came back, I found out his foot was broken, but he had finished the march. I took that guy with me.

Croatia — Sector West/Sector South

In theatre in Yugoslavia, our rule of engagement, our opening-fire policy, was pretty good. Whatever calibre weapon's fired at you in direct fire, you could return fire. In our platoon we said if it's within 10 feet, that's getting pretty close and good enough to open up. But you couldn't fire first.

Colonel Calvin's the CO of the battle group, so he gets his opening-fire policy from Ottawa. Now, Colonel Calvin has a mandate to give you his interpretation of the opening-fire rules and he did, and he did it very well. Anybody who's firing at you, whatever ammunition size they're firing, you can fire back. If the guy comes out with a 9mm pistol, you're not going to cock a .50-calibre machine gun and let half a belt go at him. So if a guy's using a pistol, you use a pistol back. If someone's engaging us with a .50-calibre machine gun, we can fire our .50-calibre machine guns. It's pretty easy to tell when you're being fired at by a .50 or an AK-47. That's a sensible policy.

Sometimes there were problems, where the Serbs would point weapons at you when you were confiscating their weapons. If they don't pull the trigger, you can't shoot. So as one guy's pointing a rifle at your head, you've got two or three soldiers behind you pointing rifles at him. Now, you know you're going to get it, but at least you have the satisfaction of knowing your three guys are gonna get the guy that plugs you if it happens. Thank God it didn't happen. When the Van Doos replaced us in Sector South, their policy was that unless you're an officer, you can't tell the troops to shoot. I'm sure when their CO got on the ground, he probably changed his opening-fire policy once he saw the situation.

It's dark. All of a sudden somebody starts shooting at you, you fire back at the flashes. If he's not firing back at you, you know you either got him or he's run away. We're not an active army. You're not going to get up and chase him because more than likely there's a little ambush set up for you down the road. After the big firefights you'd go and see what happened in the morning, and there'd just be a lot of blood trails.

Your first firefight's an awful hard thing to go through. Once that's over, then you're a lot better. I remember the first couple of times some of the guys were really scared, they kind of froze up. What I did was stand up and walk behind them. Now, at that time it was direct fire, but you could tell it wasn't going to hit you. I just knew it, but you can still hear the bullets crackin' past your head, and the guys see you standing up and they're going, "This guy's an idiot. He's right out of his mind." Then they start reacting the way they're supposed to and in a short time we were really good at knowing when somebody was shooting at us, compared to somebody just trying to pee you off. You'd hear all the cracks going above your head, but they're about 20 or 30 feet, so it's not direct fire.

Those guys were being assholes, trying to make your life miserable. It's when they hit the sandbags you've got a problem. There's always some stress happening at that little checkpoint if you're watching the bullets hit the sandbags. The two or three guys have to deal with the fire and get us on the phone. Then we come out with a couple of carriers and all the boys. But for about 15 minutes those three are on their own.

If somebody shot up one of my observation posts or checkpoints, the next day we were going to hit a house and take the weapons. We had a very successful rate of taking weapons over there, but it was very political, what you could and couldn't do in Sector West. Colonel Calvin used to hate me because every other night I'd be on the radio at 2:00 in the morning: "Get up, we gotta hit this house. We know there's weapons in there." Nobody asked us exactly "How did you know there were weapons in there?" but my directive was never to hit a house that didn't have weapons. So we made sure we didn't do that. If it meant looking in a window, or sticking your head in a basement window when nobody's looking and seeing a bunch of AK-47s on the floor, to me that's not infringing on anybody's rights. I'm there as a peacekeeper. If they don't have guns, they can't shoot each other.

There was one hit on the Serbian side that almost started a riot, and we had to pull out the whole battalion reserve to help us. I remember Colonel Calvin asking me, "How did you know there were weapons in there?" and I remember saying, "I think the wind blew the door open."

And it was a steel door. The reason we knew it had weapons is we found the steel door tied up with wire, so I cut the wire, stuck my head in and saw all the crates of ammunition, closed the door, called it in and we took the weapons. But the official version was that the wind blew the door open.

The opening-fire policy comes from the "Puzzle Palace," and people should understand when I say Puzzle Palace, we're talking NDHQ or National Defence Headquarters. Now the opening-fire policy is about 120 pages. Every situation in the world where you can pull the trigger is in that book, so if something bad happens, like in Somalia, they can turn around and say "You pulled the trigger. Right here, Section 575, Paragraph 1B: "You shall not actively engage a soldier that's pointing a rifle at you unless you've been hit by a bullet." That's how silly it is now.

I had a young soldier who stepped on the tripwire. One of my privates put his foot down and when he looked at his boot, he saw this green line that was right on his laces. It's almost invisible, like a fishing line. So we followed the line and it's on a PMR 3. If he had hit it he was going to die and probably the two behind him. For the rest of the tour he couldn't walk on grass right. It would take him an hour to go 100 feet from carrier to carrier if it was on grass. He just couldn't walk right anymore. And we looked after him. We laughed at him a bit but he knew we were joking and that helped relax him. We make fun of a thing because our morbid sense of humour is the only thing we have to protect us from the stuff we're seeing. That's the only thing that keeps your sanity.

Visitors

I hate pandering to most of the people who are coming over. They don't have a clue in the world. I'm supposed to act like you're something good, kiss you on the ass, and then tonight I'm going back in the mine-field, trying to stop my guys from getting hurt. I got a problem with that kind of crap.

Barbara McDougall had lunch with us in Sector West. I usually don't like politicians but I did like her. She was straight-up. We took her to the bunkers we had built just in case we're shelled at the platoon. The boys had made signs inside the bunker that they called a "flinch meter." It went from "I'm hardly breathing" to something like "I'm running around with my hand up my ass, babbling incoherently" and if things were really bad they'd flip the needle over to there. Now, because Barbara was there, they had it at three-quarters, 'cause flinch doesn't have to mean somebody's shooting at you. It can mean something stupid, like a politician's coming over.

She had lunch with Colonel Calvin, the RSM, company sergeant major, me and Scantlebury, one of my privates. Army guys aren't known to have the best friggin' language in the world so Skank was talkin' freely. So did I. Calvin jokingly "sent us to Siberia" and at the end of the dinner Barbara gave us her phone number in case somebody came after us for what we said.

The thing I'll always remember about her is this. The battle group had brought a bunch of wine so she could have it during lunch. She gave most of the wine to my platoon to have a glass while they were out eating their lunch and only used one bottle for us and herself. I thought that was just so decent. Skank was really fetched by her.

It was actually pretty funny. We had a rebel flag on the wall. She sat under it, and nobody said anything. Of course, two months later it's the biggest thing in the world to have a rebel flag because the Puzzle Palace decided it's a bad symbol. But that was a 2nd Battalion flag! It had nothing to do with racism. It had to do with hockey! For the whole regimental history, the hockey team's been called the 2 PPCLI Rebels, so of course we get hooked up with the rebel flag. We even bought leather jackets that they made us turn in 'cause you can't have "rebel" anywhere. It's politically incorrect! I mean, sometimes you just want to say, "Here, take another chunk of our traditions and morale and just flush it down the toilet and in 20 years tell me how good we are." Sometimes it's like that.

Now, another guy came over and they made me and a couple of the guys take all the weapons we had confiscated that week to company headquarters and put them on the ground so they could come around and have a look at them. This guy was there with his secretary, or whoever follows them around, and had this little puppy. She asked one of my guys about the dog and without blinking the guy said, "That dog sniffs out all the weapons and explosives. That's how we found all this stuff." And nobody cracks a smile. We're just standing there. She believes it and

I'm thinking, "Who are you? That's a six-week-old puppy. He couldn't find his fart if he did it."

We had one of the scopes up and I had put shoe polish around the scope hoping that the politician would grab it. The politician just walked past it; it was either the battalion officer or the battalion intelligence officer who picked it up and had a look through it. Then he looked over. Major Drew was there looking at us because now the officer has a shiner, and nobody's saying nothing, we're just sitting there.

When I was over in Yugoslavia there was a drinking policy. It was two beers per man per day. Nobody gets loaded and we could live with that. Now it's nothing. You can't have a drop for your whole tour. The generals did that in the Puzzle Palace so they can look at the public and say, "Look, there's none of the stupid stories coming back that you used to hear."

Well, that's fine for PR, but it's devastating for the frontline soldiers. If you get shelled, if you watch kids in pieces being bagged, or see civilians slaughtered and you have to clean up, trust me, at the end of the day you want a couple of beers. They don't have a right in Ottawa to tell those soldiers they don't deserve it, that they're not trustworthy as adults. None of my guys were loaded, running around doing stupid things. If you're a good leader your troops are going to respect it. Nobody's going to get hammered and do stupid things. There's not a lot of trust out there between the frontline units and the Puzzle Palace. There's a huge gap. It's like a black zone and they have to do something to correct it.

Sector South

Sector West was a lot better than Sector South. We knew we were going to get some heat when we first went over there. What we didn't know was we were eventually going to Sector South, which was right in the middle of the war.

I made a big mistake.

I was on top of a mountain with my machine gun. The crew and I had little walkie-talkies and at night we would walk the crest of the mountain and back to the machine gun. You're only talking a circle that wouldn't be much more than walking around a hockey arena, if you were at the Air Canada Centre. So one of my soldiers, Gunner Turner, and I did this quick thing at dusk. The battery was dead on the walkie-talkie so I thought, I'm not going to change it. We'll be back here in two minutes, it's no big deal.

Halfway around the trail, on the far side of the mountain, we were engaged by a Serbian sniper. Now, the terrain there had all kinds of natural crevices in the rock that sometimes were 10, 15, 20 feet deep, so I run to the first one I see with Turner running behind me. The reason we had to run, by the way, is it was a forward slope and if you're on the face of a forward slope and somebody's shooting at you, you better get down somewhere, otherwise you're not going to make it. As I jumped in this hole and turned around, I could see the splashing of the rounds right between Turner's feet. It was just like the movies. You could see them pinging off the rock as he jumped in. Well, the big Valhalla guy in the sky was looking after us that day because Turner didn't get hit.

The only way to actively fire back at this sniper was to pop up and expose yourself. So with Turner spotting, I popped up and fired two rounds. Turner would probably say they were way off the mark. I like to say they were close. After my two rounds he really had us zeroed in. They were pinging off the top of the hole we were in, so we sat down. We couldn't move. This guy had us in there, and he got us pretty scared and pretty tense. Now, the company's on the other side of the hill, but I haven't radioed them so they don't know what's going on and it's turning dark.

It took about 40 minutes for the company with the 2IC to come over the hill in an extended line and get us out of the rock formation and bring us back. As soon as the company showed up, buddy took off, so we didn't have a chance to bag the guy. After the incident Turner, who was 20, ralphed a bit. Then he said, "You know, I didn't mean to be sick." I said, "Turner, I tell sick jokes, like really bad sick jokes when I'm stressed out." That's what I had been doing. I thought Turner was throwing up because my jokes were so bad. He was a good kid. Had a lot of gonads. Most of them did. Major Drew talked to me for a while about not having a radio, but after that there's not much to say. I knew I should have had the radio.

Colonel Calvin had a couple of extra French companies and we told them, "Don't go off the road. Stay on the trail." One night they lost two guys in a minefield and one of the guys that's injured crawled about three miles to one of the Canadian positions to tell us his friend was still in the minefield, hurt. It was a really bad night. It was pouring with rain. There was lightning, thunder. So we launched a rescue operation, but we couldn't find the guy in the minefield 'cause the poor guy who's crawled three miles doesn't have a grid reference for us. All we know is they were out there and the Croats shot them up and they got hurt.

The French sent us vehicles to help with the search. Major Drew told them to follow the tracks. Unfortunately the lead French carrier kind of swerved just off the road a little bit. He hit a mine. Now, when you hit a mine and you're in a convoy or a rescue mission, the first thing everybody does when they hear the explosion is peel off left and right. Well, our guys didn't 'cause they know to stay on the road. Unfortunately the French guys peeled off left and right, and two more vehicles hit anti-tank mines. So now we've got all kinds of casualties out there. We're trying to get help and we're trying to keep the French on the road, plus we're trying to find the guy in the minefield. It was really disastrous for everybody concerned. Finally Major Drew, Sergeant Major Spellen and a sergeant went out and walked through the minefield and pulled him back.

By the school there was a cistern. Me and Danny Drew were standing up looking at the hill and they were shelling the ridge line right in front of us. It was about 500 metres away. People think 500 metres is really close. It's not close, trust me. Five hundred metres ain't close.

So we're watching this hill and this hill's just being blown apart and we're going, "God, that's so neat. Look at that." All of sudden Major Drew looks at me and says, "Warrant, what do you think'll happen if they just overshoot that hill 10 feet?" And no sooner had the stupid guy said that than in came the whine and I could feel the air change. All of a sudden we're eating dirt behind the cistern. That stupid shell hit just on the other side of the cistern and scared the living crap right out of us. The first one we thought was an accident but the next 20 or 30? Now we got a problem.

We've got all kinds of troops by the school and we had to do a really fast evacuation because at that time we weren't prepared for that type of shelling. We had no defence ready. We had no sandbags, absolutely nothing. We were yelling at them to put the kit up, get in the tracks.

"We're outta here, we're gonna pull back three Ks. Wait for the shelling fire to die down and then come back in." Well, we buggered off, and because I was the acting sergeant major, I had to be the last one out. And because Danny Drew is Danny Drew, he was with me because he didn't like to be left out of anything. I'd follow that guy through hell and back.

Now we jumped in the jeep, we start driving away and all of a sudden I remembered the boys had put some beer in the laundry bags and lowered them into the well to keep 'em cold and we had forgotten them. So I turned around and I drove back through the shellfire and Drew was actually really pissed off and telling me he was going to kill me as soon as we got back. But you gotta remember: that jeep can go 80 kilometres, 90 kilometres an hour through a barrage. The chance of a shell hitting that jeep is quite minimal really.

Well, we rescued the beer from the cistern and everybody was happy because you can't get beer just anywhere. You can't go to a corner store and buy a case of beer. When you have your beer you save it for that special time. So we went back and got it.

Jimmy Dacoste was a senior NCO, and after he got so high in the NCO world he became an officer. Everybody loved Jimmy. He was a good man. There's nothing you could say about Jimmy that would be bad. When I was at the Maslenica bridge, we were really taking a hammering by the Croats, indirect fire, but big howitzers were coming down on us, and we were short of sandbags and building materials that we needed for the bunker. My guys were cutting up these telephone poles, the transformers were already down — if you ever hear about PCBs — and we're cutting up the poles to use them as beams for a bunker. Jimmy had shown up in the afternoon and I said, "If I don't get sandbags, we're not going to make it here." And Jimmy just took off.

About five hours later these 10-ton trucks start showing up. Not only do we have sandbags but they're already full, and we've got a whole bunch of wood that Jimmy had gotten, I think from one of the officers' messes way back in the rear. He had told the rear echelon guys to fill up the sandbags: "These guys aren't playing around. There is really bad stuff happening." The boys did such a good job building that bunker the Serbs showed up to hide in it while we were in there. We took six, seven days of really bad shelling and the Serbs showed up to hide.

Matt Stopford

September 15, 1993 — On the Medak–Gospic Road

The Croatians were trying to throw the Serbs out of the Knin region and they started doing ethnic cleansing. Colonel Calvin got orders to go in there to push them back.

After the huge firefight everything was just ... worse than just stone cold still. It was just deadly quiet except for the cracklin' of the fires that were burning in the houses. And then the explosions and the screams started again. It happened right in front of us, but an agreement had been reached and we weren't allowed to go into that sector to push them back until 12:00 noon the next day.

That night, September 15, I held the crossing point, just inside the Croat line, with six guys and two carriers. It wasn't a pleasant evening to be spending out there. They had snipers up in the building, and they put anti-tank mines all around the carriers. They told us if we went out of the circle, we'd get shot. At that crossing point we were looking at about 6,000 Croatians to the north, and behind us there's about 7,000 or 8,000 Serbs. We wanted to help those people so bad but we weren't allowed to open up. If you opened up, everybody was dead. I didn't want to call their bluff because they weren't kidding. You know Charlie Company's just kicked the shit out of a bunch of Croatians, so as it's quiet, they're passing down the line what's just happened.

I was standing in front of the carrier, and we have night-vision glasses, so when you look at the building you can see the guys with their SKs and their sniper rifles all pointed at you.

If these guys in the building decide to get peed at ya, there is nothing we can do, we're just totally done. The nearest help's six Ks in the rear, there's tanks all over the place, and we're looking at 20mm cannons pointing at us. We were just two tracks and six guys sitting in the middle of the road. I never felt so naked in my life while I was wearing clothes and neither did my people. If they had decided to overrun us, we would have fired but we wouldn't have made it. See, I live with the nightmares. Sometimes I wonder if we should have opened up anyway. Then I wouldn't have nightmares. But then I wouldn't be here.

The Croatians ethnically cleansed that whole village pocket while we were on that crossing point. They were blowing up buildings, setting fires. You could hear the screams as people were dying.

Why do we have peacekeepers if you're not allowed to do anything? I mean, that's a politician talking. Well, I think maybe we should put the politician where we were, and then you tell me to wait for six hours. When they started to ethnically cleanse we called back to Colonel Calvin, who tried to get permission to get going in there early. It didn't happen.

At 12:00 noon Colonel Calvin came up with the whole battle group, and even then the Croatian general wasn't going to let us through. It was pretty tense. Calvin actually had to arm the TOW missiles — we're talking really big weapons — because they had all kinds of tanks. But we pushed them back.

Now, a soldier's job is to push the forces apart, hold the line so they can't fight each other and try to keep the civilians inside alive and safe, but in this case everything in the pocket was dead. All the humans, thousands and thousands of sheep, cattle, horses. That's what ethnic cleansing is. Anything that's alive, from a dog to humans, horses, pigs, sheep, chickens, is killed. They don't care. They're gonna kill everything and they did.

A soldier's job isn't to clean that up, but that's exactly what we ended up doing. Once we pushed the Croatians back, our job was to clean up that mess.

There's all kinds of things that you don't want to know about ethnic cleansing. There's rats, there's maggots, there's flies everywhere. You're splitting the guts on all the carcasses and filling them with diesel. You're burning all the carcasses to stop disease. We found burnt women in chairs that were still smouldering as we walked in. Women that were raped with hot pokers. The screams that you heard at night. You keep finding human bodies. Some of them are in good shape, so you can pick them up and take them to the road. Other ones you grab an arm and it comes off, and then you grab another piece and roll it onto a piece of plastic or put it in a wheelbarrow and take it to the road. Then the body crew can come around and pick it up.

When we went into the pocket I had to go find spots for my carriers. I had just come around a corner in one village and there was a Croatian with his AK, I think he was a sergeant. This fella had just thrown a bundle into the burning house. And he had on his head a pair of, not diapers, but those kids' training panties and they were covered in blood. You could see the blood dripping down his face. This guy had just thrown a kid into the burning house. This bastard had just killed a kid and he was dancing around with a friggin' pair of underwear on his head thinking he was something special.

We were going to pop that guy. Then his platoon came around the corner and they all had bundles of stuff from the house; the cutlery, the silver, anything that was worth money, they had in these bags. It was just like they'd been on a shopping trip.

They had erased the whole place. There was nothing left alive in the pocket. The only thing that we found was a horse, a big black stallion we called Lucky Sonofabitch. When we first tried to go near it, it would run away from us, but then we found if you put your rifle down, this horse would come up to you. Once we had the horse we kept him at company headquarters and everyone would pet him. It was the saddest thing. We all loved that horse, but it was the only thing left.

You read in the press about how the Serbs are so bad. It wasn't the Serbs doing it, it was the Croatians. Three years later the Croatians went into the whole of Sector South and this time instead of 4,000 or 5,000 people, you're talking 200,000 or 300,000 people. Nobody did anything to stop it. The UN didn't stop it and NATO didn't get involved. We stopped it in the Medak Pocket, but why did we do it? If foresight is wisdom, Jesus! If I hadda known they were going to do that three years later I wouldn't have put my guys across the start line. I just wouldn't have done it. But you know, I think if it had been the Serbs doing it, we would have had air support. I'd put money on it. But it wasn't the Serbs, it was the Croatians, so maybe we should keep that quiet!

We had the CDS, Admiral Anderson, come to see us. In the Medak Pocket it was quiet in the afternoon. We'd been in there for two or three weeks. Our boots are dirty, our uniforms are like crap, our flak jackets are unbuttoned, just T-shirts on. I mean, we looked like something out of a Vietnam movie and out comes a Humpty and the whole entourage, right? A million officers that shouldn't friggin' be there and, of course, Colonel Calvin and RSM McCarthy.

The CDS said, "Do you have any questions for me or anything I can help you with?" And Skank said, "Don't you think we deserve danger pay?" There is such a thing in the army as danger pay and if anybody deserved danger pay the people in the pocket deserved danger pay. Well, they were humming and hawing at this, and we blew up a captured 105mm howitzer. She was a pretty big bang. The next thing we see, these guys are running back to the jeep. We knew it was gonna blow up, they didn't. The CDS was out of there like a bat out of hell. However, two days later he called back and said we were all gonna get danger pay. So maybe there is justice. It just goes to show, if you've been shelled and shot at, you know which is close and which isn't. And you know what an explosion sounds like compared to a shell!

Home, October 1993

As you get on the plane to go home, you're giving your helmet and flak jacket to the guy that's getting off. That poor guy's coming down the steps, you give him a flak jacket that's got a few shrapnel holes in it and the helmet's all dented. Now he's looking at you like, "Where am I?" and you're getting on the plane. "Can't talk to you now. I'm leaving. In 18 hours I'm going to be in a bar somewhere having a beer. So see ya, don't want to be ya. We're out of here!"

Within 36 hours of the Medak Pocket battle, we were in a bar in downtown Winnipeg. I'm watching the guys and I'm thinking, good God, if somebody who doesn't know where these guys have been, starts giving them a hard time, there's going to be bad things happening here.

They didn't give stress briefings, they didn't give us a medical. The first thing the QMSI said was, "You guys are all gonna get a haircut by tomorrow." Wait a second, today's Sunday. How the frig are my guys gonna get a haircut? What are you talking about?

They made us sign a piece of paper that said you have been on this tour, you are not feeling any injuries, sick or ill effects from your tour of duty in Croatia. "Sign here and, by the way, here's your leave pass for four weeks. Just sign this and take that." I told my guys to put that piece of paper in their pocket. As it turned out, that was probably a smart move. Then we got our leave passes and we were gone.

The reserves were brutalized. They just got sent back to their unit: "OK, you've been away for 11 months, how was it? Let's carry on with work." In the battalion for the next little while there's a big break between the soldiers. These are the kind of bizarre things that happened between the guys that didn't go and the guys that did. You're out on a training exercise, and now you're using blanks and you've got some weird RSM looking at you going, "Why are you smoking around a thunderflash?" A thunderflash is just a small stick, like a firecracker. You light it, throw it and it makes a big bang, for a grenade. Well, these guys just got out of a place where they're smoking, putting out their butts on the head of a mortar or whatever steel is around. They're smoking in the track with the hatches down, and they're putting their butts out on that, and now some moron's telling them not to smoke around a thunderflash!

And do they keep all the soldiers together that are now trained and have done stuff that's real? Nope! The Puzzle Palace says, "We're gonna break you all up and send you all over God's green earth. That way you can share your experiences."

Well, no. I've got five privates or corporals with six months in Yugoslavia, which is probably worth 12 or 15 years of training in Canada. So there was some hard-core shit happening. These five guys are now in a platoon and they're in the charge of a couple of sergeants and a warrant who haven't done anything. I know it's hard for them because in my case I get a major that hasn't gone anywhere and I'm used to Major Drew.

The army has forgotten what a leader does. It's right in the word. Leader. You don't take 25 guys and say, "You're gonna go across this minefield and burn those cows." You get out in front of the 25 guys and you lead them across the field and then you burn the cows. If those are your orders, you can't change them. If that's what they want you to do, that's what they want you to do. But you're the leader. You go in front. I don't care if you're a warrant or a colonel or a general, you go in front. And that's where our chain of command has been screwed. Because those people in Ottawa forgot what a leader is.

The Puzzle Palace did not want the Canadian people to know that Canadian soldiers were involved in a conflict, especially after Somalia, plus the elections were just about to happen. For some reason they decided, "We're not going to tell anybody about the Medak Pocket," and you've got all these guys who did a stupendous job. We got home and we thought everybody knew, but nobody had a clue what you were talking about. We sent guys to their wives and kids and they didn't know anything: "So you had a nice time in Sector South?"

Three or four weeks after I came back from the tour I started getting really bad sweats. It was bad enough that you could wring the sheets in the morning and water would come out of them. And I started losing weight. I went straight to the army doctor and told him about it. He told me I was drinking too much coffee: "Cut back on the coffee, everything will be cool." I did that for a couple of months, but the problems persisted and then my joints started to hurt.

Now, in the infantry or combat arms you don't go see a doctor very often, and in my case, unless something was broken I wasn't gonna go see him again. Besides, I'm terrified of needles. So even though my joints are hurting and I'm starting to feel bad, I don't want to go to the doctor. But after a couple of months pass I go back and say, "This is still going on." This time I got, "Well, it's because you're stressed. We think it's stress. Just relax, take your time, you'll get better." A few months more passed and I woke up one morning and I couldn't move from the neck down, and my joints had swollen up like baseballs. I got sent to a civilian hospital in Peterborough.

And there I met a rheumatologist who told me I had a reactive arthritis that was really, really bad. The army said, "OK, see the specialist," and actually I felt a bit better as she treated me. I got put back on active duty and I got sent to Calgary and I took over another platoon out there. Then I had a relapse. I woke up and again the bones were gone. This time my eyes turned red and I lost my right eye. It's now blind.

I went to the doctors in Calgary. They sent me to the eye clinic to see a couple of doctors and they said, "It's no good, we're not going to be able to sort you out." They put me on what they call a medical-patient holding list and sent me back to Peterborough. That's where my house was and Trenton looked after me after that. Then I got a phone call: "In

22 days you're released on a medical 3-A." They came up in a car and made me sign all the papers and I was flung. That was it.

In Calgary someone had slipped a memorandum under my door, written by a Dr. Smith, that said we'd been exposed to bauxite and PCBs and some other stuff in theatre. Armed with the message, I then started to do a bit more digging. I went to DVA for help. They told me to bugger off: "It's not service related." I then started getting phone calls from other soldiers who were sick and, of course, today we know there are over 300 and they're *really* sick.

But I got caught under a clause in the military called the "Universality of a Soldier," which is the army's term for saying if you can't go to a different country right away, you're no longer employable, so we've pushed you out of the service.

Unfortunately that system made up by the Puzzle Palace doesn't work because — and I don't have to say any names — there's generals right now that are on sick leave for a year and a half, while they're releasing soldiers that are privates because they've come forward with a problem and are sick. And they've gone, "Universality of a soldier! You're gone, who's next?"

There's a bunch of guys that are sick, but they've watched what happened with Larry Black, Mike Innes, Phil Tobicoe, and a whole bunch of people, and they get scared to come forward and say, "I'm sick," because they know right away the system's gonna fire them. These guys have families, wives, kids. They can't get fired, they need the money. This is their life. "Who's gonna hire me now that I'm sick? Nobody. Obviously I've got to try and lie about it because the DVA is such a sorry excuse for a government agency, they can't even ..." We'll get there later. But the troops see what happened with me. My joints go. I bleed out of different orifices. This left eye keeps going strange but, thank God, the eye doctor keeps getting it back. If I lose both eyes that's it for me, it's done. I ain't gonna go on after that.

Now this is where I talk about NDHQ and the Department of Veterans Affairs.

I first met Tom Martineau in Cyprus in 1989. I did some time with him in Gagetown and then he was in Bosnia in 1994, just after my tour, and that's where he got shot. So you have a good friend and you read in the paper that somebody's shown up and taken his wheelchair. They were stock-taking and they couldn't figure out who should pay for it. Now it's personal. I'm thinking, if they do that to him, what are they doing to the other guys? I'm near the point where they're going to release me and I'm just getting madder and madder.

I went to Ottawa, and that was the first time I'd seen Tom since I'd heard he got shot. And we met together in a hotel and I'm sure that the rest of the hotel thought we were queer because there was the big hug and we were crying. I mean, it broke my heart. Then we went up to see Art Eggleton, who really cares about the troops and, boy, he's gonna look after us. And again nothing happened.

And it's not just Tom, it's everybody. They treat the lowest private like dirt. But if I was a general I'd have a year and a half off right now, stress leave, and they'd be looking after me. Hopefully what the guys and Tom and I have done over the last six years has changed the system. Unfortunately you can do more good if you're out than you can if you're inside. Because if I was still in, or if Tom was still in, and we did what we did with the press, I'd be able to tell you every brick size in the jail in Edmonton.

And we haven't touched on the Department of Veterans Affairs! I could do a week on those people. I mean, if they were my friends, bury me, because those people are right out to lunch. They don't have a fucking clue what we're going through or what they're doing.

Even though the inquiry is saying, "OK, you guys are sick, we made you sick, you need compensation, you need pensions, they're still saying, "You can't prove it's service related." Now, if I ever snap I'm going to Charlottetown and that's where I'm snappin', right in the middle of the DVA office building. These people should go where we've been, and then I bet you they'd be hanging from the rafters.

When I went to Art Eggleton and I told him what was happening, he said, "That doesn't happen in my department. Can't be true. There's no memorandum." It's on TV. He said that for the record. "Well, then what's this? Here's the memo we're talking about," then you give it to whatever reporter you're talking to. The next morning: "OK, the memo was an accident. The doctor was overzealous. There's only one person sick." It was me.

I wish Canadians would follow the news because you could put the puzzles together. First there was only one guy sick, me. Then there was two, oh, maybe four. Art Eggleton said, "Well, we only know of six and that's it." Six? Then, 310! Who's telling the truth now? Who told the truth then, and why did you try to cover it all up and lie? Why didn't you look after us in the first place? That's all we were asking for. Look after us. I went overseas for you people. So did my guys. Look after them, look after me. It's not too much to ask.

When the press got involved all of a sudden there's an inquiry. You watch Art Eggleton coming in and going, "We know we made 'em sick. By God, we're gonna look after them. We're gonna give them pensions, more money. We're gonna do this and that." Look, don't bullshit me. You're the same people I talked to three years ago. Why couldn't you have done something back then? They should have talked to more sick people. They should have talked to the different doctors that looked after us. They didn't want to do that. But you can't blame the Croatia board of inquiry 'cause none of those people knew what was going on. I had already talked to their bosses. Their bosses knew, not those guys.

Colonel Joe Sharpe said in the inquiry that they treated the equipment better than they treated some of the men. You've got to give the colonel full credit because he told it the way it was. I'd like to talk to Colonel Sharpe in three years. I'd love to be able to ask him, "After you criticized the army that badly, can you honestly tell me they didn't come back after you?" I'd love to hear the answer to that.

It's only since we went public and the press really put the pressure on the Department of National Defence that all this other stuff happened, you know, the stories that I've been poisoned by my own people and that I and other senior NCOs in the company woke up and found bullets on our pillows.[1] These are all things that National Defence has said about us or leaked to the press. The Puzzle Palace couldn't go after me about my career because I had a good one. You couldn't go after me because of the way I'd performed in Yugoslavia 'cause you gave me my write-up. You gave me a Mention in Dispatch, and you gave me a medal.

The RCMP said that we smuggled weapons back into Canada and we're like time bombs. When we snap we're going to go dig them out of our backyards and attack people. Well, we've all got Yugoslav army belts. Oh, heaven forbid! The belt they gave us sucked. This is a normal belt, just wider. It's not a G.I. Joe belt. It's just wide and it works. For some reason this army belt was a big issue with this RCMP guy. I was laughing when I heard him because it's just too funny. Soldiers are the most adaptive people in the world. Your kit works, mine doesn't. I'm buying your kit and I'm using it. Is there anything wrong with that?

So I've been poisoned. We've smuggled weapons. I've got a Yugoslav army belt, and people had Warsaw Pact weapons in our carriers. Yeah, we did, and, yes, we fired them. But I'm in a theatre of war here, and if my people don't know how to use the weapons that are being used against them, I haven't done my job. So we were allowed to fire those Warsaw Pact weapons on ranges so my people were familiar with them. Good idea: next time we confiscate a bunch of them, maybe we'll be able to cock the action back to see if it's loaded or not.

We feel betrayed right now by the system. We never say our regiment 'cause your regiment doesn't betray you. It's the system and it's the people in the Puzzle Palace that betray you. And they did. And they lied to get out of it: "Now that we understand the problem, we're going to fix it." Well, eat my shorts. You knew and you did nothing. Don't piss down my back and tell me it's raining. I love that line.

When the results of the inquiries came out, with people saying all that bad stuff about the army, did you hear anything about poisoning? Or about guns being smuggled? Or anything? No. Because they started to tell the truth. I've said this for four years. They were the easiest people to win against 'cause all I had to do was tell the truth.

When you're 17 and you join the army, you're not grown up. People are gonna teach you. Somebody asked me when I came back if I had any heroes. I want to say Don Cherry so bad 'cause, jeez, I love him on *Hockey Night in Canada*. But military guys? Danny Drew, Jimmy Calvin. I would say any senior NCO that instructed me, or master corporal or corporal when I was younger. It's because of them that my character is the way it is today. Without those guys I probably wouldn't have done what I did.

We all signed contracts and mine was indefinite. And my contract is that I will go places, do horrible things, possibly die, get nightmares, come back. That's my part of the contract. I did that. So did my guys. To the max they did that. The government's job is, if any of us are hurt, sick, broke, shot or whatever, to look after us. If we come back dead, then you look after our families. That's your side of the contract. I think they forgot that.

We have to quit being stupid and tell the Canadian public the truth, tell them what we've been through. Be really honest about our equipment, and yeah, it's going to embarrass somebody, but if you don't embarrass them, they won't do anything. Before we went public I went right through the chain, up, up, up. Somebody's gonna do something. Always having faith. When that faith is broken by them, it's like somebody's torn your heart out and just tossed it away. That was my life. You guys talk about it as a career. That was my soul, my life. I love what I did. I still would love to do it. But the people in Ottawa have taken my heart, thrown it on the ground and jumped on it about eight times. If you are a mother or a wife, you should think twice before you let your people go and do what the government wants them to do. If I had a kid, he wouldn't be joining.

I lost a family over this. And my mom and dad figure I just haven't come back yet.

NOTES

1. The conclusion reached by the military in May 2000, after an RCMP inquiry, was that WO Stopford had been poisoned by some of his soldiers. Although the soldiers were identified, no one faced serious punishment in the case. A special review group was called in June 2000 at the direction of the CDS to investigate alleged misconduct and leadership deficiencies of Canadian Forces members serving in the Canadian Contingent of UNPROFOR in Croatia, Operation Harmony (ROTO 2), from April 1993 to October 1993.

From the Report of the Special Review Committee Operation Harmony, June 16, 2000:

> The issue which has attracted the greatest public attention and concern is the allegation that soldiers serving under former warrant officer Matt Stopford had attempted to poison him. (1) A number of soldiers in his platoon felt that his aggressive leadership style could endanger their safety. It appears that amongst the complaints exchanged by these soldiers concerning their difficult circumstances, there was a great deal of rumour and innuendo about such possible poisoning attempts. However, the report also went further and identified witnesses who stated that they had either attempted or witnessed attempts to administer naphtha, visine and coolant to WO (retired) Stopford by placing these substances in his coffee cup. The report concluded that at least three soldiers had placed such substances in his coffee cup.
>
> No evidence was brought to our attention to suggest that WO (retired) Stopford's current medical problems are related to the ingestion of such substances or, indeed, that he ever did actually ingest such substances. We make this observation in light of the unfortunate difficulties that he encountered in attempting to obtain his full pension upon leaving the service. His apparent statements to the media suggest that he does not believe that soldiers serving under him would commit such acts. There is no evidence to indicate that LCol Calvin, Major Drew, MWO Spellen or WO Stopford were ever made aware of the attempts to harm WO (retired) Stopford through tampering with his coffee.

The Department of National Defence told Matt Stopford that if he didn't like the findings, he could take the department to court. He didn't and he did. He is suing the government for withholding information that prevented him from receiving proper treatment. Meanwhile, his health is getting worse.

TOM HOPPE

Sergeant

Tom Hoppe is one of Canada's most decorated soldiers. If he was in the United States he would have had a ticker-tape parade all the way to the White House. He would have met the president and he probably would have gotten the Congressional Medal of Honor. But he lives in Canada and nobody gives a shit.

Jordie Yeo

I grew up in Vancouver, joined the reserves in 1982 and joined the military in 1984, I guess for the challenge, getting a chance to travel and do something for the country.

In the recruitment process and going into basic training, everything happens so fast. They throw you on a plane, you pull in at 5:00 in the morning in Cornwallis and you wonder where you are. After that you really don't have any time to think, you just go with the flow like everybody else. I guess you wonder if you're gonna make it through because people do wash out. People get sent home for one reason or another, and of course the instructors are always reminding you of that. That is in the back of your mind, so it motivates you to do well.

The training has changed quite a bit over the years. When I went through you started with a large group and you finished with a smaller group. People that really weren't cut out to be in the military left. This would allow you to have people that wanted to be there. They really wanted to be soldiers. That has changed. You always try to do the best with the students you have. You try to develop them and you want everybody to make it, but there are some people that are just not cut out to be soldiers. And I've found that on some of the courses that I've done it's been difficult to let people who shouldn't be there go.

On the other hand, I've had soldiers come through that other people didn't find were good soldiers. Now, I'm not a guru, but with the right kind of motivation, they've improved. It all depends on the supervisor they had before, what their knowledge and background was and how they treated that individual. But I've also had soldiers come into my patrol when I was the last guy that was assessing them and they didn't make it.

I think camaraderie is a very large part of the military and it's very important. Going to the field with the boys, doing the job and then having a beer later on, that's important because it makes a better team environment. I stuck around because I enjoyed the job, but camaraderie was a big part of it.

Yugoslavia

Bosnia was my first tour in 1994. It was a peacekeeping mission, you were going to do convoys and observation posts. You start gearing up for that and you focus on going and doing the job. You're excited. You're wondering what the hostile situation's like, if there is any. It's a challenge, but you're a little bit scared too, and anybody who says they're not scared is lying.

Ray Wlasichuk, our CO, had been there and had a full understanding of what was going on, so a lot of our training was based on his experience and a lot of the feedback that we got was based on his experience. But a woman can tell you everything about what it's like to have a baby, but you still don't know what it feels like. That was the same thing. We were briefed on it, but until you actually get in the country and set foot in there, you don't know what the feeling is.

I was a sergeant in the Strathcona battle group, but I went over as a TOW detachment commander. Now, that's an infantry job, but because of the shortage, the infantry could not man that position, so they retrained us to do it. I was in charge of eight people, including myself. I had a master corporal and I had two vehicles and there were four people in each vehicle. I commanded one and my master corporal commanded the other and we worked as a patrol.

The TOW is an anti-tank missile system that has a range up to three kilometres. The vehicle is an armoured personnel carrier that has been refurbished. Inside, it houses the missiles and it has a turret where the missile system sits. It has a crew of four: a driver, a commander, a gunner and a loader. The missiles always stay the same but we carried a lot of small arms ammunitions and smaller anti-tank weapons, hand-held anti-tank weapons too, depending on the mission. The platform that it sits on and the missile system itself is good. The optics are good and the missile is good. I found the vehicle to be a bit slow for the application. There's a lot of weight in it when it's loaded down. We were hit a few times, but the rounds didn't go through the hull. We were lucky, we didn't hit any mines, but I have seen similar vehicles that have hit mines and they took their toll on the vehicle. The big thing with the vehicle was that it was slow. It was just a bit underpowered. There are better systems on the market, but it worked.

The rules of engagement were, for lack of a better term, confusing. We were put into an area where there was a war still going on. We're in a war zone, and I can put a magazine on my weapon but I can't put a round in my chamber till I go through certain assessments. Is it effective fire or not effective fire? Is effective fire the bullet one metre from you or 10 metres from you? When someone's shooting at you, I don't see how you can decide if that's effective fire or not. They're not just shooting one or two bullets at you. In my experience they were shooting quite a few of them. It's a different case if a sniper shoots at you because by the time you find him, he's gone. But if you're in the position where there's an actual exchange of gunfire, by the time you go through the loading and radioing in, your hands are tied. We did have a rule of engagement called self-defence, and if you felt your life and the lives of your members were threatened, you could use lethal force. I was very supported by my CO and by my squadron commander on the decisions we made.

I consider myself a soldier. Peacekeeping is just an arm of what we do. If there's peace, why are we keeping it? We had a job to do over there, to aid convoys trying to bring food and medical supplies to people who needed it. That's an important role. If you've got to do that in a war zone then you have to do that in a war zone, but don't tie my hands. I'm the guy on the ground and I'm responsible for seven people as well as myself, and I should make the decision to fire or not to fire. That's why I'm being paid as a senior NCO and that's why I was trained as a senior NCO: to make those decisions. I can't have somebody who's miles away, in New York or wherever these decisions come from, telling me that I can't shoot. Part of a senior NCO's job is making those decisions.

We had four patrols on the trip. You'd do 24 hours on this observation post, then come back to camp and you'd be on what they call "quick reaction force." You'd be on standby if there was ever an incident where the CO needed to move a squadron out or you had to go somewhere very quickly. Then you'd stand down for a certain amount of time and move back up. If you were heading out, you'd have your orders the night before and make sure all your vehicles and weapon systems are in order, all the guys are in form.

You get up, have breakfast and get in the vehicle. You leave the gate and drive down or up the hill and you relieve the other patrol and they go back to camp. It becomes a routine, it becomes a job. You always think of what could happen, that's part of your decision-making process, but you just go out and do the job and attack the challenges as they come. If a sniper shoots at you, of course the old adrenaline gets going pretty quick. But once that winds down you carry on. You put it behind you and you move on.

Driving up through the town of Visoko, it was relatively safe. Once you started getting up to the confrontation line, which was on the hill overlooking Zvornik on the Serb side, we had a lot of sniper fire. The Muslims would drink heavily and then they would take potshots at us. The Serbs would take potshots at us, but most of them came from the Muslims and we're on their frontline. I never figured that one out. At nighttime there would be firefights or small arms fire between the Serbs and the Muslims, but that would happen during the day too.

I've got two vehicles to be concerned about. Where's the fire coming from? What kind of fire? What's the threat? How am I going to deal with it? What's my escape route? Where do I fall into the rules of engagement? So there's a lot that's going on at the time and that's where the teamwork comes in because you don't have time to train. You've got to know what you're doing. This whole thing wraps up into one big, neat package where the loyalty, comradeship and the training aspect is so important because if you're not ready for it when you get out to play the game, someone's gonna die. And this is where you need soldiers that are there for that sole reason. We're all expected as soldiers to do our job, we don't question that. We know that being shot at is part of the job and we're not going to bitch and cry about that because that's what we have to do. But we've got to be trained for it and we've got to have the right equipment for it so we can execute that job properly. Otherwise it's like sending a fireman in without any water to fight a fire.

My patrol was called the shit magnet patrol because every time we went somewhere, something happened. I don't know how true that is, but it was the opinion of the battle group at that time. We did have a lot of things that went on, and maybe it was just bad timing or bad luck or good luck, however you want to look at it. There were a number of incidents that happened and we were under fire quite a few times.

July 4, 1994

I received briefings from the squadron commander that the incident rates and exchange in gunfire between the Muslims and Serbs in our area of operation, Romeo One, had increased. Since we were on that position, sitting on top of the hill, we were in the way. My vehicles are right up on the trenches of the Muslims, so if there's any fire coming, regardless if it's aimed at us or not, we're in the way, we're gonna get hit. And our tents were situated behind the trenchline and down, so any rounds that went over the trenchline would be coming over our heads. They don't stop once they hit the trenchline, they keep going. If you're on a playing field in a football game and you're in the middle, between the teams, you're gonna get hit.

Because of this increase of hostilities, we were told that the CO had authorization to fire mortar illuminations from the Canadian camps to try to quiet things down. Half an hour after our troop leader had explained that situation to me, the Muslims and the Serbs started going at each other. The Muslims started it off by firing a hand-held anti-tank weapon into their own town and then blaming it on the Serbs. Then the firefight started. The CO authorized a launch of a mortar illumination, like a big flare, and both sides scurried into their bunkers 'cause usually what follows that is high explosives. But that wasn't the plan. It was just to get them to quiet down, and they did. That was about 10:00 at night.

At about 2:00 in the morning the Serbs started a firefight, and when the Muslims exchanged gunfire, we were sitting there on the hill, counting. One of my jobs was to inform our command post what was happening, how many rounds were being fired, who was doing it and so forth. I counted roughly 700 small arms and machine-gun rounds and two anti-tank rounds that were fired. We got hit by small arms, but nobody got hit by the anti-tank. The Canadians fired 13 rounds of paraflares to try to do the same thing that we had done before, and the jets were called in. They did a flypast and the whole thing quieted down. We went back to camp at 6:00 in the morning and the next patrol came up.

July 14

On the night of July 14, probably about 11:30, we had two vehicles on top of the hill. One was watching two OPs that were in the low ground, manned by Canadians. It was parked right up on the Muslim trenchline. The other vehicle was parked about 50 metres away, overlooking the Muslim trenchline and the Serb side, and in the centre, about 20 metres down behind the trenchline, were our tents, surrounded by sandbags. We have one guy in each vehicle in the turret watching through the therms, and we have a guy walking around. As we're right on the Muslim trenchline, you have Muslims walking back and forth too, so we have to make sure that they don't get into the vehicles. So you have three people up and the other five are sleeping.

All of a sudden this hail of machine-gun fire, must have been about 200 rounds, just came flying over. That lasted for a few minutes and then it quieted down. One vehicle was hit with a few rounds and the individual that was doing the roaming around between the two vehicles almost got hit. He was face down in the dirt.

We'd been in that position long enough to know that things can happen very quickly and things just didn't feel right. So we stood to, and got everybody into the vehicles except for myself, Jason Skilliter and Darren Magas. We were out where our tents and the sandbags were. Master Corporal Ward was in the vehicle over to my left, which was looking into the valley, and he backed it off the hill. The other vehicle had three people in it. We had a can with a headlight in it that we'd shine on the UN flag so they'd know that the position was occupied by UN, and all of a sudden the machine-gun fire started again and the light got hit and got spun around and lit the whole front of the vehicle up. It was getting wracked. It was just a cloud of dust.

The Serbs were firing at us but the Muslims were shooting at us too. This was confirmed by Master Corporal Ward because he's got thermal imaging so he can see at night where it's going on. So we returned fire. I fired maybe four or five rounds. Jason had a small light machine gun and he fired a five-round burst and it quieted down for a few minutes, which gave me a chance to send in a situation report. Then I sent Darren up to get the second vehicle, with three people in it, back off the crest and as soon as he walked around the corner of the sandbags the dirt kicked up right in front of his feet. The Muslims were targeting him, so he came back in. Then the Serbs were shooting. My gunner and the other vehicle that was on top of the hill returned fire, 50, 60 rounds at the Serb, which kept him quiet. Then two anti-tank rounds came in near the second vehicle and Magas decided on his own to try again to get up to it. I went behind the sandbags and started doing my situation reports.

Darren got to the vehicle and got it down to the lower ground. I had my back against the sandbags, talking on the radio. Skilliter ran out toward the vehicle with Darren and the other guys in it, and when he looked around, 200 metres up the Muslim trenchline, there were two Muslims shooting at the sandbags that I had my back toward. When he saw that my life was threatened, he fired a few rounds and he fell short, so he just walked the trace and finished those two guys off, which allowed me — and I didn't know this at that time — to get into the vehicle.

As we were driving off the hill past the one Muslim bunker, we had the turret turned around so my gunner can see as we're leaving and watch our back. This Muslim stood up and started firing, shooting into our back ramp. The vehicle comes equipped with smoke grenade dischargers, which gave us a smokescreen for cover as we left. I could easily have made a decision to have him shot but I didn't see the need for that. This is often referred to as "The Night That Never Happened." I don't really know why.

We went back the next day to pick up our equipment. The sandbags were three-wide. The bullets went through the first two and then halfway through the other one and stopped maybe a couple of inches from my back, but I didn't know that. The only time you hear a bullet is if it's crackin' over your head or hits something hard in front of you.

We had to meet with the Muslim commanders at their position to explain what happened. We did not have confirmation that two of their individuals were killed, so we had gone up there. When you fire 16 rounds out of a light machine gun, you're going to have some trace of it. When you fire six smoke grenade charges, you're going to have some trace of it. I had thrown a trip flare because our standing operating procedure was that any tents or anything that was left behind would be burned so they wouldn't fall into other people's hands. Of course, it didn't work. It was a faulty trip flare. They work 99 percent of the time but that one time, for whatever reason, it didn't. It was gone. Everything was cleaned up.

We had sleeping bags and food and of course we leave everything behind because we're worried about radios and night-vision equipment, that's important to take with us. All of our sleeping bags had been taken out, but the Muslims had piled them all in one tent saying, "We never touched your stuff and we put two military police guys on there to make sure nothing was stolen." And all the food was gone. They tried to say that it wasn't their fault, they would never shoot at us, why would they shoot at us and interfere with our guys? The only thing that they didn't clean up was one of the smoke grenades that had fallen on their trench position. They accused us of that. Why would we do that to them since they were such nice people? And they got this whole political propaganda thing going saying it was the Serbs. That wasn't my concern. My concern was me and my seven guys.

After these incidents at Romeo One they attempted to build another observation post, better fortified, but it finally got closed down and in August we got moved to the edge of Visoko, into a parking lot where we built a big observation post with walls. It was on the edge of a road we called "Sniper Alley." Our job there was basically to observe the hillside. Convoys were using that road quite a bit and civilians were using that road. If the sniper activity increased, we could warn the civilians, because of the optics we had, by hanging a red flag on the road so they could wait by the observation post before entering. If UN convoys or other UN patrols came through that area and they got attacked by snipers, we would be in a position to retaliate or to provide cover. We had one guy at the gate and one guy in the observation post. This is a big compound and we were there for two days at a time. We were always getting rounds coming over the observation posts but they were fairly high.

Across the street we had a cemetery with a wall and about 80 metres down the road was the cemetery gate with big cement posts. I was just coming off a shift one day and I stuck my head around the corner and there were three kids there and they were being pinned down with sniper fire. You could see the rounds kicking up. So I radioed in, and they said, "Wait. We're assessing the situation." And I said, "There's no time to wait."

I said, "OK, I need a driver," and Bombardier McLean, an artillery guy that we had with us, volunteered and jumped into the armoured personnel vehicle and pulled it out of the gate. Fire was coming this way, and I just ran alongside the vehicle and when it got to the cemetery gate he dropped the ramp and I ushered the three kids into the back of the vehicle and we turned around and went back. They were Muslim kids and they were being sniped at by both Serbs and Muslims.

You don't think about it. You just go and do it. Once again it's a team effort. I had my guys backing me up. We all did the job together. But you know, heroics can be in the line of stupidity too. There's a fine line. But we always took it seriously. I always believe you take the worst-case situation and you prepare for that. If it doesn't happen, that's fine, that's great. But if it does happen you're ready for it. We're in a war zone. We're here. This is not a game, this is not an exercise, this is the real thing. And that's the way we viewed it within our patrol. I had excellent guys and because of their training and their professionalism, we were able to get out of these situations.

Home

I'm not one that likes the limelight. My guys should have those medals on their chests too. If I'm the most decorated guy since Korea, so I've been told, what about the guys who aren't as recognized, who did the job? How are they being recognized? They aren't. If you don't know my actions and I'm well publicized, then you don't know the actions of the guys behind me who got me those medals.

Nobody cares. It's just another day. I don't expect to have a ticker-tape parade but a call from my own unit saying congratulations would be nice. I haven't got one letter from the CDS or from the minister. I've received it from certain individuals, but from the military as a whole or the government as a whole, no. I don't care if I get a letter from the prime minister because I've got one from Prince Charles, and that's fine, but the recognition I want is from my military family. I know that it's my job as a soldier to do the work that I did over there, and I don't question that. I don't bitch about it. I did it. But at the same time, if I'm willing to do that for you, with no questions asked, the least you can do is recognize my efforts. Or if I get hurt, look after me.

When you come into the military you're trained to think in a certain way. You're separated from civilian life. I think a lot of people in the military don't realize that you need to be deprogrammed when you re-enter civilian life. You need to be retrained when you get back. It's a simple thing.

We never got a proper debriefing when we got home. There's still no proper debriefing in the military. They should talk about what combat stress is, what one may go through and what one may feel, which is all normal. It's a normal reaction to an abnormal situation. You start feeling withdrawn, you start having mood swings. You're agitated, you don't sleep well, and anxiety is higher. You feel almost like you're having a bad attitude toward the military.

There are a number of things that contribute to it, and I learned this through reading about it and talking about it and going through some therapy myself. The big thing is seeing little kids that are helpless. If you're a person that by nature wants to help people, it's hard because you can't fix it.

Somebody should have told me and my guys that this is what you're going to feel, or this is what you may go through, and not five minutes before we get on the plane.

But there's a lot more to it than just seeing the horrors that were there. It's the disillusion at not getting the recognition. No recognition from the Canadian government, no recognition from the military, no recognition from the Canadian public on the job that we did over there. Why did we do what we did? Why did I put my life on the line?

There are programs that are available out there. We set one up in a place that I was posted to. We set up a debriefing program for the people coming back from an operation. We had permission to use an outside person for that. This program was a mixture of the South African and Israeli models and it worked quite well. We briefed the leaders on what combat stress is, what to look for, some of the feelings an individual might have, where the support groups are, where the help is, how to deal with your family again. And then they brought the troops in and you sat down with your troops and you went through a questionnaire and you talked about it and you left it at that.

A lot of guys don't come forward because they think they're going crazy — "I shouldn't be feeling this" — when it's all perfectly normal. It's just learning how to live in society again, to live a normal life. Canadian society didn't change, we did. We left Canada and went over there, and then we came back and now we have to adapt. You've got to work on these issues, but if you don't know what the issues are, then how can you address them? "My family's breaking up and I'm starting to drink, but I'm not gonna talk to anybody 'cause I'm in a green uniform and I shouldn't feel this way, I shouldn't have emotions." I went through that. It's quite normal. No, you're not crazy. Yes, you're in a uniform but you're not a robot. You do have feelings.

And the leadership itself has to be informed. It boils down to leadership. Know your men and promote their welfare. As a leader you have to understand what stress is about so when one of your soldiers has it, you know how to deal with it. They're working on it. They are trying to make efforts to change it but they still have a ways to go. Having gone through the last four years looking at this and seeing what other countries offer, they should have had something in place for eight weeks after you come back, no questions asked, doesn't matter what's going on, the unit goes through a proper debriefing. It would save them soldiers in the long run because a lot of good ones have left the military.

As soldiers we are expected to do a job and we don't question that. We understand that there's danger attached to that. There's time away from our family. Our family understands that we may get hurt. We may even lose our life. We understand that. I don't think any soldier would question that. At the same time I expect that same dedication from the military. When someone gets injured, physically or mentally, they're taken care of and their family's taken care of. They're retrained, their paperwork's all in order and they walk out the gate. It's not a hard solution, it's a simple solution. And that's all a guy expects. He will do anything for you if he knows that he's being supported.

I'm accountable on the line. If I don't do my job and somebody gets killed, I'm accountable for that. Well, somebody at home better be accountable too.

Loyalty goes up and down. I'm responsible for my men, have loyalty to them, but I have loyalty to my superiors and I would expect that my superiors have loyalty to me too. We look out for each other. I know it's not fair to paint everybody with the same brush because there are good leaders in the military, but I've been let down when it comes to the loyalty side by some individuals. Because there was no recognition from my own military for the decorations that I have, you don't know the seven guys behind me that got me those decorations. The recognition side of it is very important because in a sense it ties into the loyalty.

In the last four years I've tried to improve the way they deal with debriefings for stress and to advocate change to make it better for the next guy coming up. If there's a problem, there should be a solution. That's part of leadership, but there's a connection missing. And that's in Ottawa, in NDHQ.

I may be challenged on that, but I'm the guy that's gone through it. I'm the guy that works with people that are going through it, so I understand it. If we have problems then let's work on them and try to put it back together again.

But it's hard when people don't listen, and even though I was supported by certain individuals who were on tours, other people weren't that interested in my efforts. I don't know if they let me down because they didn't understand what I was going through. I'm not in the minds of the people who are up in HQ. But what I do know is the soldier on the ground, and there's a very large gap between Ottawa and the guy on the ground.

There's always that issue about equipment and money and who makes those decisions. Well, I'm the end user and I want something that's going to work. We went over there and we didn't even have flak vests. We used flak vests from previous tours. We used helmets from previous tours. We'd get on the truck and there would be the helmet and the flak vest from the last tour and some of these were falling apart. This is not a million-dollar tank. This is a personal helmet! And that says to me that you're not looking out for my welfare. That's what it says to me. You're not looking out for my welfare and you're not looking out for the men's welfare. Now the helmet issue has been addressed and the flak vest issue has been addressed. But in 1994, when we went over there, that was not the case.

The military's been my family for a number of years and I'm pretty disillusioned with it. It's a family and it's like a dad kicking you out or disowning you. It's hard to take. The only support that I had was myself and a few friends in the military. Individuals, not the system, and it's made me a stronger person because I had to do it on my own. Of course, because of that, I no longer will be with the military.

Remembrance Day to me has always been very important but it's changed because of what I've seen and what I've gone through. A lot of guys gave their lives, and I'm not on the same level as a Second World War veteran, but I understand now some of the personal loss. When you think "Second World War," it's a bigger, bigger picture, a bigger deal, and maybe we didn't come home with a conclusion, but our regiment did a good job over there and we achieved a lot.

Defence Minister Eggleton, in response to a question in the House of Commons, asked, "When was the last time that Canadians were fighting on the ground?" Well, I would have to say, in my experience, July 4, 1994, July 14, 1994, August 31, 1994. And that's just me and my guys. There are a lot more dates than that.

RAY WLASICHUK
Colonel

Ray's the smartest man I have ever met in the military. He's one of those pied pipers. You'll only see a few of them in your whole career and you'd follow them off the end of the earth.

Tom Martineau

As a teenager growing up on the Prairies, I knew there was a much bigger world out there and the army was one way that I could see some of it. It was an adventure. I joined as a private, as a reservist, and spent two years with the militia in Winnipeg. I joined the regular force, still in the rank of private, and carried on up to the rank of corporal. For a number of reasons, and with a lot of support and encouragement, I sought to become an officer. What the army gave me was an opportunity to take responsibility and to have accountability for your actions.

Lord Strathcona's Horse is one of Canada's oldest cavalry regiments. It's just celebrated its 100th year since its deployment to fight in the South African war in 1900. It has been involved in both world wars, the Korean conflict and throughout all of the UN operations.

I've been in the military now for 27 years and I'm a veteran of two tours in Bosnia. I was a monitor on my first tour in 1992–1993 along the Adriatic coast, Montenegro and then in northern and central Bosnia. It was the middle of a war, there was a lot of fighting going on. There was political confusion. There were criminal elements involved and you literally had to fight to stay alive.

It was a humanitarian-based mission, so I was heavily involved with people and the victims of the war. I was living in the towns and villages and operating in those areas at the same time that the atrocity of ethnic cleansing was going on. Being moved out of a place that would get shelled or burned and then moved on to somewhere else was a very stressful way to live. At night you had to go back and fend for yourself and get enough rest to relieve the stress that you'd built up in a day so you could come back strong enough to continue to function week after week, month after month.

In a monitor-type mission, an unarmed mission, all of the tools that you have been given in terms of how you can stay alive and still do your job are for the most part denied to you. I was walking around in a white uniform in the middle of a war for six months. You fine-tune your survival skills and take no chances, no particular risks. You can't even defend your interpreter, so you have to be clever and watch out for yourself. This teaches you to be far more diplomatic than you would be on a heavily armed mission.

I was very thankful for that experience with the European Community because, just one year later, it helped me train 850 other soldiers to take back with me.

Yugoslavia

We deployed the Strathcona battle group into the same area that I had been working in, so it was familiar country to me. I recall the feeling I had when I was first driving back into central Bosnia for my tour as commanding officer with UNPROFOR. There was a coldness that just went down my spine when I went through some of the villages that I had been in before, and found them all but destroyed, with nobody around. There were so many lingering questions I had about the welfare of those people we had put our lives on the line for.

We had an impressive fleet of some 232 vehicles, all in various states of repair, or in some cases disrepair, because of the heavy use that the vehicles had undergone. We'd even taken over some of the vehicles that were deployed in Somalia. They'd come straight off the ship from Somalia and we used them after painting them white. We had long-range weapons, stand-off systems, direct-fire systems, and each and every one of the soldiers was skilled and armed.

Because we had fairly heavy guns on the vehicles, and based on the rules of engagement, we needed a very accurate system that would have minimum collateral damage. But our weapon system was so inaccurate in the way that it fired, and because most of our deployments were inside small cities, towns or villages, it was seldom, if ever, employed. Now things are better. We've got a thermal-imaging system that allows us to operate at night, better communications and a very accurate weapon system. There were very few of these in place for our tour in 1994, so we had to make allowances. We knew the equipment that we had and what its limitations were and we made up for those limitations.

We were concerned about light armour in some of our vehicles, so we covered that by building bunker systems or protected areas to deploy them in, making use of man-made structures or natural obstacles. We had restrictions on the amount of work we could do at night, so we'd work as much as possible during daylight so we wouldn't be caught in a situation where that limitation affected us.

We would have to go back to Korea to look for some sort of parallel to what we were faced with. Three sides fighting, each with different causes and strategic intentions, with thousands and tens of thousands of UN peacekeepers playing a significant part. We were not necessarily trying to stop them from fighting — there was no agreement to do that, they were in a war — but we were trying to prevent untoward damage to the civilian population, the infrastructure and the industrial base, and to address humanitarian needs.

So we were *not* trying to stop the fighting that was going on. There was no political agreement to allow that to happen. It was still an open agenda and there were strategic goals that were being pursued by the warring parties. We had to learn where we could function and do an effective job and where we could not. Clearly getting in between two clashing tank forces or infantry forces wasn't the place to be, nor would it do any good. We'd get forced into becoming party to one side or the other and we didn't allow that to happen.

We were deployed on all three sides. The Canadians were the only UN battalion group in 1994 that had troops deployed on the Serb side, the Croatian side and the Muslim side. It was my initiative to do that because of the need for impartiality and, despite a lot of reservations on the part of some of the UN people that were involved, it actually worked out quite successfully. We managed to make major strides in our mission through a balanced relationship. It brought us closer to the conflict, though, and there was a risk in doing this. We ended up getting in between two or three parties at a time with Canadians on one side, Canadians on another and the warring factions just continuing their battles.

We were still in Visoko sorting out all our equipment and preparing to be deployed out in the area. There was a young private in the Princess Patricia's Canadian Light Infantry that was assigned to us, and he was working on an observation post that was a security post for the camp. A drunk local soldier from the Bosnian army walked by, had his machine gun and fired it off into the air. Not specifically at the observation post, but in the area. The response from the Canadian, who was taught only to use deadly force where it's necessary, resulted in the private taking aim six inches above the fellow that was staggering around and putting a bullet just over his head. He had every right in the world to kill him and I commended him for his action to, first, return fire, but, second, to avoid an unnecessary death. If you can't justify the death of one of the belligerents, you can expect that a brother, an uncle or a grandfather is going to come back and return the same to you the next day.

This went on every single day in our particular area. We had 800 square kilometres, and we averaged between 60 to 120 firing incidents per day and we never reported it if it was only small arms. We only reported .50-calibre or heavy-calibre weapons and greater. Engagements of heavy-calibre weapons, mortar fire, tank fire were a daily occurrence for almost every day of the 180 days we were there.

Two buses a week were allowed out of Sarajevo. We'd do all the escorts for those very volatile missions. People were killed on the buses from sniper fire. We'd do prisoner exchanges, body exchanges at the end of some of the battles, reconnaissance. We were a force that could move into an area and come back with information, so we'd go into some of the remote villages in the mountains and find out the state of the people, if their roads were mined, if they had any water. Then we could come back and organize aid.

We had managed to force the fight out of the towns and the villages and into the open fields. The three parties could never agree to do that, but it happened through personal influence with their commanders. They realized the benefits they would get and some of the resources that I could make available to them if they did co-operate. This was peacemaking to the limit that we could, with the limited mandate that we had. It was in the broadest of terms and it was entirely open to interpretation.

As our mandate was to promote the cessation of hostilities, we worked very hard to stabilize the area that we were in. One way to do that was to try and influence the humanitarian aid agencies to deploy with us under our protection. We had found that if we could get a limited water supply working in a town, if we could clear the mines off the roads that people were using, if we could influence the mayor of the town to have the confidence to go into his office, bring in his staff and work under a more secure environment, it paid off because the town now liked us.

They had already been into their war for almost two years, and they would do things now to protect us because we were doing something for them. Our soldiers were able to take great initiatives in schemes that they would develop. They'd say, "OK, I can help. I can help a hospital over here on the other side, and that will result in them letting me fix up a school someplace else." Or they would open up an evacuation route for refugees in return for something that would be done on a reciprocal basis with the other side. It was very clear that the humanitarian aid agencies aren't equipped to go out and take great risks sending doctors, truck drivers, ambulance services, disability services into some town that's in the middle of engagement. What the regiment is able to do is move in, provide that leadership to co-ordinate things between the two. They all hate each other and nobody can talk and make arrangements except through you, and we did this day to day, to the point where we had almost everything deployed in the regiment that was possible.

We had a system of rotating troops through areas so that they had a chance to recover, rest and relieve some of the stress that had built up. We also built in opportunities for our soldiers to deploy into other areas, to conduct unique humanitarian-type missions, to get personally involved, at all rank levels, in some project. It could be the care of some old man someplace who never gets seen by any of the aid agencies, or the convoys that we used to run into Sarajevo that we were never asked to run. When the soldiers went on those, they went out, brought all that good into the city and pulled out of there with no casualties, safe, then they had a feeling of mission success. For the six months that we were doing this, we had anywhere from 12 to 18 operations a day. That personal satisfaction motivates those same soldiers to go home and — when they're asked, "Are you ready to go a second time?" — to come back.

October 3, 1994

One night, at the beginning of October, I was writing to a friend about what we'd gone through and the good things that had happened to us. I had just finished writing "... and I'm very thankful that we have had no serious casualties," when I was disturbed by my operations officer, who said something urgent was going on.

I went into the operations centre and, sure enough, almost at the time that I was writing the letter Warrant Officer Tom Martineau, who was working in Romeo One with Recce squadron, had been shot by a sniper. When I received the report from my staff that we had a soldier hurt, I had no idea that it was Tom 'cause you wouldn't transmit that sort of open communication — it might be picked up by others. We had to quickly establish a way to get him safely back across an active confrontation line at night, and the UN does very few operations at night. They're difficult to co-ordinate and it's a much higher-risk operation. It all makes sense when you see it in the daytime, but when this happened it was already dark. We were into fall. It was very hard to get him back because a vehicle just can't go roaming around at night without the two sides knowing what's going on.

To understand just how close you are to the fighting that's going on, these aren't battles in the towns and villages that are fought using binoculars. Our soldiers were right on the frontlines. Warrant Officer Martineau couldn't have been any more than 20 metres from a major

Serb bunker system and entrenchment line. It was in a critical route and area directly across from the Muslims, with the Canadians all mixed in between. It's confusing.

There was an OP on top of our building that overlooked the Serb side and the Muslim side, and when I'd given my direction about what had to be done and put the surgical team on standby, I went up to the roof. By this time we'd received a coded message that told us who it was, that it was Warrant Officer Tom Martineau.

I had known Warrant Officer Martineau in a number of ranks and positions over a long period of time. We'd been friends and comrades. We were two soldiers that had served together and had a close understanding and respect for each other. I watched with dread at the slowness of how things were going. I could see the blinking blue light of the European-style ambulance going up to the position. And then the agonizing wait, watching the ambulance come back slowly, returning over the line. There was still some firing going on but nothing that impeded their progress. I watched the light slowly approaching our camp, and when the armoured ambulance arrived I helped unload him and went into the field surgical team. They were trying to determine what was wrong with him because there was a hole in him but there was no exit hole, and they weren't sure what they were dealing with. Warrant Officer Martineau, who was conscious at this time, was in agonizing pain.

I was an observer, not to the operation but to the process, because I had other responsibilities that I had to tend to as a consequence of this, but I checked on him routinely. During my checks down with the surgical team I found our medical surgeon, a very qualified, very good surgeon, referring to his manuals outside of the operating room because he was running into so many new and unfamiliar types of injuries, which were all internal. I credit him and his team for having saved Warrant Officer Martineau's life that particular night.

I had a number of limited options that I could take. I could retaliate, return fire, but I wouldn't be sure if that would be effective or not. I could unleash a considerable amount of lethal force if it was necessary. But was I making judgments based on anger over the incident and was it actually rational and could the situation be controlled? I took the more controlled approach, which was dealing with both the Serbian and

Bosnian army side and taking the issue up with their commanders, their mayors, their local people of influence, just to make sure that they knew that I had a soldier who was precariously injured and that we wouldn't take any more of it.

We did investigate the shooting to determine where it came from. It came from the Bosnian army side, and we identified the exact trench-line and everything else that had to be done. I didn't receive much support at the UN to actually do something about it.

It's the luck of war. You don't know if that act of sniping was committed when one of the belligerents was under the influence of alcohol, or if he was under orders and it was just a one-off event.

There's not that much a commanding officer can do to correct the outcome for a seriously injured soldier, other than what I owed to his family for an explanation of what had happened and to ensure that he had the best support from us. But I did find it personally frustrating that, even though we knew who did it, where it came from, and we were going to our government saying, "Here's what has happened," we weren't getting any results. There was still the same amount of firing going on in the same areas, with us indiscriminately being targeted.

I took my frustration out on paper and sent a letter to my member of Parliament in Calgary, telling him how many times we'd been attacked by Muslim forces and questioning whether or not the role that we were being asked to play was appreciated by Canadians at home and whether there was a political awareness of the situation over there, the way it was on the ground. I gave him the background, that this was the 13th Canadian soldier that had been shot by the Bosnian army, the 13th attack on our battle group, and that this was from the same side that we were actually there to help.

I'd heard about Canada initiating a $10-million grant to the Bosnian government to help out their efforts, and I made the point that, as this was being done at the time that they were shooting our soldiers, I found it very perplexing. I made the suggestion that something should be done about it and he was good enough in his response to say that he understood and he did take it to Ottawa. He raised the issue in the House of

Commons. It was recorded and answered and he was good enough to send me a copy over to Bosnia, just to say, "Look, I'm doing what I can." I felt some relief, but I don't know if it ever satisfied the soldiers who were really close to Tom.

He was a tremendous soldier. He was one of the fittest soldiers that we had in the regiment. Lively, a great sense of humour. When we were out in the field and it was cold and rainy, no matter what we were doing, he could always get a laugh and a chuckle out of people because of the force of his great character. He was well liked by his regiment. He was respected and he took good care of his men.

My concern was that, because of the anger developing in the men, they might take the situation into their own hands, which would have made the situation that much worse and that much more dangerous for them. But they were already experienced soldiers by that point. They were five months into their tour, they had another month left to go. They realized that there was some target out there, somewhere in the dark, at a long range, and if they were just to take it on their own, or do something to relieve that frustration, it would result in a far, far worse situation. So they had to be patient and have confidence that we would do everything that we could.

Tom'll be hurting for the rest of his life. But he's been strong, as I would expect any soldier to be, and it's in all of our hands, my hands, to be responsible for his support. The individual responsibility to the soldiers and their families that get hurt is part of the role of a commanding officer and something that never leaves you.

In areas that were tense, it was difficult for the soldiers to rationalize the actions that they had open to them. It was frustrating because we weren't entitled to use the rules that we had available to us to protect civilians. It was only our own soldiers, our own property. But morally we had an obligation to do something. We found ways, through trench systems and other ways, to get people moving in these dangerous areas a little more safely. But there was frustration: "Why can't I just put my marker on that particular target and blow it up?" That's what a soldier's trained to do. A soldier has got that response, that he returns fire in a war situation without question, and he does it immediately. If he realizes he can't handle it then it eventually works its way up to my level.

Most of the time the soldiers took action which was correct and appropriate and were commended for it after.

On the edge of town there's a famous stretch of road which was covered by Bosnian army fire and by Serb forces in a number of dominating areas. It was a major civilian traffic route between a Croatian-held area, a place called Kiseljak, and the town that we were in, which was Visoko. That road was essential, but heavy disruptions could happen when they would engage the convoys using that route or engage civilian refugees using that route. This was the place where Corporal Gunther from the Van Doos had been killed a year and a half before. We deployed into that area and we set up our own antisniper operations, which had a dramatic effect on reducing the number of casualties, but it didn't prevent someone on one side or the other taking a few shots at innocent civilians just as sport.

I let it be known to both sides that our responsibility was for the protection of the convoy routes and if it was civilians that were walking on that convoy route, then they would be entitled to our protection too. I went back to the Serb side, where we believed that the fire was coming from, and explained that they were receiving protection on another route that was important to them. At the same time they're attacking a route that was under our control on the other side. I said, "You can't have it both ways." We eventually came to an agreement and the amount of sniping dramatically decreased.

Tom Hoppe was commanding a missile detachment and was in a two-car position covering the high ground where the Serb positions were. There was a cemetery in behind the position with a number of stones and a little mortuary and a funeral home, which was a very busy place. Some children were walking along the road and started playing in between the cemetery stones. When the firing began Sergeant Hoppe and his crew started to receive fire and see fire going over their heads in toward where the children were.

With no hesitation, he took direct action. He got one armoured vehicle, didn't take the time to get into it himself, deployed it across the road, running beside it as the bullets were following him and the children. He got them loaded safely into the back of the armoured carrier and brought those children to safety at his own peril. There's no question that he saved the lives of the three of them. As a result of his actions on that afternoon, Sergeant Hoppe was awarded the Medal of Bravery.

Before that incident Tom had been at an OP where the situation was becoming worse. There was a high level of violence and a lot of confusion at night. They were receiving a tremendous amount of fire, and it became clear to me that it was necessary to withdraw him from that area for the safety of his patrol. They had done the best they could to maintain their position and they maintained it as long as they were ordered to. They were exposed and something had to be done.

The withdrawal out of that position proved to be most perilous. As they were starting to pull out, they came under sustained machine-gun fire from a nearby Bosnian army trench. One of Sergeant Hoppe's crewmen used his machine gun and assaulted the bunker and essentially saved all of their lives. I was particularly proud of them because they reacted with all the war-fighting skills that we have trained them to use. That's an important factor in understanding why peacekeepers have to be trained as soldiers.

Sergeant Hoppe took control of the situation and brought them down a slope into the town before the Bosnian army forces could react. Had they realized at that point — they probably had already been drinking — that some of their own had lost their lives at the hands of Canadians in proper return of their fire, there could have been some retaliation, so the call was made to pull out. He got things moving quickly and I credit him for saving the lives of that entire patrol.

He's our highest decorated soldier since the Korean War. *Maclean's* included him in the "Top 10 Canadians," and I was honoured to see his name again in the *National Post*'s "Top 20 Canadians of the Century," on the list with the likes of General Currie. But I found there was very little recognition from within the Canadian Forces itself. The soldiers actually coined the nickname "The Fire and Forget Battle Group."

The most frightening personal experience that I had in Bosnia, and one that helped make me that much stronger for others who were to follow, was being pinned down on the edge of a minefield, with a Croatian tank force coming in to close in on a small city called Gornji Vakuf at a time that the Bosnian army was holding the line there. It was, for a moment, terrifying.

As we were moving through, our vehicle would raise a little bit of dust and people would come running out of their homes, trying to get to their well for water using our dust for cover, and you'd see them being shot as they were doing that. We were trying to get through on the breach of this road, which was an authorized route for us to go through. It had been mined and a soldier was being attacked for trying to open it up for us, and a number of shell and tank rounds were going off around us. One hit immediately to my rear on the outside of the vehicle, but there was a house there, so I had partial cover from the firing. The next moment half of it was gone. I had to maintain the appearance that things were going to be OK because I had a young driver with me. I also had concerns for the safety of the party that I was escorting. Before long we got some help from the British. I felt like I had aged a little bit just based on one incident. It taught me just how much adrenaline you can build up in a series of terrifying little events. I still remember all the details. I can smell smoke. I can smell the burning that was coming off the vehicles. I hear things. It's almost like a movie that keeps running over and over in your mind.

But on the positive side, it shows what you can do under fire. That you can still react and maintain control. When you live with violence going on around you, you take action. We would protect ourselves by putting ourselves into armoured vehicles. We would improve our procedures, our drills, our security routines. You can overcome the ever-present danger and carry on and — at considerable risk — do your job, which is what Canadians expect of their soldiers.

We had a visit from the Treasury Board, trying to justify why we received such a high rate of risk pay. I don't believe the gentleman who came over was looking to take something away from the soldiers. He really did want to be informed and wanted to see for himself so that he could speak in the same language the soldiers did to the people where he worked.

As we were going into the Serbian city of Ilijas, which was just outside the perimeter of our camp, the town came under shellfire and we pulled over for a few seconds until it had subsided. It wasn't heavy shelling, six or seven rounds, and we were due to see the military mayor of the town of Ilijas. We parked in an apartment block complex. Four children had been out playing and had just been killed there. People were shattered, crying, and there was a lot of noise. The bodies had been removed but there was glass and things were still smoking. To get to where we were going, we had to walk across the area where their blood was, where they had lain on the ground. I believe he reported back about the conditions that we were under.

The Media

It was very important for the soldiers to be recognized for the work that was done. It was extremely difficult, because of the conflict in the area, to get much media coverage.

I didn't feel that there was much being covered nationally or that there was a good understanding of what we were doing. One way that I knew I could make an impact and avoid any sort of screens or filters was by establishing a good relationship with our local media from the area in Canada where our regiment was garrisoned. That resulted in human interest stories, where soldiers were receiving newspapers or notes from their wives or families saying, "I read about what the unit did today. Great work, keep it up." That was probably the most important thing, that local recognition. It was one way to not have to go through a whole system where they filter out your emotions and your words and any of the bad experiences. It was also necessary just to stick to your guns. If you believed there was a message to get out, you'd find a way of getting those words to the public. But, I mean, we were all under gag orders. That wasn't going to help our cause any.

In some cases we make it very difficult for the media to get the information. Perhaps we live with suspicions of what their motives are. In my own experience, where media people were trusted, shown what was going on with complete honesty, they responded very well, and a lot of soldiers' families back here in Canada got to learn, through the media, some of the things that their sons and daughters were doing.

I believe we were winning the battle with the media because we brought them in as part of our team. We brought the media into our camps. We lived with them. We put them through the same risks that we had with our soldiers in a realistic environment where they could report and see what was happening. There are thousands of good stories that have come out of all of these operations in the last few years.

Home

It's normal for the commanding officers of the battalions who are returning to Canada after six months of operations to report to the headquarters in Ottawa and provide a report, just to give a firsthand view to senior decision makers. There were three of us that had gone in at the same time because there were three units coming out of Bosnia on the same tour. We had all reported in and I was advised that we were going to have approximately 30 minutes each, including questions. We quickly found out that we were limited, in total, to one 30-minute time period. They couldn't spare the time for us. I never had a chance to pass on my concerns about weapon systems, my concerns about the acts of the Bosnian government or the Bosnian army, in particular, or to try, along with other battalion commanders, to influence how our troops are deployed or how they're supported.

I put a lot of work and effort into making sure all of our lessons could be handed to our successors in that mission area. That, I think, was accomplished successfully and acknowledged by the regiment that had taken over. There were so many things that were going on in that period of the 1990s that maybe the resources just weren't there for two or three different missions at the same time. The lessons learned came out slowly over the years as we wrote and encouraged other people to write and make changes to our doctrine that would allow for that knowledge to become part of routine procedures.

It's always been frustrating for me because it was hard to get people to understand and realize the importance of the new knowledge that we had gained in this post–cold war type of peacekeeping mission. I had visions that many of the people I was briefing were thinking of far different situations, like Cyprus.

I never really had time to get some help or try to resolve in my mind what the impact of that first mission had done to me, as I quickly turned around and took over another battle group. I think all soldiers, or all good soldiers, like to have an image of themselves as energetic, robust, hardened — a soldier who can go anywhere and do anything. I found that, once you started going everywhere and doing anything, the stress levels increased to a point where they became too difficult to deal with and symptoms started to occur.

I've learned that the battle to help myself on this was too big for me to do personally and I'm still, years later, dealing with some of the issues. I'm very thankful to a supportive mental health care system within the Armed Forces that's now helping people like me. I'm also getting help from some very good friends like Warrant Officer Martineau and Sergeant Hoppe. We all support each other. Our families have been able to support us and our regimental families have been able to support us.

I guess I found out I'm just human. I'm not some kind of hero superman that's invincible. They're very, very personal emotions that come out and take years to resolve. I found it very difficult to deal with the continuous, cumulative stresses that had built up over the years. When you return home, when you finally feel safe, where you can take the time to think and gather up your experiences in your mind, post-traumatic stress starts to open up into new and sometimes scary areas. We've been helped through it by the knowledge that it's a natural reaction to an unnatural situation that we were in. It takes a great deal of personal effort to work out some very difficult problems, the flashbacks, or a feeling, or a smell that you don't wish to smell again.

It's very difficult to have people understand exactly what we have gone through and I don't expect them to understand. But when we're relating those stories either to ourselves or close family, the strong feelings and the strong sensations that you have out of those experiences seem to increase in intensity. I didn't have time back then to become highly emotional about any of the situations that I had to deal with, and some of them were very miserable. But I did have to take the time to think about them when I got home, and I actually said that I wasn't going back again. And that's where my struggle still lies, getting that care so I can return to what I was before.

Soldiers have impressions of how they appear to others, and they'd be described as physically fit, robust, having great levels of endurance, someone who can be counted upon in any time and in any situation. What I learned was that it certainly wasn't true of me. I have been able to perform to the level that was expected and beyond for a considerable amount of time, but I'm not the same soldier. I don't feel I would ever have the personal strength to go back and do some of the things again that I did in Bosnia. It would be impossible, and I think would endanger myself as well as endangering others.

The last decade has seen Canadians deployed on more missions than ever before. They vary in intensity or violence and the risk that goes with each one. We've gone off to war, but we had forgotten what that was like, except for training exercises somewhere in Germany or in the training areas of Alberta. I above anybody should have known everything I needed to know about post-traumatic stress disorder, and how a human being reacts to the situations we were faced with. We should have had critical, instant stress debriefings but we just didn't have that basic knowledge. It was available in psychiatric journals but it wasn't something that the military focused on. What we have now, within our leadership and at all rank levels, are people with experience, and we're very aware of it now.

People like Warrant Officer Martineau and Sergeant Hoppe have done a lot to change the system, and there are other caring people out there. I think we'll find, as time goes on, more understanding about what the nature of our business is, something which we knew very well at the end of the wars we've been involved in, but have forgotten. I feel confident that the system is getting better and that a lot has been done to address the care of our wounded, the care of our soldiers. There is much more awareness than at the time when I went through the experience.

Leadership

I learned through my own experience and self-education that leadership is the ability to take care of your soldiers. For each and every one of them, at all rank levels, from my level down and up, they must be confident that their leaders are going to take care of them, whatever perils that we put them into. I've lived by that. I believe the calibre of leadership is very good right now because of the amount of experience we've gained on actual operations that involved such an intensity of conflict. It has made better men, it has made better leaders and we're benefiting from that now. We have a core of highly experienced people now that will carry on.

But soldiers need to feel a sense of accomplishment. If they're going to take those risks, and take themselves away from their families, they have to understand that it's for some greater good. It's got nothing to do with pay or anything like that. It's personal satisfaction that their risks were worthwhile. And everyone who was going over there was putting their life on the line.

The responsibility to pass on a lot of what happened and what was learned is the duty of soldiers and leaders who have gone through it, and we've tried to encourage them not to be afraid to go out and talk about their experiences and what they've done. But it is very hard, you know. Our families still can't really understand what it was like over there.

Canadians need to learn again what it is to have a commitment to our military. I've spent a lot of time lecturing to different groups and organizations about the experiences that we had and the difference between our good life here in Canada and what was going on over there. These were often very difficult presentations to do emotionally, but I think they had a tremendous impact. People's reactions were almost disbelief that such a thing could be going on. I think that's due to a lack of experience, thank God, with war here in Canada. Our battlefields have been removed by time and are much more distant.

TOM MARTINEAU
Warrant Officer

In Cyprus we had an old warrant who was past his prime. It was New Year's Eve and the warrant went off to party and told us that all the troops had to stay inside, just in case something happened. Tom and I got all dressed up and we snuck anybody who wasn't on guard duty that night or on the OPs through the green zone into the city, and we went off and had a good time and came back before the warrant found out. We were pretty near the same kind of breed.

Matt Stopford

As a young kid I was always in trouble with the law and I was headed nowhere real quick. I sat down one day and I discussed things with my mom, and we came to a decision that it might be a good idea if I joined the Canadian Armed Forces. I went down to the recruiting station in Hamilton, Ontario, wrote the tests, and went off for my basic training in Cornwallis, Nova Scotia, the 15th of September, 1977.

When I first joined it was a little bit of a culture shock. I mean, I had no discipline in my life. I was in a family with three other kids, two brothers and my sister, and then my mom remarried, and we brought in a stepfather, stepsister and a stepbrother, so we had a bit of a clan there. There was some discipline from my stepfather before I joined up, but once I joined the military, there was a lot more discipline than I ever expected. At first I didn't like it. There's a lot of people screaming and yelling at you, telling you what to do, what time to get up at, what time to eat, wait in line for this, wait in line for that. That was difficult to accept because I was a bit of a renegade, a rebellious child. But after a certain point in basic training I got over the hump, and I realized that I was capable of doing this.

Out of my military experience I learned more about me than I ever would have had I not joined the Canadian Armed Forces: how strong I was physically and mentally, how far I could go, what my weaknesses were. That's what I liked the best about the military. Obviously they saw something good in me. I was successful in basic training and I went to the unit, January 2, 1978, and started my trades training with my regiment in Calgary.

I was the youngest soldier in my regiment when I went to it. At the Christmas dinner I sat up with the colonel and the RSM because I was this little boy still wet behind the ears. I didn't feel like that on the inside, but physically I was 17 and I always felt like I had to compete a little bit harder than the other guys. And I benefited from that. I was put on courses at a younger age than everybody else and I did well on the courses. Every once in a while, everything's going fine, then all of a sudden you fall face forward, steppin' on your dick. Well, I did that a few times. I was always scrappin', you know, that egotistical G.I. Joe "green, mean, fighting machine" attitude.

In basic training a soldier learns rank structure, drill, how to march, how to salute. Once he goes to his regiment he learns trades training. Trades training, or TQ-3, is the same as basic training, but it's geared toward the job you're going to be doing — armoured, infantry, artillery. Once past that he goes on to his unit and he's a fully trained basic soldier.

My job was to train my men, prepare them for combat. The number one job of a soldier, especially a fighting soldier, is to train and prepare for war, not UN peacekeeping missions, not jailbreaks, not forest fires. Their number one job is to prepare for war.

In Gagetown, New Brunswick, at the combat training centre, each trade has its own school. That's also where you get all your phase training for officers. I was teaching CLC, combat leader courses. A soldier with four to six years gets that first leadership course. You learn how to instruct a little bit, you learn how to teach drill. After that I advanced up to 6-A courses, which were tank crew commander courses, then phase training courses, which are officer training courses. Basically the training patterns for the officers and men are the same, they're just called different things. During the last two years of my time in tactics squadron in Gagetown, I was teaching officers how to be troop leaders. I learned a lot of things from my students and I always used to tell them, "I'm not here to fail you and I'm not here to pass you. I'm here to record your performance. You'll pass or fail yourself. I'm just here to write it down."

I benefited a lot from being in Gagetown. I loved being there. It was probably one of the best jobs I did, other than having men under my command in a fully operational theatre like Bosnia. I loved instructing. It's very rewarding, after 40 minutes, to have people leave a classroom knowing a little bit more than they did when they walked in. I wanted to really know my subject matter when I went in there. I didn't like making mistakes and I hated saying to a student, "Hang on, I'll get that answer for you."

Near the end of my career in Gagetown, I'm still at the rank of sergeant, but I became a course warrant. I wasn't an instructor anymore. I was taking care of all the students, taking care of all the instructors. It was an administration job. I had to feed them, I had to pay them, I had to transport them, had to get tanks out, had to get tanks in, get all the supplies for all the instructors.

I loved it. I ate it, I breathed it, I tasted it. I couldn't get enough of it.

In the summer of 1993 I returned to the regiment. I was made a troop leader because we were short of officers. We got a six-month warning order that we were deploying in April 1994 and I was given a troop and we started training. When I went over there I was still a sergeant, acting troop warrant. I got promoted to warrant officer over there.

Yugoslavia — 1994

I went into Bosnia with the advance party.

When you do a UN mission like that, you don't all go over as a big group, you do it in "chalks." The first chalk's called the advance party, which arrives a week before the others. We learned what was going on for a week so that the other chalks coming over — Main 1, Main 2 — are dealing with guys that know what's happening.

It was hot. It was really, really hot.

In Split, Croatia, there was no problem. Then we started driving inland.

You start hitting the towns and one of the first towns you see is ethnically cleansed. You don't understand it then as well as you do a couple weeks into theatre. It took time, once you were inside the country, to know what the hell was going on. The first trip in we didn't see a lot of bodies. But it doesn't take long to figure out that this is the real thing. You're thinking, "Holy shit, I'm playing with the big boys." And there's no rules. It's not "911, William Shatner, come give me a hand." No rules. The Canadians are in the middle of the fire in Visoko, where all three warring factions come to an arrowhead. You knew right away, this is it. This is the real thing. No more horsing around boys. No more horsing around.

Nineteen ninety-four was UNPROFOR. We're in white vehicles and wearing blue helmets. After that the Americans assumed leadership of it and it was IFOR. IFOR, just two tours after us, went over with no white vehicles, no blue helmets, no UN forces, a NATO force. With the UN's white vehicles and blue helmets, you've got a bunch of guys going around as targets.

The big first task Colonel Wlasichuk gave me was to take the first chalk of 12 RBC back to Split 'cause our guys were coming in. I was given the specific route I had to take. You've got 120 guys, 45 vehicles, taking them through a war-torn country. I had officers and captains and majors, but I'm in charge of this. The drive usually takes five or six hours, but you've gotta go through the towns, and you're getting shot at by snipers continuously. Just out of Tuzla, the bridge is gone. How am I going to get these guys to the coast? There were some Brits and French waiting around because they wanted to get on these tank pontoons that are a

Soviet piece of equipment. You drive a tank or personnel vehicles onto it, two little tugboats push it through the water and land it. Then you drive the vehicles and the personnel off.

The Spaniards were in charge of these pontoons.

I've got this Spanish guy in the 12 RBC who's in this chalk going back to Canada. I said, "Go down and talk to these guys. Get them on our side." He finds out that a couple of the Spanish guys knew English, so I go down there and I'm telling them I'm a UN leader and I'm going to Torremolinos with a friend of mine, and Spanish women are great, and the country's wonderful — I'm just blowing smoke. But they gave us these pontoons first, before the Brits and the French. So we cross down the river, get off and carry on over to Split.

Now that was a command decision I had to make and I had a bit of a problem with the major. "Why don't we just take another route through the mountains?" he asked. And I said, "No, we're going to do this." This is where you can either be a hero or an asshole. You get all those people and those vehicles across the river and carry on, you're a hero. One of those pontoons sinks, career comes to an abrupt end. I was lucky that day. None of them sank.

On the way back it took 14 hours, and it was the road movie party from hell. We pick the Strathconas up. We do the little helmet/flak jacket exchange, put them on the trucks and start heading out. Our trucks are just tarp vehicles, not protected at all. We're in the back. Now, when you move a bunch of vehicles, they don't all go in a row, they go in packets. One packet gets lost. They don't follow the packet in front of them and they start driving through some other mountainous terrain. I can't even get a hold of these guys on the radio. I don't know where they are now. They might end up in Hungary. And we're in excellent sniper territory.

I briefed everybody: "When you go for a leak, when you get off the vehicles to have a piss break, don't leave the hard-packed surfaces. This country is mined." For the ladies, of course, we had a little port-a-potty in the back of a vehicle called the Bison, and so they had privacy. But these guys were walking right over the guardrails to take a leak. "What don't you understand? The little upside-down triangle means it's mined. Piss on the road, right?"

The vehicle which fuels everybody breaks down, and another driver fell asleep and he takes out a fence. He's trying to call the local police department because they don't understand how UN insurance works over there. You've gotta pay them right there. The local police come and they're sorting out the problem with this guy's fence, people are crowding around the vehicle, and we've got the mechanics going up trying to fix up the bowser because vehicles are gonna run out of gas any minute now. Anyway, we get it all sorted out and I get all my little ducklings back in the trucks and we start up again. About three kilometres outside of Camp Visoko, we started taking sniper fire from a machine gun.

When we finally get into camp, the cooks are ready to feed us. I'm totally exhausted but I got all the vehicles back, and no one got shot.

Canadian soldiers are the greatest peacekeepers in the world not because of the results of what we do. It's because we do the same job as everybody else with half the gear. You come off the plane, and a guy hands you his flak jacket and helmet. You put it on, and hopefully you get a helmet and flak jacket that fit. He gets on the plane without that equipment and flies back to Canada. You got guys on the tarmac in Croatia exchanging combat kit! Who gives a shit? He's going back to Canada, but we're the ones going into the trenches. I'll tell you what I'd like to do with that combat kit.

The French were just down the road in Sarajevo. They were well equipped. They didn't have flak jackets on, they had clay jackets on that stopped bullets when you got hit, and they had proper helmets. We had flak jackets on that the Americans wore in Vietnam in the 1960s. Now that's OK if a grenade blows up 100 metres away, but I fired at a flak jacket on the small-arms ranges in Calgary before I left, and those bullets just ripped right through that jacket like nothing. I found out exactly what happens when you're wearing the jacket and you get shot. We shouldn't have been wearing those jackets.

I had a really good troop over there. I took some young kids over there to Bosnia, but they were all men when they came home. They wanted to order stuff out of magazines and I had to tell them, no, it's not Canadian issue. These guys wanted to bring their own combat vests over and they're getting told no. The young soldiers know what's happening to them. Most of these guys have got Grade 12, some of them a couple years' university. They're not idiots. You can't bullshit them. And they knew they were going over to a fully operational theatre and look at the equipment we've got!

We name all our vehicles after cats. Leopard, Cougar, Coyote — well, that's not a cat — but the Cougar, the AVGP Cougar, is a piece of junk and should not have been in Bosnia-Herzegovina. They were purchased in the 1970s and the reason why was because the upper echelon in the Puzzle Palace in Ottawa couldn't decide what kind of tank to buy. It was a tank trainer for guys in our trade to hone their gunnery skills on until a real tank purchase was made. Well, that real tank purchase didn't happen, so that's what we were in Bosnia with, tank trainers!

The Cougar is a six-wheeled armoured vehicle. Now I think the Swedes put water cannons on them and use them for riot control. We use them for armoured vehicles. The Scorpion turret is a very, very primitive gunnery system. It's all hand controls, it's not an electric turret. Its 76mm cannon is very inaccurate. It can't fire on the move. It has to stop to engage a target. After you fire it rocks for an hour and a half before you can re-engage another target because the graticule pattern that the gunner looks through to engage the target is moving around. If the factions over there knew it couldn't fire on the move, I think we would have been taking a lot more shots.

We did have some equipment over there that was a big deterrent. I mean, TOW missiles can really screw up your weekend. But that Cougar? It was good against small arms fire and that was as far as it went. Mind you, it was fast. It's hard to hit a fast-moving vehicle and it had speed. And it's a good swimmer. It does well going across the water. It had an eight-mile-per-hour ability. But toe to toe, man to man, the Cougar wouldn't have a chance. So why were we sent with it? Why is the sky blue?

Rumour had it — and I believed the rumour — that they didn't want to send Leopard tanks over there because we didn't want to look too offensive to the warring factions: we're Canada, let's hug a tree, let's hug somebody and the problem will go away. That's why the Leopards didn't go. Had I been over there in a Leopard tank, it would have been a lot more difficult getting around because the terrain in Bosnia is very mountainous, like goat trails, but I don't think anybody would have shot at us.

They wouldn't have screwed with us nearly as much as they did with those AVGP Cougars. It was crazy. Some of the warring factions over there could have taken us out in a New York minute with our equipment.

Peacekeeping

In Tom Martineau's dictionary there's no such word as peacekeeping. That is a bullshit word. In Cyprus, that was peacekeeping. You've got a buffer zone, a demilitarized zone keeping warring factions at bay. Bosnia-Herzegovina wasn't peacekeeping — or Croatia or Kosovo or Somalia or Rwanda. None of those were peacekeeping missions. They're war monitoring and you're in it, baby, you're right in the middle of it. You smell it, you taste it, you feel it, you hear it and you see it. There was no peacekeeping in Bosnia. But we got, "Don't protect yourself. Don't shoot at anybody." Good peacekeeping!

People think peacekeeping is when you hand the little kid a candy and you hand the mother some flowers. That's not the way it is. You're picking up bodies, you're seeing guys getting killed on a daily basis. Your own men are getting shot at. Guys are getting killed left, right and centre. It's death, death, death. You're seeing old people get executed, you're seeing children being thrown into fires and burned to death. You're seeing towns getting ethnically cleansed overnight. You want to stop it, but that wasn't the mandate. Humanitarian aid, baby. Bring food, drop it off at a goddamn warehouse so the local warlord can come and grab it. He's got all the guns and threatens any of the civilians that want any of the food. Take half the rations up to the frontlines for the troops and then sell the rest of them on the black market, and if anybody says anything they're gonna get a bullet in the head.

You've got to understand something. The warring factions were shooting their own people. One of the tricks was to get the elderly. Then a doctor from Médecins Sans Frontières would come. They'd whack some of their own people to get more medicine! Where do you think that medicine went? Do you think it went to the guy that was sick or the kid that was yellow with jaundice? They didn't get any of it. It went to the frontlines for the troops.

Our rules of engagement were bullshit. Rules of engagement over there were under Chapter VI of the United Nations Charter. If you get fired at directly, not just close by you, you can return fire if you can see the target and there's not going to be any collateral damage. How many times is this guy allowed to shoot at me before I can engage him? The soldiers don't go over there with a warmonger mindset: we're gonna get some trophies, we're gonna shoot some people. No soldier has that. But you shoot at me, I'm gonna try and blow your head off because I'm not going to give you a second shot to shoot at me again.

We had so many briefings before we left. "You can be charged with murder. You can be charged with manslaughter. You can be charged, you can be charged." Why are you telling me this? I'm a soldier going into a war. The most scared person in war is a soldier. You don't know if the next one's gonna hit you in the head or just come by you. I mean, if you get shot at you should be allowed to return fire.

The British and the French were pretty good at it. You shot at a British or a French soldier and you're shooting from a building, they blew that building up.

October 3, 1994

We're in a place called Ilijas, which was Serb-held territory. Now, the first OP, called Romeo Two, was just inside the Serbian-held territory. As negotiations went on, the Serbs gave Ray permission to put an OP further in. That was called Romeo Five and that was my OP. To get to this OP you went along the main road and then there's a little goat trail you had to take up this hill. Once you got up there you were looking down into a valley. About three kilometres away was a town called Breza, which was in Muslim-held territory, and Muslim forces were just in front of Breza guarding the town.

So you've got Muslim forces on a bit of an escarpment, and you've got Serb defence forces here, up on the escarpment, and a gully in between, 800 metres or so, where the Muslims and Serbs had trenchlines. Now, the escarpment came to a bit of a tit, and I was back from that about 150 metres up on a higher knoll, so I can watch the Serbs down in front of me and I can watch the Muslims further out. We had a bunker system there for protection but we also had a tented living area. It was about a 75- to 100-metre walk down the hill, behind our position to the living area and this bunker system.

I'm in the crew commander's seat of the Cougar, here on the left in the turret. On the right is the gunner; he has all the hand controls for the gunnery system, and I have a hand control to actually move the turret. I can override his hand controls. So if I was giving out a fire order and the gunner's going the wrong way, I'd just override him and then bring him onto the target. In behind me here is a 59-round ready rack of ammunition, 76mm bullets, that go in the gun. The crew commander loads the gun. Up front on the left of the turret floor is the driver and up front on the right is the engine. In the back you've got spots for tools and grenades and pyrotechnics.

We had this vehicle in a static position, which is a nice little target. But we're UN, white vehicles, blue helmet, doing our thing.

The Serbs had a spotlight that night. They were turning the spotlight on, finding some Muslims, shooting at them and then shutting the spotlight off. They kept on doing this, so then the Muslims started engaging the Serbian bunker system in front of us and if they were to shoot over top of them, those bullets were hitting us. We had a spotlight shining on us to show that this is a UN vehicle.

So these guys would turn their light on, they'd find the guys running around, *boom boom boom*, shut the light off. This kept going on for a couple of hours and we started taking fire at our position. So I phoned my command post and said, "Listen, we've got to get our shit together. Someone from there better start talking to someone from here 'cause I'm taking a lot of heat." The Serb area commander came out to the position, and I dismounted from my vehicle. I told him, "Your men are shining their spotlight on the Muslims, shooting at them and then they're shutting the spotlight off. The Muslims are shooting back at you guys and the bullets are going over top of your bunker systems and hitting my vehicle and that's not making me a happy camper." He said, "I'll go down and talk to them."

Well, I guess he ragged them out. "Tomski's up there. You're shooting and so Tomski's getting shot at here and you know Tomski's good to us." We had really good relationships there. All my men got along with all the Serbian men in the territory. These guys aren't real soldiers. They're guys from the town who used to be bakers, candlestick makers and train operators and busmen and taxicab drivers, and now they're wearing uniforms with guns and protecting their own little terra firma. We all had lives and wives and kids and houses, so we got along with them, we could relate to each other. We had a couple of little parties for each other, not parties to celebrate but just to show friendship. We're here to help the whole situation, not to be enemies.

The Americans had CNN making the Serbians seem like the worst guys in the world. All three warring factions were shooting at Canadian soldiers, all kinds of UN soldiers. All three warring factions had good people, all three warring factions had assholes. All three warring factions were ethnically cleansing, but any time the Muslims wanted help, it was there. If the Serbs wanted help, even if the Serbs were attacked in Canadian positions, there was air.

I went back up to the position and we started taking more fire. The spotlight hadn't gone on again, so here's the problem: the Muslims are now shooting at our spotlight and they're gonna say it was the Serbs. I mean, it's a no-win situation over there. Who threw the first rock first, and how many rocks did they throw? It's like dealing with two-year-old kids fighting over a toy. So I radio in that we're taking fire. Now they're going to try and get a hold of the Muslims and say, "Listen, we know the Serbs aren't shooting at the spotlight. Stop shooting at our UN vehicle." We had an infrared scope to observe the infractions that were being committed, and I was standing up in the turret trying to pick up muzzle flashes.

Then Marko, who was the commander down at the Serb OP, came up with coffee, this Turkish coffee the Serbs used to drink. He came through the back of the vehicle and he handed us the coffee, and my gunner, Sean Tracey, handed one up to me.

That's when I caught the bullet. I spilled the coffee on Sean and then fell and caught myself in the turret. I didn't hear or feel anything. I just caught myself with my elbows, and it felt like I had fallen asleep and I just woke up. And then there was just 20 seconds or 30 seconds of disorientation. Sean — young kid, only 18, 19 years old — was in the gunner's seat and he's saying, "Warrant, are you OK, are you OK?" I looked at him and I can see a little bit of fear in his eyes and I'm thinking, holy shit, what happened? I realize I've been hit and I can't feel my legs. Here we go. This is it. And that's when I started making a whole bunch of deals with God.

I said, "Sean, get on the field phone. I've been hit. Get the guys up here right now." So he gets on the field phone. If guys are talking on the radio and someone says, "No duff. No duff. Over," that means everybody get off the radio, this is not pretending anymore, it's serious. So no duff was called and Sean says, "Get the fuck up here. The warrant's been hit. The warrant's been hit." My guys were out of that tent and up that hill and 75 metres became three metres. A bunch of guys in khaki boxer shorts and combat boots and helmets and flak jackets and rifles coming up that hill like shit out of a goose.

My 2IC, Master Corporal Phil Friday, was there and starts assuming control of the whole situation. All of a sudden my training kicks in. You're told what to do when you get shot: relax, breathe deeply, don't panic, you don't know what your injuries are. So I'm like, "OK, stay calm. Stay calm. You're gonna get through this," and they get on the phone with the command post. When it's an emergency situation, everybody wants to confirm 15 times, so I grabbed that radio. "Listen, I've been fucking hit, and it fucking hurts, so get the fuck out here and get me the fuck out of this vehicle so I can save my life!" "OK, we got ya."

Marko has taken off back down to the Serb OP. He's grabbing his guys now to come up and help me and they phone Major Mjrc, the area commander, to come out. So our guys are on top of the vehicle, the Serb guys are coming up, and now you got about 300 guys on top of this vehicle trying to haul me out. Some of them are falling off, which is about a six- or seven-foot drop, and they're climbing back on. So there's a bit of commotion going on. We're still hearing some small arms hitting the front of the hill. We're still getting shot at. And these guys are risking their lives with my own men, trying to get me out. There are some Serbian soldiers that are heroes to me.

The Serbs had come up to the position with a nurse. They wanted to take me back to a Serbian military hospital, but Phil Friday says, "No. He's going back to the Canadian hospital. Thanks for the invite."

"But it's closer."

"No, no, no. He's Canadian. We're taking him back home."

187

Everybody's figuring out how they're going to get me out 'cause I'm not four foot two. I can't feel my legs anymore. I can't push with them, I can't understand why I can't push with them. I'm confused and I'm sitting there thinking I better just sit here and relax. So I start kind of giving orders, and it felt like I got punched in the stomach. I'm losing my wind and I can't breathe. Every time I say something, I'm grunting it out.

Then — and it really was a phenomenal feeling — I just relaxed. I started looking up and it was a clear night that night, and I'm looking at all the stars and that's when I started talking to God. "Listen, I don't know what the hell you got in store for me. I don't mind dying but I don't want to die in this country. Take me to Canada, I'll die over there. I just don't want to die here. Get me back to Canada. I don't want to go home in a pine box."

Then the commotion comes back and the guys are hauling me out of the vehicle and down the hill. They're carrying me down on a stretcher, down the hill, and the ambulance is still on its way out and they rip my clothes off. I'm starting to slowly go into shock now and I'm looking at their eyes. I want to see their eyes when they look at my wounds. The size of their eyes is going to tell me whether I'm in deep shit or I'm just in shit. A couple of the young guys are cutting my combat shirt off, and they open it up and they had eyes on them as big as saucers. I'm thinking, "This is not good. This is gonna leave a mark. This is not my idea of a good night."

"OK, boys. Let's remember our first aid training. We've got an entrance wound, let's find the exit." Then my legs got really sore. "Don't touch my legs. My legs are sore."

It was funny. "Warrant, we can't find an exit wound."

"Make one, do something. There's gotta be an exit wound."

Well, they couldn't find it 'cause the whole left side of me's blown open. So they put field dressings on me to stop the bleeding and they got me prepped. I'm on the stretcher still and we're waiting for our ambulance to pick me up to take me back to Visoko 'cause we had an FST there.

My buddy Darryl Peters comes out in the Bison with the medic and he's screaming and yelling at everybody, "Get him in there. Let's strap him in and get him back." I remember looking up at the Serbian nurse and she had that look of sorrow, like she really was looking at me with compassion. I'll never forget that. I asked her, "How long ago did I get shot?" and she said, "It's been about 20 minutes." That reassured me: "Then I didn't get shot in the heart."

When I was in the vehicle, I was talking to Sean. "I don't think this is a good scene, brother. This is gonna leave a mark and I'm not feeling good. I've never had this sensation before and I think —"

He goes, "Warrant, you're not going to die."

"Listen, if I die, you gotta tell my son, write a letter, do something, word has to get to my son Justin that his daddy loves him."

Then a Rolodex goes through your mind of everybody you ever met in your life and you start to think, "OK, I'm out of here. What a way to go." I had so many things to do, so many places I had to take him, but you're not upset at the time. It's quite easy to be upset about it now because you realize how close you came.

They rushed me back to Visoko, and Ray was right there, watching the blue light coming in all the way from Romeo Five 'cause you could see it from the top of the building. This was 10 days before we're going home and one of his men gets whacked right now. They put me in for pre-op, and the last thing I said before I went in for my operation — I don't remember it but he told me later — was, "Don't worry, Colonel, this is gonna be a piece of cake."

When the doctor unzipped me he says, "Has this soldier had a splenectomy?" and they're looking at my medical file and saying, "He hasn't had one." The doctor says, "Well, where's his spleen?" And then he sees it. He reached up inside my torso and pulled my spleen out of my shoulder and threw it in the trash can, I guess, or whatever doctors do with organs. Then he clamped everything, filled up my kidney with a foam they use — I guess it would be like the same shit you put in a tire when it gets flat — and he told the colonel, "Keep your fingers crossed. The guy's in really bad shape."

It was artwork what Dr. Macdonald did with me. The bullet went in and out of my left arm, left triceps, point-wise, and then it went flat when it hit my chest, ripped the side of my chest open, broke off a rib, went in behind my heart and in and out of my left lung. Then it took a different route and went down and split my left kidney in half and went across my torso. It ripped my spleen out, which is in your lower left abdomen, and threw it up into my left shoulder. And then it hit my spinal cord, my thoracic 12th vertebrae. If you were to feel your ribs down where they meet at your back, that's your thoracic 12th. The bullet crushed it and lodged right in there. And that's where I lost my legs.

The morning after they threw me on a Puma helicopter, flew me to Split and then from Split up to Zagreb, where there was an American MASH unit. I stayed there for four days. I remember bits and pieces, but you're on morphine and you don't know what planet you're on. There's only one memory I have from the hospital in Zagreb. One night I woke up and I ripped all the tubes out and I flipped myself out of the bed. I was still quite a big guy then, I was still strong. I crawled on my elbows over to a desk, and I reached up and I grabbed the desk and I pulled myself up. Then all the nurses and the doctors come running in and I've left this trail of blood from my bed. I'm on the phone trying to call my mom. Of course, I don't know who to call or how to get the operator, anything like that, but I'm just on the phone, trying to call my mom.

Home

My mother was four foot eleven; she always said five feet but she wasn't. I measured her 100 times. Four foot eleven, Irish mom. The information that came from Bosnia after I got whacked was inaccurate. I had told everybody, "If I get whacked over there, don't phone my mom. Phone my brother, he can break it to Mom."

So they phoned my brother and my mom was over there that night. They're havin' a couple of beers and Pat answers the phone. He said, "Tom's been shot. They said he got shot in the arm."

After five days John Kernaghan from the *Hamilton Spectator* came up to the house: "Do you mind if I do a story?" Hamilton boy gets shot in Bosnia-Herzegovina, war-torn country, blah, blah, blah.

So he's sitting down talking to her at the kitchen table, and the whole family's there. My mom says, "Well, he got shot in the arm, we heard about that. And they moved him to another hospital. But why can't I talk to him. When is he coming back?" John Kernaghan had a friend in the press over in Bosnia who had told him what was wrong with me, so he says, "Your son was shot in the arm, and then the bullet went into his chest." He gave the details of all my injuries. "And they don't think he's gonna make it." Well, I mean, she passed out.

I remember the first time I realized that I was alive and that I didn't die, I wanted to make an amendment with the Lord. He's kept his bargain 'cause I haven't died in Bosnia. He's got me back in Canada. I remember saying to Him, "Listen, I gotta make one amendment to that last contract we signed. Let me see my son turn 18 and I'll go the front of the line. No questions asked." He's seven now so we'll see what happens.

They flew me back to NDMC in Ottawa. Of course my family was there, front and centre. Mom was there and she was running those people around that hospital. Major-General Mom! She had all these signs up in my room: "Don't Touch Legs, signed Major-General Mom," "Don't Touch Bed, signed Major-General Mom." It was funny as hell. She had people rockin' and rollin' in that hospital. My mom used to say to the doctors, "OK, I want to know the exact truth of what happened here."

I was a paraplegic. One day I'm an excellent athlete, good runner and can hop, skip and all those things, and now I can't feel anything from about halfway up my ribs down. I can't go to the washroom by myself, I can't get an erection, I can't walk and I'm in 100 percent pain from the hypersensitivity. Not my idea of a good time.

I was in the ICU for 16 days, I think it was. And the bullet's still in me. They're not going to take it out because it's lodged in the spine and the spine is swollen and you don't want to go in there and start screwing around 'cause you're gonna screw with the nerves. OK, we're gonna leave the bullet in, so now we've got to worry about infection. Infection of the spinal cord.

My mom's running around that hospital jacking people up, going for all these interviews with the hospital staff and they're blowing her off. Well, you don't blow my mother off. One day the doctor comes into the room.

"Warrant, your mom's telling all the doctors what to do and she's ordering staff around."

"Yeah?"

"Well, do you think you could have a little talk with her?"

"You guys have pissed her off. What do you think I joined the army for? It was to get away from her. Now you've pissed her off, you want me to sort her out? You guys pissed her off. Deal with her."

We were happy I was alive for a while, and then I said to myself, "OK, enough of this, I need a challenge. Tell me I can't walk again. I dare you to say that. Tell me I can't be home for Christmas. Tell me. I need something to sink my teeth into." I was still with that hard-core, rah-rah attitude. A lot of people don't like it, but I'm glad I had that attitude and personality because I think it got me walking again. I was one of the top-shape guys in my regiment as an older sergeant, as opposed to the young whippersnappers, and here I am lying in a bed, watching my body disintegrate in front of me. I mean, it's leaving.

I couldn't walk and the hypersensitivity in my legs was so bad they couldn't even put a sheet on my legs. They had to use a cage to put the sheet over. Even if you opened the door too quickly and the wind hit the hair on my legs, they'd have to give me a morphine shot. You couldn't even look at my legs. People would look at them, they'd hurt.

One day a nurse came in to bathe me. I guess she was having a bad day and she was kind of taking it out on my legs. I grabbed her wrist, just shy of snapping her forearm, and I said, "Don't touch me like that. If you touch me like that again, I'll throw you right out this window." She starts getting pissed off and says, "If you want to experience pain, why don't you try having a baby?" Well, how am I supposed to relate to that? Unbeknownst to her, the doctor had walked in behind her, and he put his hand on her shoulder and — I'll never forget this — he said, "If you're going to experience the pain he's going through, your baby would have to be 600 pounds. Now please remove yourself." And out she went and he finished bathing me.

In my case the DVA was there for me, front and centre. I know that it's not there in a lot of cases, but with mine they were pretty good. Mind you, my injuries are pretty obvious. I had physioterrorists and occupational terrorists. That's what I called them 'cause they always bend things till it hurts. "Does that hurt?"

"Yes!"

"Well, it's good for you."

I was joking and carrying on in the hospital. This isn't a good situation, but I like getting the positive out of everything, so I'm having fun. At Christmas I stole everybody else's decorations and put them all up in our room. It's really hard to move around a hospital in a wheelchair with this big Christmas tree and a blanket over it.

I had my bad days. I was going through a lot of tests where they hook up electrodes to your brain and then down your extremities and through your spinal cord. They put in a pulse and see how long it takes to get back. The normal person's was wham, wham. Mine was whoosh, whoosh. Very sluggish.

And then one day my right quadriceps flickered. I tried to tell everybody at the hospital but no one really believed it. I said, "No you don't understand," and while the doctor was standing there it flickered again. Then he said, "You know, getting shot was nothing compared to the road you've got ahead to learn how to walk again." So I went down there on those even bars, and I'm just draggin' my feet behind me, and I said, "Look, Mom, I'm walking."

The occupational therapist would come in on a Friday and tell me what we'd start to learn next Monday. Then I'd practise all weekend, so when she came in Monday I'd have it aced. I always kept her behind my schedule and she used to get pissed off: "You're supposed to rest this weekend." Here I am a biathlon champion and it's taking me an hour and a half to put a sock on. But I worked hard, with that hard-core, olive-drab attitude, and then one weekend I said, "I want some canes." I practised the whole weekend, walking. I walked to the washroom and I walked back to my bed on canes. Then I just started walking the halls of the hospital. Every day. One day it would be 20 feet. Then 30 feet, 40 feet. It didn't look that good.

My son said, "Dad, you walk like a duck out of water."

"How many dads you know walk like that? You're a lucky boy."

When I was in the hospital they forced a TV on me. They said it was available and that "We want you to watch this TV at night. We don't want you losing your marbles. There's funds available for you here at the hospital to take care of things like that for you boys coming back from Bosnia." And I said, "I don't care about the TV, I'm learning how to walk again. I'm going to walk, walk, walk. Let's stay focused here." And they said, "No, no, the TV's just here to relax you." Anyway, they gave me this TV.

A week after I was home they sent me a bill for it. I'll never forget what that bill was worth: $118.76. I started crying. I broke right down. And that was just the first in a series.

The System

I went back to Hamilton, Ontario, with my mom and dad, and they're taking care of me. They weren't even going to release me from the NDMC in Ottawa until the wheelchair ramp was built. That was one of their stipulations. When they looked it up in the book, I wasn't entitled to a wheelchair ramp 'cause it wasn't my private residence. Well, when was I supposed to go on the house-hunting trip? When it was finally decided that I was going to get this wheelchair, different area commanders were trying to figure out where the money's got to come from. Why don't you assholes figure it out later? OK? Because right now I'm the poor prick without the goddamn wheelchair. When I went home I had the wheelchair.

They want me to come up for my checkups to Ottawa, so I've got to get my wheelchair, get to Toronto, fly up to Ottawa. When you have a spinal cord injury and you go up and go down in a plane, it is extremely painful. On one trip to Ottawa they wanted me to return the wheelchair for stock-taking. It took 14 months to get another wheelchair after I turned the last one in.

And this is when I started seeing the problem with the system.

There's the McMaster hospital rehab centre here in Hamilton, and one of the top spinal cord research doctors, Dr. Joanne Bugaresti, is there. Why can't you just transfer me? What's the problem?

One person grabbed the reins when I got back. Ray Wlasichuk, my colonel over there, took care of me when I got back, but he was limited. He can't go too far above him. Outside of him forking over the money out of his own pocket to buy me a wheelchair and wheelchair ramp, what else can he do? But he was there front and centre for me, fighting for me every day. Phoning me wanting to know how I was doing, how I was getting along.

Ray came over to my house. "Tom, I've got to explain something to you. You're not with the regiment right now because you're disabled. I want to generate another position for you. I want to get you posted to CFB Toronto." So I became a part of CFB Toronto, but they don't know who I am. I phoned there for a bit of assistance. No one has my documents.

I wanted a letter from some captain at CFB Toronto. "This is what you got to do for me, Cap. Write a two-sentence letter for me so I'm allowed to drive again." I hadn't been insured in over a year and we're in Ontario, so we can only imagine what I'm going to be paying for premiums. "So will you write me a two-sentence letter saying that the whole time he was injured, he was still insured under the Canadian Armed Forces vehicle insurance program, so that when I buy a vehicle, I can actually drive around in it?" It took six weeks to get that letter 'cause he was golfing.

So I said, "Screw this."

To actually go anywhere, to get into a vehicle, was difficult because I was still in excruciating pain. But I drove all the way to Toronto and I walked into the office of the administration officer: "Where's the base commander's office?"

"Who the hell are you?"

"You've got a minute to get the base commander and the RSM and any other bigwig down here to this office. You've got a minute. And then I'm gonna find out where his office is and I'm gonna bust right into it. The MPs won't get here quick enough. And I don't give a shit what he's doing." The base commander happens to be Colonel Fox, the brother of General Fox, who was honorary colonel of the Strathcona Regiment.

"Who are you?"

"I'm Warrant Officer Martineau, and you've now got 45 seconds."

So she flies out of there and gets the base commander. He comes running down.

"What seems to be the problem here?"

"I'm Warrant Officer Martineau, Colonel Fox. I've been having a lot of problems with your staff on the base, and here's the list."

I'm halfway through my list, and he says, "Oh my God, how long have you been posted to my base?"

"Since June."

He looked at the administration officer and said, "How come I don't know about this?"

He didn't even know I was on his base. Are there 600 of me like this here? All I was asking for was just someone to do their job. They always said, "Any time you need anything, just give me a call." Bullshit! The problem is the system doesn't exist. There wasn't a system in place to take care of us. And the military just wouldn't recognize that they had a weak system.

I called General Roméo Dallaire. He said the reason why I was having so many difficulties with administration was because I was one of the first wounded. How does that hold water? There's 10 guys been killed, and I was the 45th wounded. Even if I was first, or 101st, why is there not a system in place to take care of us? I told them that the Armed Forces are in the business of getting us hurt, but they should get out of the business of taking care of us. "You're not good at it," I told him.

I ended up calling Roméo Dallaire a fucking asshole. How dare he tell me that?

The commanders of the Canadian Armed Forces lied to me. They told me that I'd be taken care of. But not only have you lied to me, you made me lie to my own men. What if it was one of my men that got shot and went through the crap I went through. I was a 20-year warrant officer. What are you going to do for the young corporal or private with a wife and a new baby? If you're going to treat me like shit, I can imagine what he's not going to get. I was so pissed off.

I had people from CPP disability writing me back after I applied for it. "We don't think you qualify for CPP disability. We don't know how your injury stopped you from working." Hello? Then I find it's not really a doctor that looks at the paperwork, it's an insurance agent. I phoned them. "What janitor looked at my report?" I mean, where's your leadership? I'm just a number in a computer. I'm damaged goods. Thanks for the 20 years. No, you don't get a watch.

I couldn't believe my own government was actually trying to trip me. I went to Ottawa. Art Eggleton looked at me funny when I said to him, "We went over there and fought a war for you. We came back and you treated us like Third World citizens."

I turned it into a positive. I started helping soldiers out. You taught me to know my men and promote their welfare. You taught me to take care of my men. You taught me how to look after them. Well, maybe you just created a monster. Maybe the wrong soldier got wounded. Tom Martineau started the whole shitball, I'll take full responsibility.

Now I've got 60, 70 soldiers ringing my phone off the hook and I'm telling them how CPP disability works, DVA, and how the system works. How they have to get to their family doctor, get a letter and then go see the DVA doctor. Then you get a pension. Then you can start seeing a psychologist and get it taken care of. Tom Martineau now knows exactly how the whole system works. But nobody told me anything. I had to figure it out step by step.

I called Art Eggleton a fucking asshole because he's the minister of national defence trying to tell me how the system works. When's the last time you got shot, Art? You're telling me how the system works? You've got generals and MPs coming on TV saying that Matt Stopford was poisoned by his own men and "we're so worried about his health." Why did they say that in 1999 and not in 1993 when it happened? You're telling me in the Parliament of this country that Matt Stopford's being taken care of? I've got you on video telling me Matt Stopford's being taken care of. And all these guys with PTSD. Stress? I'll show you stress. What are you going to tell me now? What physical and mental stress is? I'll show you stress. Don't tell me about your paper-pushing, bureaucratic, red-taped bullshit. I've got no time for it anymore. I've got no faith at all in our governmental Department of National Defence system. It's bullshit.

Then I've got Rick McClellan, the chief social worker of the Canadian Armed Forces, doing interviews with these soldiers that got wounded about how they're being treated. He's got staff quitting 'cause they can't believe the stories they're hearing about an organization that they all belong to. I said, "Rick, give me that report as soon as it's done." "Yeah, no problem, Tom." I get lied to again. Guess who sent me the report? Dave Pugliese from the *Ottawa Citizen* downloaded it off the Internet and mailed it to me. What am I, red-flagged? People start getting scared of you 'cause you're on TV talking and speaking your mind.

What's the problem here, gentlemen? Nobody can handle the truth? I'm only talking about the facts. I'm talking about what happened, not what could have happened, not what should have happened, not what we all want to happen. I'm telling what happened. You can't handle the truth. You're big, tough paper pushers. Don't bullshit the home team. You wear the uniform, I'll talk to you. You don't wear the uniform, shut up. I know how the politicians work. I know how it all works. Do I know what it's like to be a politician? Nope. Do I know what it's like to be a cab driver? Nope. Nurse, doctor, lawyer? Nope. Garbage man? Nope. Soldier? Yup.

I can't talk to anybody about it unless I talk to someone that was there with me. That's why I started getting tight with Ray Wlasichuk. We're best of friends now. It's not colonel and warrant anymore, it's Tom and Ray. Ray's going through his shit and then you've got Matt going through his crap. I started travelling to all the bases and talking to soldiers about what I went through. Remember me, Warrant Martineau? Big green fighting machine, G.I. Joe? Well, guess what boys? I got some bad news for you. I'm broken. I'm broken physically and I'm broken mentally, and I'm telling you right now your family and your friends are more important than your military career. And if you're experiencing anything like I'm going through right now, seek help.

I'll tell you about the day I knew there was something really, really wrong with my mind. I was down on Main Street and John in Hamilton and it was the middle of the afternoon. It was a beautiful day. I was in my Jimmy and I'm at the light and the light's red. And all these people are walking in front of my vehicle. And all I wanted to do was just push on that gas and run all those people over. Now, that is not normal, you're not supposed to think like that, but I was physically fighting with myself to keep my foot on the brake.

All the pain I went through physically isn't one-millionth of what I went through mentally. If you have physical pain you take a morphine shot. When you have mental pain, how do you run away from it? How do you run away from your own mind? Well, the answer is not very good. And I almost tried it, probably on six different occasions. A 9mm right through the top of your head. That's how you run away from the pain of your mind.

And nobody knows where to go. People in the NDHQ in Ottawa don't know the phone numbers to give me to seek the help I need. It was just a bowl of spaghetti and I was in the middle of it. I felt I was the first guy in the Canadian Armed Forces ever to get shot.

I don't even think Art Eggleton is the problem here. He can't be the problem. The prime minister's a bit of a problem. I mean, Doug Young, Collenette, Eggleton? When's the prime minister going to step in and say, "Listen, when are you guys going to get this portfolio sorted out?" You know, I'd like to apply for the job.

We have a political system and a military system. The problem is that you have civilians dictating to soldiers how to fight their wars, how to fight their battles. That's not right. You've got to put it back in the hands of soldiers. The soldiers have to make those command decisions. Political figureheads shouldn't be making decisions for military ground troops. It's like the UN. The UN loses paperwork in their Jell-O. If you're gonna have a war, it better be Monday to Friday, 8:00 to 4:00, or you're gonna get an answering machine.

Defence has gone from crisis to crisis and they're excellent at crisis management. But we don't have an infrastructure to take care of the soldiers. Someone's got to go in there, grab their balls and say, "Listen, I'm going to sort this all out. Leave it up to me." If maybe we could just have one or two people in Parliament say, "Wait a minute. We've asked a lot of all of our soldiers, going back to the Boer War, World War I, World War II, Korea and all of our UN peacekeeping conflicts, and we're asking a lot of these guys now." How many lives do you get? Everybody only gets one and if you put that at risk to help people all over the world, you should be taken care of if anything happens to you. Our politicians are going to be barrel-chested with their chins up, their chests out and their stomachs in, taking international peacekeeping compliments from the world, so I think we owe it to our soldiers to better equip them and take care of them. When they do come back, if they happen to have their legs blown off or a bullet in the spine, or are sick with physical injuries and mental injuries, we owe it to them to take care of them.

The press was good with me, but it's sad when you have to use the press to get something like this done. This should have happened internally with soldiers. We shouldn't have had to go on TV and badmouth Art Eggleton. I know it's not really all his fault. I know somebody's got to be bullshitting him, but he should be doing something about it.

I know they're making efforts now, I know the efforts are coming. Rick McClellan's got the Care and Wounded Cell up in Ottawa. When Tom Hoppe was talking about putting these little cells all over the country to assist soldiers and help out with the DVA, he said, "You know, Tom Martineau's one of the reasons why we got the cell here in Ottawa. He pushed and pushed and pushed and he called a bunch of people names."

If my son wanted to join the army, how do I tell him no, it's not a good idea? What if he wants to. Isn't it my responsibility as his father, and as an ex-soldier, to make sure that the system's in place and operable, so that when he wants to pull on that great Canadian Armed Forces uniform with that Canadian flag on it, and go out on a peacekeeping mission to help people, wherever it is, I know I've made the system better for him? And Matt's kids and anybody else's kids that are going to be coming up through that system?

My mom said two things to me when she was dying that I'll never forget — you know when you get cancer and it hits the brain, you don't know what kind of story you're gonna get. She'd seen a T-shirt when she was down on her last trip to Florida and she says, "Out of all the people I've met in my life there's only one person who could have worn that T-shirt."

"Who would that be, Mom?"

"It was you."

"Oh, that's nice," I said 'cause I don't know where she's going with this story.

"Do you want to know what that T-shirt said?"

"Yeah."

"That T-shirt said, 'If you're not living on the edge you're not living.'"

The other thing she told me was, "You always talked about those young soldiers and how you loved to take care of them. Don't give up that fight with those bastards in Ottawa. You've got to take care of those soldiers."

So, yeah, that's the way I see it.

People have called me a hero. I don't think I'm a hero. I think the guys that are heroes are the guys that come back in pine boxes. They made the ultimate sacrifice for this cause, and I don't think this cause was worth it. It really wasn't.

The best thing I got out of the military is that I learned a lot about me. You made me a man at a much earlier age then I ever expected to be. You made me a soldier and you made me someone that understands life really well. I got to do things in the military that I could never have done in any other job in the world. Then you sent me to Bosnia, in a fully operational theatre, and called it a peacekeeping mission. It wasn't a peacekeeping mission, it was a war.

I stuck to my part of the bargain. I signed a contract saying what I was going to do and I did it and I never complained about it. You taught me a lot of good lessons and when I applied those things I got good results. Then I got shot and I lost my legs. I came back and you treated me like a piece of shit because the leadership didn't apply those lessons to me. I had to apply them again, for myself, without any help.

Too many people think soldiers are machines, that they're robotic. They fight, they go out and shoot bullets, they get shot at, they kill people, they get killed. Well, there's a human being behind that uniform. It cries. It laughs. It jokes. It drinks beer. It has sex. It makes kids. It gets married. It has moms, it has dads, cousins, nieces, nephews.

But I'm only talking for the guys in the trenches at 2:00 in the morning who are cold, wet and hungry and pissed off, and as soon as this exercise is over they're gonna put their release in 'cause they've had enough. Those are the guys I'm talking about. I'm not talking about the guys that do a 20-year career and never go further west than Loblaws.

Every soldier in this country that does what I did knows what I'm talking about. I don't think civilians understand, but word will get out.

PETER VALLÉE
Sergeant

I was 17 years old when I joined up just out of high school. My grandfather and great-grandfather had been in the military, so I figured I'd give it a shot. It was the best thing I ever did.

The Royal 22nd Regiment is the French-Canadian regiment, and to be perfectly honest with you, all my best friends are in that regiment. If I could say I have a family, it's probably those guys, and the guys in the Royal Montreal. For 12 years these were the only people I was with, and probably the best people I'll ever meet.

In the Royal 22nd we pride ourselves on doing things a little differently than most. We like to follow our own rules. We don't break them, we just bend them a little. It's not carved in stone as regimental history, but that's the way we do things. It's different from the English regiments. The PPCLI or the RCR or even the Strathconas or the Dragoons all have their own way of doing things. The Van Doos maybe stand out a little more because we're French Canadian, and proud of it. There's rivalry between everybody; between the three services, between individual regiments;

inside a regiment, you'll see that there's rivalry between the companies and the platoons and the sections. But more often than not this is good, competitive rivalry that makes people proud of where they are.

I left the Van Doos in 1991, after I had done a full tour in Germany, but I stayed on as a reservist and I was contemplating whether I should go back to school when Bosnia started up. In order to augment the regular force battalions, they took on reservists that had some background experience, and there wasn't any question what I was going to do. I got a phone call at home from the Royal Canadian Regiment and they asked me if I was volunteering to go to Bosnia. I said, "Of course. That's why I joined the military!" They said, "OK, pack your bags. In two days you'll be in Gagetown." And I packed.

I had an idea what was going on. I read up a bit and I got some feedback from my friends from the Royal 22nd Regiment 1st Battalion, who had been there on the first tour of Operation Harmony, so I got some idea about what things were like over there.

The First Tour — October 1992

At the beginning of the tour we were in Croatia: Lipik, Pakrac, Daruvar, those areas. There was fighting everywhere. Then the fighting spilled over into Bosnia, and they wanted a Canadian contingent there, a Canadian presence, and we had to find a place to set up shop. After three months we finally set up in Visoko.

We weren't there to pick a fight. We were there to do a job. We were there as exactly what it says, the United Nations Protection Force. And to monitor the demarcation lines between the various factions, patrol the sectors and to protect some of the civilian elements they had there. We weren't there to pick a fight with any of the factions, even though the factions often resented our presence.

But it depends where you are. If you're in a sector where you're protecting the Croats, they'll be glad to have you there. The Serbs won't want you there. If you're in a sector where you're protecting the Serbs, the Croats won't want you there. You know, everybody's got an excuse. But I've been in all of them during my three tours, a Serb, a Croat and a Muslim sector. It doesn't matter where you are, the guy on the other side's not gonna like you because you're preventing him from getting what he wants.

Of course, throughout the whole war there was a lot of jockeying for position, a lot of moving the frontlines. It was a little complicated because you had the civilians mixed up in this. I mean, it was a big mishmash of people, and certain belligerents were trying to move into certain parts of the city, move back into their own places that they had before they were taken away from them, and you had women, children, civilians mixed up in that. It was a big quagmire.

Sarajevo

In Sarajevo we would patrol the Serbian and the Muslim frontline. We would escort workers, help out the refugees at the airport, along with other armies, other units. One day we were escorting some workers to the frontline and there was firing going on. I was a corporal back then, I was a C9 gunner, and the driver took good amusement at watching me flip from one side of the vehicle to the other with my C9 trying to find this guy who was taking potshots at us. The civilian workers, though, didn't find it funny at all. If you feel that your safety, or the safety of the people you're trying to protect, is in jeopardy, then you return fire. I mean, if you don't what's the point? Stay home and eat doughnuts.

On March 15 we had gone out to do some escorts. Just routine escorts, for guys to get the electricity, the plumbing back up, stuff like that. We would escort these workers to, or close to, the frontlines to provide security and maybe a little bit of cover so they don't get their heads blown off. We had a platoon strength of vehicles, and we were rolling back into the airport. There was fighting going on in front of us so everybody put their heads down. Some of the guys up front pulled out M-72s, rocket launchers, and got ready.

I cocked my weapon and, being the person that I was, stuck my head up. And I heard what's called a "crack and thump." I don't know if you've ever heard a bullet go over your head, but it makes a very distinctive sound. And that round went close to my left ear. I slumped down in the bottom of the vehicle. I shook my head a little. I knew what had happened but now I had to react. I couldn't stick my head up because the drill was to be down, so I couldn't stick my head up to see what was going on and actually do something about it, but I did. And nothing came of it. The vehicles were moving, and we were in motion until we were in the airport. When I got into the building where we were staying my ear was ringing. I figured it would go away. It didn't. My hearing's been bad since then. It was close.

If you're being shot at you're gonna know it, you're gonna hear it, and anybody who's been shot at will be able to tell you the same thing. When a bullet goes off, it's a high-frequency sound that you hear. When you hit a hammer on a board, it's a low tone, but a round, when it breaks the speed of sound, will be a higher tone when it's passing your general direction. It'll zip over you on a range — not that they shoot at us in the army — and you can hear this crack and thump. That's why they call the exercise "crack and thump" — 'cause that's exactly what it does.

There was one instance when we were going into Srebrenica, one of the first times, and it happened very quickly. It wasn't funny at the time, but I think back now and it was pretty funny. We were going through a Serb town called Zvornik, rolling through, and of course we went up into the hatches in the APCs and something happened. I turn around and I see my friend go down like this, in a clump in the bottom of the carrier and he was clutching his stomach. My first instinct was, Christ, he's shot. I open up his hands and I see a big rock, and his eyes are big, like loonies, and he's pissed off. A minute after that happened I received one right on the side of the head and I thought I had been hit.

I cocked my weapon and I pointed it up to these buildings. And what do I see? I see a bunch of kids throwing rocks at us. At the time I was seriously pissed off. You know, a four- or five-year-old kid is not going to throw a rock at anybody for fun. Somebody told them to do this and they knew we weren't going to shoot at any kids.

We established a presence around Srebrenica, around the perimeter of Srebrenica and did patrols, observation posts. We confiscated weapons, provided medical help for the people there, evacuated casualties and refugees who needed medical attention, as best we could. Srebrenica was a town that was held by the Muslims but surrounded by the Serbs. It was in the hills, and there wasn't a long system of highways over there. It was a day and a half drive to get back to Sarajevo or Visoko.

The Siege of Srebrenica

I understand that the UN expected us to resist with all necessary force in order to hold on to Srebrenica. If the Serbs had decided to come over the hill, realistically we would have fought them off the best we could, but we were a short company, maybe 70, 80 guys and some medical support staff, and we didn't have an abundance of ammunition. We didn't have any huge fire support. We didn't have any artillery support to be able to mount an offensive against these people.[1]

We knew we were cut off. Golf Company was there, and one platoon of Hotel Company. And that's basically it. For a month. We established our patrols and observation posts and weapons caches as best we could. We washed when we could. We were on rations the whole time. Bottled water, of course, no services whatsoever. We were absolutely outnumbered by the Serbs, but our UN presence helped, I guess, to get them to a standoff. You had Muslims living in Srebrenica and up and around Srebrenica. Some of them were living in shacks, little shacks close to the mountains, in the mountains. It was a strange sight.

I went into one of the old buildings in Srebrenica and I picked up an old travel brochure. To think that people actually travelled here at one point in time, and here you have residents that basically look like they've come out of the sewer. It was really bad. By the time we left it we pretty well looked the same way.

The 2nd Battalion of the Van Doos came to replace us, and they took a few days to get in and negotiate — the Serbs were always screwing people around, jerking people off — it took them time to get in. These fellas were in Canada maybe two days before, saying goodbye, and the next thing they know they're trucked into Srebrenica and they see 70 really tired and hungry guys who have had a pretty hard six and a half months. Our uniforms were dirty, paint was chipped off our helmets, we'd lost weight and we were tired.

And these fellas came off the plane, you know, brand-new combats and shiny new helmets and basically looked at us and said, "Jesus! Where the hell have you guys been? What've you guys been doing down here?" They were pretty shocked.

We know what happened on July 11, 1995, in Srebrenica. The Dutch contingent was there, and they basically got rolled over by the Serbs. We were pissed off because for a few years we had kept Srebrenica, kept it going and kept it safe. It's given over to someone else and they lost it. I don't know who's responsible, but they should hang that sonofabitch.

On the last day of our tour we sent out two sections to two observation posts. One was my section with Sergeant Deveaux. The other was Andy Achtenburg and his section. Routine observation posts at night, little sand bunker up there, looking out. All of a sudden there was fire going on around our sector, both observation posts. And I hear over the radio, "Man down, man down." We knew Andy's section had been hit, and of course we were trying to figure out what was going on.

Afterwards we found out that Andy got shot up in the legs. They patched him up as best they could and a good buddy of mine from the Van Doos met them halfway and picked him up in an ambulance and tried to get him out of Srebrenica, but couldn't. They finally got him out and he was on the flight home with us. Same flight. He was in a stretcher, though.

The Second Tour — October 1993

I actually didn't want to leave. My first thought when I got home was that I wanted to go back. I came into my regiment, the Royal Montreal Regiment, and the 1st Battalion was going to Croatia. An officer pulled me aside and said, "They need volunteers." I said, "Put my name on that list." He said, "OK, you leave in a week for lead-up training, then you're off." Lead-up training at that point was lasting a few months. After we had finished all the bureaucratic swan dance, we had been back about four and a half months, ballpark. I think I had maybe five or six days off.

A good number of the soldiers had been to Sarajevo on the first tour with 1st Battalion Van Doos. My platoon warrant officer had been in Somalia not long before. So they knew what was going on. Some of the younger troops hadn't been in that kind of a situation. My experience was welcome in that platoon. You had more reserve augementees, good ones. A lot of different people from different regiments were called upon to fit into this organization. The 1st Battalion Van Doos was an excellent battalion.

Sector South — Gracac

We basically set up a demarcation line between the Serbs and the Croats during our tour. We didn't have one casualty during that tour. We didn't loose anybody. When you look back, the mission itself was good. Of course, during the tour we're not always saying that, eh? We had a hell of a lot of fun too. A lot of it had to do with our company, Delta Company. Major Stalker was a company commander. Excellent, excellent guy. He contributed a lot to what this unit has done.

One day I was at company headquarters and one of our OPs had received a couple of mortar rounds close to it and I had a feeling where it might have been coming from, so I decided to take a jeep and driver and see what I could find, sniff around a bit. I told everybody I was going to go visit some of the B Company OPs, but that's not what I was going to do. I wanted to see what I could find, without a map, see what I could conjure up. I drove in to where I thought a few Serb units might have been. However, we went in a little too quickly. I drove directly into a Serb mortar pit.

Well, they looked at me in amazement and I told that driver, in the plainest English anyone's ever heard, "Put it in reverse and get out of here." As we did that two Serbs stopped us. They spoke Serbo-Croat. I whipped out a map and started talking to one of them a bit in French, which I knew he didn't understand. And in between the words I was telling my driver to put it in first, leave his foot on the clutch. So when the two guys came a little closer to us and further from the front of the vehicle, I told him to let go of the clutch and step on it. As soon as he did that, I cocked my weapon and turned it back and these guys were ready to shoot us. Of course I pointed my weapon to the back of the vehicle and made sure that we could get away. At least we had cover fire. These Serbs, they were gone, they were running.

So we got away from there and made it back to our headquarters, and I reported what had happened and that I had found a Serb mortar pit. But I knew that wasn't the end of that because one of the UN observers who was floating around (he was a Canadian) had gotten an official protest from the Serbs saying that this particular individual came into our mortar pit where he wasn't supposed to be. If he ever comes back, armed action will be taken against him, which means that they're gonna wipe us off the face of the map. But we sure did find that mortar pit. And I didn't get in trouble for it, remarkably.

The Third Tour — Visoko, 1995

I always said, "I'll go back as long as the war is going on," and my next opportunity was to go back with the 3rd Battalion of the Van Doos in 1995. I put my name in and while I waited I was an instructor. I taught various courses around the Montreal, Quebec City region, and waited it out until my third tour.

The 3rd Battalion never really existed. It was basically a part-militia, part-regular force battalion. It was kind of a bureaucratic con job for a deployment into Bosnia. They had all these characters coming from I don't know where, from various companies and different postings, and they all came out to form a battalion. You had the regular three- or four-month lead-up training but what it lacked was the unit integrity that the 2 RCR and 1 Van Doos had, or even 2 Van Doos or 2 PPCLI had. All of them had been working as a unit for years on end. And I think things kind of got mashed up.

This wasn't done because they were running short of troops. I think it was that somebody had the idea to form a battalion this way, by putting together various companies and making a battle group for four months. "OK, away we go. Let's boogie." But the unit integrity wasn't there. There was a lot of in-fighting. When the boredom set in they had to find stuff for us to do. There were all kinds of activities, you know, beach parties or casinos, thrown about here or there to keep people busy.

On my last tour the war was ending and we were confined to the camp by the Muslims for four or five months. Some of the guys from A Company were taken hostage. They weren't mistreated in any way. They were basically taken as a political tool to get the UN to stop what they were doing.

What was frightening to me was that I was going to have to spend the remainder of my time in that camp. That was frightening because I hated being in a place like that and not being able to do my job. That burned me up like you wouldn't believe. "You can't leave. You can't go." Boom. That was the end of that. I think it would have been good if we had maybe imposed a little bit of what we were made of. We were highly capable of it in any circumstance.

It was suggested the command structure wasn't quite sure enough of themselves to take on the Muslims who blockaded the camp at Visoko, but I'm an NCO, so I'm not going to say what the officers should or shouldn't have done because I wasn't in their shoes at that time. But if they thought that they couldn't, in that battle group, accomplish the task that they had to accomplish, they should have stayed home. If they don't think they can accomplish the parameters of the mission, put somebody in there who can, not somebody who says, "We'll see when we get there."

You're in a war zone and we have to remember that Canadians are not peacekeepers. We are foot soldiers able to act as peacekeepers. As soon as we are in harm's way, as soon as somebody attacks us, there's no longer a peace to keep. You use your ability as a foot soldier to deal with that situation.

I don't think anybody really knew what was going on. It's impossible to predict war. You can be thrust into a situation one day, and maybe a week later it's turned into something else. And of course you can't just take your stuff and go home. You have to sit there and deal with the problem, and I think, after working with other armies, there was only one army that could deal with it in the best way possible. It was the Canadian army. The individual Canadian soldier has got a weapon that you can't buy. He's got a weapon that most other armies don't have, and that's brains. That'll take you a long way in a place like Bosnia.

If you're going to go into a place like that, you're going to expect that people are going to die. People are going to get hurt. That's what war's all about. That's a fact. That is war and we can look at it from any angle we want to. You can train, you can prepare, you can have the proper equipment, everything, but some things are going to go wrong.

To the best of the Canadian military's capacity, we got what they could give us. It's easy in hindsight to say we should have gotten this and we should have gotten that, but it was kind of hard to assess the situation and what was going to happen. I think the military establishment learned a lot from Bosnia about what it's going to need in the future for a situation like that.

I look at it in from one angle. I'm sent there to do a job. These are the tools that they're gonna give me and I will accomplish that job to the best of my ability with what I have. I didn't really have the time to sit up and say, "We need this." If it's broken, let's fix it, and when we get back we'll get a new one.

The people who joined in the 1980s, people from all walks of life, you know, were a little more down to earth. Youths these days, 16, 17 or 18 years old, don't necessarily think the same way we did and they're not as hands-on as we were.

People asked, "Why'd you do three tours?" Because I was happy most of the time that I was there. To me, I had the best job in the world. I was doing my job as a soldier. That's why I joined the military!

You have to understand, I was 17 when I joined with not all that much going for me. The military has informed me about who I am, what I can do. It certainly helped me in probably 85 percent of my second career. I wouldn't be a pilot today if I hadn't been a soldier, if I hadn't been taught the way I was taught, the discipline, the hard work, the getting up in the morning. I left because there comes a point where you have done everything you wanted to do. Things get repetitive, a little monotonous. I don't have a family. I don't have anything of that nature, so I could afford to try something else and see what other capacities I had.

It was a big shock when I got out, when I left the military. Immediately I went to Africa for a month and I came back. I finished up all my pilot licences and then I jumped right into civilian life. And the shock was that you're not around a whole bunch of guys. It's hard to describe the intensity, especially in Bosnia, of what that's like, being around a whole bunch of guys, that big family, getting this done and getting that done. You know, camaraderie. In civilian life everything is more individual. In the military, if I wanted something, I knew where I could go and get it. In civilian life it seems everything takes a little bit longer and you can always do it next week. I wasn't used to that system. I wasn't used to "Well, wait till tomorrow." Where I came from there was now.

There were a few people in the military I admire, the guys that trained me when I was a buck private in the Royal Montreal Regiment and in the Van Doos when I got to Germany. I could think of probably a dozen of them. NCOs, warrant officers, sergeants. Even an officer.

One thing that would be great would be to actually educate our country about what our military does, all the things that all of us have done, all the soldiers. There are people, I'm sure, that don't even know what happened in Cyprus in 1974, the Congo, Korea. Some Canadians don't know that Canada was even in Korea. Educate them about what happened, not just about us, about Bosnia, but about everything before. They don't know.

The Canadian public is very supportive and they're interested. But you feel you shouldn't talk about it because they're so clueless about all of it it's almost laughable. It's not, but almost. Jesus! If I'm in a civilian context, at some civilian party, talking to people, they'll say, "What's it like, really, to go through that and then to come back here?" It's not part of their reality. It's just a flash on the news. They can watch it on television, and all they have to do to forget is turn it off. I won't talk about it, *ever*, because immediately you're the outcast. It's not a great icebreaker at parties.

The memories don't haunt me, you know. They don't haunt me. It's just what happened there. I could sit here and talk for two weeks about the memorable incidents I've had on my tours. Probably the most memorable of them is a look I saw on a kid's face.

We were going through a town called Tarcin, going to pick up some supplies with a deuce, one of our convoy trucks, and we had to stop just short of the village because there was fighting going on between the Muslims and the Serb element. Now, of course, when you'd stop you'd have kids roaming around, trying to talk to you, or get food or cigarettes off you.

She lived in one of the houses right by the village.

I'll never forget the look of horror on that child's face when a mortar hit the village. That look. I'll never forget, never forget that look on her face.

213

NOTES

1. In March 1993 Vallée's platoon was among a small number of soldiers sent into Srebrenica under Major Poirier to reinforce two sections from the RCR. During this time the Serbs cut off all access to the town. The Canadians were relieved by Dutch soldiers and in 1995 Serb forces took Srebrenica and massacred thousands of citizens.

JORDIE YEO
Master Corporal

I had been in the militia for quite a few years when I heard that the regular force was looking for people to go overseas. I didn't know what was actually happening at the time, but I decided to volunteer. I figured I'm a master corporal and I've been trained for this. This is what I've looked forward to, and it's a worthwhile humanitarian cause. I went to Quebec City to join the 2nd Battalion of the Van Doos in Valcartier, on January 23, the day after I got married.

Our training for Yugoslavia was pretty messed up because all of it was done in wintertime and we were showing up there in the summer. It was one of the coldest winters I had ever experienced. Being on the .50-calibre range and having the freezing wind blow wasn't too pleasant. The next thing we knew we were packing up our stuff and we were going. When we arrived in Yugoslavia, it's plus 30 degrees. I remember the front door on the Airbus opening up and the officers getting ready to walk out, and the heat just hit them.

THE CHANCE OF WAR

Yugoslavia — 1993

When we arrived in Visoko we saw these odd patterns on the cement. The patterns are impact zones. The mortar hits and makes a circle and then the shrapnel tears away little bits of the concrete or asphalt around it. The locals used to call them "Sarajevo flowers."

As we were driving to Srebrenica, we passed one area where we could look down into a valley and there was a lake at the bottom and it was emerald green. I remember looking at it and saying, "This reminds me so much of British Columbia. It's so beautiful, it's so gorgeous, so pristine." Then you drive for another 15 or 20 minutes and arrive in this village where everything was burned out. No roofs on the houses, people lying in the streets, and there was this incredible smell — a smell that you can't really describe because it's a mixture of burning flesh, rotting flesh, human feces, urine, decaying bodies, smoke and fire and gas, diesel, you name it. It was a stench that was unbelievable and it just hung there in the valley.

The Serbs didn't particularly like the fact that we were showing up. We had to argue and banter our way in through the villages. They knew if we were going in, the troops that were there, the Patricias, were leaving, and that meant that we were going to be fresh.

Srebrenica

Srebrenica wasn't a village. There it would be considered a city, but you'd drive out of the city and there'd be these little villages with 10 houses and some farm fields. It was a Muslim enclave that the French had started and the Canadians had taken over. I understood that originally it was a resort village. It must have been beautiful at the time, but when we arrived all the valley sides had been clear-cut, so you just had these bare, brown, muddy valley walls with bombed-out buildings all around. The Dutch took over from the Canadians and I'm not exactly sure what happened. From everything I've read, the Serbs and the Croatians started shooting at the Dutch and the Dutch gave up and walked away. As a result, the Muslims we had been protecting, the majority of them, got slaughtered. When we found that out a lot of the guys got really upset.

At the time we arrived I was in my mid-20s and there were no men our age, other than UN peacekeepers. None. Just women and children and very old people.

The winter before we arrived it had gotten so bad for some of them that they had actually taken their corncobs after they had eaten the corn, and they had ground these up and made different types of suet or a substance with some water. And they would eat this. The problem is that it's so rough that it actually cuts your intestines, so they would be bleeding from their sphincters.

Médecins Sans Frontières had set up a small hospital in the middle of Srebrenica. They had these European-style garbage cans that are rounded on top and on four wheels and these garbage cans were just filled with body parts, gauze that was filled with blood.

The other thing I remember very clearly is that there were no birds.

Often when we were away, driving through villages, people would stone us because everybody believed we were trying to help the other side. Sometimes it would be Muslim villages, sometimes it would be Serbian villages and sometimes it would be Croatian villages. They didn't understand that we were there to help everybody. We had no political agenda to stop one particular group. Our job was to keep the Muslim enclave safe and to get rid of weapons and disarm the civilians so it was safe for us as well.

A lot of people were being shot at. Most often it would be us, the peacekeepers. The first time, we were filling up sandbags to build ourselves a bunker, using gravel from a parking lot. The shots came from a mountain top that was about a kilometre and a half away. But they weren't shooting at us, they were shooting near us. This was their form of entertainment.

So we're filling up these sandbags and potshots are ringing off the walls of the buildings that are nearby and I'm really starting to get scared. I reacted. I ran. I mean, what human being wouldn't? And I was told, "Listen, the more you react, the more they're going to shoot."

"Yeah, but what if somebody messes up and they actually shoot and kill us?"

"We usually just ignore them, they get bored and they stop."

"So how many shots are they going to take at us?"

"Well, they usually take about three or four."

Then all of a sudden, just like it had started, it stopped.

Under our rules of engagement, unless somebody dropped from being shot, we weren't supposed to shoot back. I found that very frustrating. Other tours had officers and commanders that would say, "Well, you know, that's nice that Parliament said that, but screw you, my men come first." Quite often we should have shot back and we didn't. We just stood there. In a lot of cases it caused us to lose face. It actually made things a lot worse. If we had been better equipped and better armed we could have made a bigger difference a lot faster, and there would have been less people hurt. Less Canadians, I should say. Unfortunately there would have been more people hurt on their side.

George Skett, the section commander that I replaced, was piling up sandbags and suddenly he was being shot at. So he looks across the field and he sees this guy standing there. He's waving. George looks at him through the binoculars and the guy's still waving and then disappears. He thinks, OK, maybe it's not him, and he continues piling sandbags. Then another shots rings out, so he turns, picks up the binoculars and looks, and sees the guy and he's waving again. He was screwing with their minds. We look at it now and it's quite humorous, but at the time George was getting quite upset. Here's this bozo that's having fun by playing with their lives.

On the top of the hills that encircled Srebrenica there were small OPs that the Canadians had set up. We had just finished building up one of the OPs and we heard a boom. One of my guys in the OP is in the turret watching and he says they're shelling down in the bottom of the valley on the opposite side. We were watching and we noticed it starting to come toward us. We figured that whoever it is that's shelling the area is probably going to try and kill the cow that was grazing below us, along with the farmer. It wasn't that at all. They were making a point. We had just finished building up our defensive position and they started walking the mortars up the side of the mountain and they stopped a few metres away from our wall of sandbags.

When we started building up our defensive position on top of that mountain, the Muslim locals came over and asked, "Excuse me, could you do us a favour?"

"Yeah, no problem."

"If you find any human remains, can you let us know, please. There are two or three guys that we never found after an attack and we're not sure where they are."

The soil was a red clay that was very, very thick and the mortar rounds would just come in and hit, and if it was muddy, the person would disappear. I can't really imagine what it was like in World War I, but from everything I've read, I guess this was similar to the conditions that they faced. A body would just disappear into the mud.

There was another time we were filling up sandbags for the ammo collection point. We had been rotated to another OP and I got a radio call.

"You know that big mound of dirt that you were filling your sandbags from?"

"Yeah."

"Well, it's a mass grave."

They were finding body parts and lots of them.

The Kid with the Grenade

My job at the beginning was taking care of the stockpiled ammunition and weapons that we had received. We would remove all weapons from the surrounding area in Srebrenica. I was the 2IC of the section, so the health and welfare of my men was paramount. One of the OPs had a patrol that would go into the mountains to make sure that people had no been harassing the little homes nearby. And they would bring anything in that they had found. We were stockpiling it.

The ammo collection point was surrounded by barbed wire. We had modular tents and we had the ammunition in behind corrugated steel and sandbags. This kid came up.

"Canadish?" He has his jacket on and he put his hand inside and says, "I have grenade."

"OK, what do you want for it?"

"Trade garbage for grenade."

We weren't allowed to give garbage. Our garbage was supposed to be taken away and disposed of, but they would use whatever they could out of our garbage, scrounging through it for salt and pepper and even the plastic bag that held the garbage. So I said, "Well, maybe." The kid says, "One garbage bag for grenade." A grenade is dangerous. It doesn't care who it blows up, so I tell the kid OK. We had three rows of barbed wire and I toss the garbage bag over and the kid starts laughing at me.

"Ha, grenade. You stupid. I'm not giving you grenade. I'm going to throw grenade when you guys sleeping, kill you all."

"Give me the grenade."

"No."

So I tell the private that was inside the turret of the M113 to give me his rifle. There was another kid now beside the kid I had just bartered with and he spoke English. He tells his friend, "Listen, the Canadian soldier's getting pissed off." And I said, "Tell him that at a count of three, if he doesn't give me the grenade, I will shoot him."

The kid's telling him and he's walking away and I raise the rifle. "One" — kid's laughing. I cock the weapon — "two ... " I lift the rifle up, point it straight at his chest. He goes, "OK, OK," and pulls out his hand. He has a bottle of hand cream. The kid had a bottle, like an Avon bottle with a metal top on it. It looked like a grenade behind cloth, but it wasn't. The kid was willing to jeopardize his life for a plastic bag and garbage.

You're seeing little kids with fingers cut off because the soldiers don't want to see these kids grow up to be on the opposite side. You see an eight-year-old boy with his index finger cut off. The brutality's insane. And you ask them, "Why are you fighting?"

"Oh, I am Chetnik."

"What do you mean, you're Chetnik? You said yourself that your mother was Serb and Croatian and your grandmother was Muslim. How can you say that you're purebred Serb?"

"Oh, I am Serb."

"No, you're not. You're part Muslim, part Serb, you're haberdashery. You're Heinz 57." It's like a Canadian trying to say that he's 100 percent Canadian. There's no such thing as 100 percent Canadian.

On a couple of occasions we actually started to run out of food and water because the different forces wouldn't let our convoys through. It would take roughly a day for the convoy to get there if it hadn't been stopped by whoever decided he was the leading whatever in the area, and depending how much *slivovitz*, or as we called it, sleep-in-a-ditch, he had had. He may be in a good mood or he may be in a very foul mood: "Nobody gonna go through." And whether we're United Nations guys bringing medical supplies or a farmer with a cow, the guy doesn't care. We were the ones that were giving them the majority of the medical aid that they were getting. Not once did I ever see our doctor ask for anybody's nationality or their ID card. You were hurt, from a child to a colonel of a different force, he didn't care. He's a doctor first of all, and he was in the military second. His main objective was to help people.

I found it very odd that as a multinational force with international backing, some drunk-yesterday farmer can turn around and dictate to us what we're going to do and when we're going to do it. That was the part that was difficult to accept. The Government of Canada has sent us here, the United Nations has sent us here, yet we're powerless.

I ended up being the section commander because my section commander left for his two-week leave in the middle of his tour. I made the decision that it was my responsibility to take out most of the patrols for the simple reason that it was dangerous. Everybody in my section were my friends from my regiment in Montreal. If something had happened to them, I wouldn't have been able to live with myself.

We were just a two-man patrol, which in the Canadian Armed Forces doesn't really exist. But we just didn't have the manpower. I found this a little bizarre and I made a complaint. I also said that I didn't particularly like the fact that we were doing this every night at the exact same time and I was told, "We can't send you out any later because by the time you get back it's getting very dark and once it starts getting dark, we're in a no man's land." But when you're bopping around with a big blue helmet on your head, you're a very visible target for a very far distance. Even if the rest of us is in green, my brain-box is still covered by that blue Kevlar helmet. That made me nervous.

We did rotations to different observation posts in the mountains and basically our job was to make sure that the Muslims in the enclave were safe. For anybody to say that they weren't afraid to go out on the patrols, they're either lying or they don't want to admit that they were scared. You never knew when somebody was going to booby-trap the trail.

When we were walking out we used to do a large route that was sort of meandering all over the mountainside. It used to take, on a good night, about an hour and a half, two hours. and it was uphill, big time. The roughest part of the patrol was the beginning. It was an almost vertical climb, and then the path ran up and down the mountain, and then went across a field to this orchard. We'd have on our flak jackets, and we'd be wearing our big, funny blue helmets. We'd have one individual with a C9, a light machine gun, and I had the common infantry rifle, the C7, which is the Canadian version of the American M16. We had a radio, water, some food and a couple of bandages.

On these patrols we were looking for mines, booby traps, and quite often I was looking for fresh graves. If there was a fresh grave that meant either that the family had been attacked the night prior, or somebody had been attacked previously and had eventually passed away, or, on occasion, someone had actually died from stress or old age. You could tell whether or not it was a young person or an older person from the size of the grave. The number of times that I saw graves that were only three or four feet long was too many. The country's future. That really bothered me.

We were looking for any visible signs that there was activity in the evenings 'cause every night we heard gunfire and could see the tracer rounds. And we knew that if it wasn't being fired at us, it was being fired at somebody else. The day prior to the attack my platoon commander had gone out with my 2IC and had found some trip mines. They're like a pineapple on a wooden stake. There's a small pin, a cotter pin, that goes through the top of it and a small, thin wire that goes across. They had found several of these where our patrol route had been, so they shortened our route. But in shortening it they stopped the route and put the turnaround point in the middle of the open field near the apple orchards.

July 23

The next day Jeff Melchers was with me and I decided, instead of stopping in the open, we would stop before we got to the orchard, at the edge of the wooded area. At this point the trail had been bulldozed at a 90-degree angle into the side of the mountain, so you had an earthen mound on one side. We stopped at the wood line so that Jeff could have a cigarette and I could have a slug of water. We were just standing there talking when we heard a single shot. Then we heard some rustling in the woods. Jeff started getting a little nervous. I was very nervous: "Let's grab our stuff and get going."

No sooner do we start when I see something move in the woods to the left of me. Then I saw bright orange. I felt a large, hot flash all over my body and I saw bright orange. Then I was face down and all I see is grass. I hear Jeff behind me and he's screaming. So I roll over and I see Jeff sitting on his butt holding onto his arm. I said to him, "What's wrong?" and he goes, "I've been hit. I've been hit." I try to get up and that's when I realize that I'm in a lot of pain. I mean, I'm in a shitload of pain. My legs were killing me and my butt was killing me, and we were getting shot at by a lot of rounds. "Tell me where you're hit." He tells me that he's hit in his legs and I can see blood starting to ooze out of his fingers. I tell him to move his hand and there was a little squirt of blood that starts coming out, so I take a field dressing and put it on his leg. I ask, "OK, are you going to be able to move?" and he goes, "Even if I'm not able to move, I'm going to get up and we're getting out of here."

So we got up and started walking toward the open field. We were hugging the side of the mountain as we went because higher up was where whoever it was was shooting at us. We couldn't see them, but they couldn't really see us either because of the dense brush. When we got to the edge of the wood line we couldn't go any further because we could hear the rounds going by. At one point we fired back, but we had no idea who we're firing at because we have no idea where they are. They were at the very top of the crest in a dug-in position. We knew roughly where that dug-in position was from previous patrols, but where the people were that had thrown the grenade and started shooting at us, I had no idea at all. So we were stuck.

I called on the radio and — this was the most horrifying part of this — I couldn't reach my observation post where my guys were. But I did get the command post in the middle of Srebrenica. I told them, "This is a no duff situation. You've got two men down and we're on the trail." I'm told to wait, and I start explaining again to somebody else on the radio and they said, "Just hold your position." So we did. And it seemed like hours and hours went by, but it probably was a very short period of time.

A lot of the guys were in the downtown area at our headquarters. They scrambled into the armoured personnel carrier and drove up the mountain to try and get as close as they could to us. The guys tried coming up the hill in our big, huge, white M113, which is a box with giant tractor treads and huge Red Cross symbols on it. Once the snipers saw it, they started shooting and these things are light-skinned vehicles. I mean, you start shooting at it with things that are larger than a Mont Blanc pen, and it punches through it like a hot knife through butter. So they had to go back and try a different route. They got as far as the brush line on the opposite side of this field and because there was no cover, they had to stop.

They finally pinpointed exactly where we were with the references, but they couldn't get to us because these other individuals didn't want them to get to us. I can just about guarantee that it wasn't the Muslims because they were the people that we were always saving. Whether they were Serbs or Croats, I can't say, but they knew we were peacekeepers. Giant blue helmets. We were pretty obvious!

Jeff was getting very scared and I didn't know how serious his wounds were. The next decision was quite hard. I gave him my rifle and I took his machine gun and I told him, "OK, Jeff, you're a small guy" — he is five foot seven maybe, max — "you can run across the field." The mound of earth would almost cover his entire silhouette. So that's what he did. He ran because his life depended on it, and he made it to the opposite side. Our troops heard scrambling, and Jeff comes crashing through and they're pointing their rifles at him. "No, no. It's me," he's yelling.

They were saying that they were going to wait a little longer to come and get me, so that twilight would start coming. The sun sets very quickly there because it's hidden by the other side of the valley. After Jeff had run I was so nervous I started picking up the spent brass casings. I had decided, "I'm not leaving anything for these assholes to have, nothing!" I was looking down and my combats were a very dark green, and I could see a puddle of blood at my left foot. I actually thought my right leg was much worse because my combats were pretty much torn open and I could see most of the bone of my right leg. So I decided, I'm not waiting. I tried standing up. That didn't work. So I took the radio which was in my bag, it's like a little schoolbag, put that on my back and slung the C9 around my neck. And since I couldn't walk, I just said, "I'm going to start crawling." I was behind the earthen mound and they wouldn't be able to see me except for my blue helmet that would bob up and down. So I started crawling across the field.

About halfway across I was exhausted and in so much pain that I collapsed. It was six months to the day that I had gotten married and I decided that there's no way in hell that I'm going to die there. No way! I was crying like crazy 'cause I just didn't know what to do. I didn't know if I could continue, but I said, "No, I'm not staying here." So I got back on all fours and I continued crawling. I've heard conflicting reports about how far I crawled, anything from 100 to 200 metres. All I know is it was too far.

I got to where the end of the trail was, but now I had another problem. When the two guys who had come down from the APC and were waiting in the brush on the other side tried to get up, the enemy had a clear sight of fire down this road. They could see us and whenever they got up, they started shooting at them. So I told them, "Listen, I'm going to throw you my stuff and then I'm going to hop across."

I took the C9 and heaved it with all my strength into the bushes. Then I took my bag with the radio and everything else in it and I heaved that as hard as I could over to them, to make myself light so I could go a little faster. I told them that on the count of three I was going to make a run for it.

I got up and sort of hopped as fast as I could over the dirt and dove into the bushes. Before anybody could react and start shooting, I was across.

They tried to pick me up and fireman-carry me, but I'm not exactly a little flyweight and the flak jacket probably put me over 200 pounds. Because the terrain was so rough, they weren't able to put me on a stretcher and there was just not enough room to manoeuvre, so I put my arms around their shoulders and grabbed onto their flak jackets and lifted my legs and we walked that way. We had a Muslim guide who was directing us up the side of the mountain to the waiting troops and the carrier through an area that may have been mined. We had to stop quite often so they could rest and I remember the lieutenant-colonel looking down at me and saying, "Jordan, just relax, take your time" 'cause I had started crawling again. I said, "There's no way in hell that I'm going to stay here and wait for you guys. If you want to stay, you stay. I'm going. You can walk beside me, but through hell or friendly fire, I'm going to make it to that track." At that time I didn't know how badly injured I was and I didn't know whether Jeff had made it back to the carrier. They told me he had, but did they say that just to keep my morale up? I wanted to see him for myself. So that's what we did. I'd crawl and they'd walk beside me until they could catch their breath, and then I'd grab onto them and we'd continue walking.

Because I'd got shrapnel wounds to my buttocks, I was lying on my stomach in the carrier. They had the hatches open on the M113 so that they could have two guys on the top where the C9s were so that if anybody fired at us, we could return fire. And we were driving through the apple orchard on our way to the headquarters area, and every once in a while we would hit these trees and these stupid little apples would come down and they'd hit me square in the ass. I was thinking, "Oh my God, can it get any worse?"

Twenty minutes later we ended up in the makeshift hospital we had down at Srebrenica. When they found out what was wrong with me they had to call Airevac and the only available helicopter was a French medical helicopter. The surrounding forces weren't letting anybody land but they took a chance and had the helicopter come in, and it landed on the soccer field. Nobody fired at it when it came in, so we got into it and started taking off and I remember the helicopter making some serious moves. It was being shot at and I looked up at the French medic and told him, "Listen, I'm in a lot of pain," and he goes, "No problem, we can fix that." All I can remember after that is waking up as they took me off the helicopter to put me into an armoured personnel carrier to bring me to Visoko.

From there I was taken into Croatia. They had to negotiate passage onto the runway into Croatia. The first plane that the Canadian Armed Forces sent over wasn't configured properly for the transport of people, so they had to send another plane. We were flown, Jeff and me and one Med A and one nurse to Germany and then back to Ottawa. It took quite a few days.

Tracie, my wife, found out I had been hurt through a phone call. Same thing with my mother. When they phoned each other they had received conflicting reports. My wife was told that I was gravely injured and my mother had been told, "Don't worry. He got hurt but he's going to be OK." So they're both freaking out.

Once people found out that I had got hurt they tried to do the best they could for me. My colonel, Toby Glickman, was on the phone constantly once he found out that I was being shipped back home.

Home

Because of Colonel Charles Buckley, one of the best doctors I've ever seen, and a couple of other doctors, they were able to save my left foot. My heel was destroyed and they rebuilt my foot and saved my leg. I walk with a limp. But I'd rather walk with a limp and have a foot than walk with a limp and have no leg!

When we were back in the National Defence Medical Centre — great place, it's a tragedy that it was closed — people started complaining about Jeff and me. The nurse comes over, ward nurse, a sergeant, big, huge, massive guy, and he goes, "I have a problem here."

"What's that?"

"People have been complaining about you guys."

"What do you mean? We're quiet. We're just sitting in our room."

"People say you smell."

"What do you mean we smell?"

"Well, actually, you guys *do* smell."

The smell of Srebrenica, the smell of mass death, had gotten into our hair and into our skin.

When I was at the National Defence Medical Centre, I got this paperwork while I was still in bed and it said that my contract had been cancelled — according to Department of National Defence, yaddah, yaddah, yaddah, subsection whatever: "Because you are no longer in an active theatre of operations, your contract is no longer valid and will now be terminated. Thanks for coming out." I was all drugged up on painkillers because they're reconstructing my left foot and my right leg was in a cast, and I couldn't truly understand what was being said in this paper. I was on so much Demerol at the time that I was like, "Yeah, whatever, man." It meant that they weren't going to pay me anymore.

My brother-in-law was a medic at the hospital. He finds out about it and brings it up to the base RSM, and the base RSM freaks. I mean, here's two guys that just finished getting hurt in Yugoslavia on active duty. It's not like we were joy-riding on snowmobiles in the Yukon or somewhere, having fun just putzing around.

The RSM had to rattle some chains. "Listen, you just finished using this kid as a poster boy for the Department of National Defence. We had almost every newspaper and almost every major television studio on the tarmac greeting him when he showed up in Ottawa, and now, a couple of days later, you're cancelling his contract? What's wrong with you people?" The next thing I knew my contract was reinstated and I continued to be on the payroll — for the time being. I had my contract cancelled quite a few times after I got out of hospital.

I lived on Sherbrooke Street in downtown Montreal. Just getting up and down the stairs with my crutches was difficult enough, but they were making me go do physiotherapy at St. Hubert air base, about 20 minutes, minimum, away by car. At first my regiment, the Royal Montreal, was transporting me back and forth, but sometimes they weren't able to find a driver. Anyway it was the 2nd Van Doos' responsibility. At first they had said that I was going to go back to Valcartier, near Quebec City, but my colonel had talked them into making sure that I stayed in Montreal: "That doesn't make any sense. His family is all in Montreal. His mother, his father, his brother, his wife, everybody's there."

I read a report in the newspaper that the Canadian Forces denied that the helicopter had been shot at. They probably said that for the same reason that they said my incident was an accident. I could understand somebody shooting a rifle, one or two shots by accident, but you don't throw grenades by accident. There was another incident that was reported as an accident. Daniel Gunther was at an observation post in the driver's compartment of the APC, and the next thing the guys heard a big bang and they grabbed all their stuff and started loading into the vehicle when they realized that the big bang had killed Corporal Gunther. It was also initially reported as an accident.

After I was injured and was back in Canada I felt the Van Doos didn't really want anything to do with me. And that's the way I sometimes felt about the Department of National Defence too. But any type of press coverage they wanted they'd say, "Could you please do this?" I was on the CBC, I was on BBC, CBS, I was on *The National*, I did newspaper interviews. They even asked me to go to the Montreal Children's Hospital to carve pumpkins with the kids for PR. They asked me to do all kinds of things.

On the other hand, they're telling me, "We don't really see a reason to pay you anymore." I'm still going to physiotherapy. I'm walking with a cane. I'm having a hard time getting up and down the stairs to my apartment. I'm lucky I live on the second floor 'cause I don't have an elevator in my building. And you're saying, "Excuse me, but we're not sure whether or not we should be paying you?" When I was paid I was given a piece of paper that said, "The minister of national defence hasn't quite decided whether or not your case is legitimate." What, did they figure I was downstairs in the basement of the Royal Montreal Regiment faking all this paperwork? That I somehow managed to sneak my way over to Yugoslavia, stuck a grenade in my sleeping bag and blew myself up and then decided to shoot myself in the ass with my own rifle?

Why is it that the Department of National Defence and all the politicians that are sitting there getting their massive salaries aren't trying to take care of the people that they're sending over to do their dirty work? Because they're the ones who came up with the idea to stop the fighting. It's not like a whole bunch of privates in the junior ranks' mess decided, "Well, you know what? We've been practising being soldiers for an awfully long time now. There's this thing in the Balkans, looks like a lot of fun, let's go over there." I mean, if they feel that it's not that important to even thank us, don't send us. It's not our war. A lot of guys were asking, "Why the hell are we here? We go back home and nobody gives a shit."

Nobody bothered to check to see how many people coming back had any type of psychological trauma, or whether anybody was suffering from post-traumatic stress. Everybody was asked, "Are you OK?" "Oh, not bad. I'm having a couple of nightmares." "OK. Thank you. Bye." That was your psychiatric evaluation after your tour of duty. When I first came back I used to have a lot of nightmares.

I used to get very upset with the Canadian public, hearing people whining about things like their cable wasn't working, or the city's too noisy, or they have to wait a little bit too long in the emergency room. Well, get a grip on yourself. For me, that was a wake-up call. We're spoiled rotten. We're very lucky. We have some shortcomings, but compared to a lot of other countries we're fabulous. Canadians lead a very sheltered life. We don't like seeing other Canadians hurt. We don't like seeing our soldiers in any kind of war action and we believe that everybody in the world should be nice and peaceful and quiet, just like Canadians are. People don't like seeing their brother, their husband, their cousin, their friend or their boss being sent into an area where they're going to get hurt.

A friend of mine was on a bus with a couple of other guys he had served with in the Black Watch. They were going out to Concordia University and they were talking about their experiences in Yugoslavia. Some people on the bus were listening in. When the two guys had gotten off, one of the civilians said to another, "That guy's so full of crap. He served in

Bosnia? Yeah, right. Look at him. He's young. No way he went to Bosnia. There's no Canadians in Bosnia. What the hell is he talking about?" Yes, we were there. Canadians died in Yugoslavia. There's a bloody monument there with the names of dead Canadian soldiers on it.

Unfortunately I had to leave the militia because of my injuries. They told me they could always remuster me as a clerk, but according to my medical categories I couldn't even be a clerk. To add insult to injury, I signed my papers in March, and on April 1 of the same year they came out with a pension for reserves and I wasn't entitled to a cent. A lot of people have said, "Why don't you fight it?" The fight's not in me anymore. Every single time you have to ask and continue to ask, you start feeling like you've become a burden. You feel like you're begging. It's very degrading. We are supposed to be taken care of by the military and by our insurance. The insurance was a joke. I was paying into the program and they told me because I didn't lose any digits, and because I hadn't lost part of my leg, I wasn't entitled to a damn nickel.

I did get a little recognition by Parliament with Tom Hoppe, Matt Stopford, Tom Martineau and Peter Vallée because the Reform Party asked why the Canadian public hadn't recognized us and Parliament stood up and started clapping. But my mother had died before that time, and it had really bothered her that it seemed like nobody cared.

I can truly understand what soldiers from the United States who were in Vietnam have gone through. They came back and people hated them or just ignored them. That's what happened to a lot of Canadian soldiers. Just about every single guy that's in the Canadian Armed Forces has done some sort of tour of duty either in Yugoslavia, Haiti, Rwanda, Somalia and we're doing this because the Canadian people and our politicians believe that it's the right thing. If it's the right thing, then how come when we come back home nobody says, "Good job"? I would really like somebody to sit down and explain to me why.

The bad press that the Canadian Armed Forces has had in the last few years, since Somalia, is very unfair. You're talking about a very small group of individuals that were uncouth and not professional. But for every one soldier that wasn't professional, you're talking about thousands that were. Yet the press and the public seem to love to use us as whipping boys. I would like the Canadian public to realize that we do a lot of good.

When we were in Yugoslavia we helped handicapped children and adults in a mental asylum get a certain standard of life back. They were sitting in their own excrement, they didn't have any food and they were being picked off by snipers for fun. Canadians walked in and stopped all that. Guys, instead of getting a couple of hours of sleep, were going and volunteering to clean up the asylum and feed the handicapped people. These guys were never thanked. The Canadian press turned around and said that these soldiers were sleeping around with the nurses and the patients. We were in a foreign country, taking care of people who have psychiatric problems and mental deficiencies, not because we had to, because we wanted to, because that's the type of people real Canadian soldiers are. They care. They're not just going to turn their back and walk away and say, "It's not my problem."

Well, this is your problem. It's your country and the soldiers are your people. They do what the Canadian public wants. If you don't like what they're doing, then talk to your politician. Tell your politician that you don't agree with what's happening. Stop sitting on your hands eating your Pringles.

EPILOGUE

There was a collection point near this mound that we found out was a mass grave. And every single morning there was this really old man, I mean he looked old enough to have known Jesus himself, and a very young kid, roughly the same age as my daughter is now, about three years old. And everyday they'd walk hand in hand, and it was kind of funny because the old man was so old that he couldn't walk fast, and the young kid was so young that he was unsure of himself and he couldn't walk fast. Everyday they would walk past us.

In our rations we would get little candies, so the guys would give them out to the little kid and then the little kid and the old man would go and sit on top of this mound of dead people. The little kid would go through the grass and find four-leaf clovers and run over to his — I assumed it was his grandfather — and they'd eat the candies that we'd given them. Every morning they'd watch the sunrise. Sun would rise, and then they'd thank us and they'd walk away. And it's upsetting me because the thing is, Srebrenica was overrun, and I never knew whether or not these two lived. Harmless old man and a young kid.

Jordie Yeo

GLOSSARY

2IC   Second-in-command.

Airevac or Medevac Terms used for medical evacuation by air in helicopters or fixed-wing aircraft.

AK-47   Soviet automatic assault rifle.

APC   Armoured personnel carrier.

AVGP   Armoured vehicle general purpose.

Beaten zone   The section of the target area where the rounds
from rifles or machine guns impact the ground.

Binders   Brakes on an armoured personnel carrier that has
tracks rather than wheels.

Bowser   A fuel truck.

C6	A machine gun.
C7	Canadian version of the American M16 rifle.
C9	A light machine gun.
CAR	Canadian Airborne Regiment.
CDS	Chief of the defence staff.
Chetniks	Serbian resistance group during World War II, now an extremist group, which was active during the civil war. It is currently connected with the far right Serbian Radical Party. The word chetnik is often used simply to refer to any Serb.
DVA	Department of Veterans Affairs.
Frag grenades	Fragmentation grenades.
FST	Forward surgical team.
Green Line	In Cyprus, the dividing line indicating the buffer zone separating the Greeks and the Turks (so called, reportedly, because when defining the boundaries on the map, the British officer in charge drew the line with a green ballpoint pen).
Gurkhas	Nepalese Hindus noted for their love of battle. Many Gurkhas have served in the British Army since the early 19th century.
Howitzer	A weapon used for high-angle firing of shells at lower velocities than a gun.
IFOR	Implementation Force, the NATO force which replaced UNPROFOR.
JNA	Yugoslav National Army.

JTF 2	Joint Task Force 2. The Canadian army's elite and very secret anti-terrorist unit.
Kukri	A curved knife, broadening toward the point, used by the Gurkhas of Nepal.
M1A1	Abrams tank. Upgraded version of the U.S. army's M1 Abrams main battle tank introduced in 1985. The M1A1 was followed by the M1A2 version.
M72	A fibreglass tube housing a 66mm rocket.
M113	A U.S. built Canadian armoured personnel carrier.
Med A	Medical assistant.
Militia	Citizen soldiers; army reserves.
MPRI	Military Professional Resources Incorporated.
MSR	Main supply route.
My Lai	The village in Vietnam where American soldiers from C Company of the 11th Brigade murdered 300 unarmed civilians on March 16, 1968. Exactly 25 years later, on March 16, 1993, Clayton Matchee of the CAR murdered Shidane Arone in the Canadian camp in Somalia.
NATO	North Atlantic Treaty Organization.
NCO	Non-commissioned officer.
NDHQ	National Defence Headquarters, Ottawa.
NDMC	National Defence Medical Centre, Ottawa.
No duff	The radio code words used to get people off the air because a serious incident has occurred.
OP	Observation post.

PMR 3	Serbian antipersonnel mine.
PPCLI	Princess Patricia's Canadian Light Infantry.
PTSD	Post-traumatic stress disorder.
Puzzle Palace	Soldiers' name for NDHQ and sometimes Parliament.
QMSI	Quartermaster sergeant instructor.
R22eR	Royal 22nd Regiment.
Rangers	Elite army unit with some similarities to Britain's SAS.
RBC	Régiment Blindé du Canada. The regular army's francophone armoured regiment.
RCR	Royal Canadian Regiment.
Recce	Reconnaissance platoon.
SAS	Special Air Service. The British Army's elite special forces unit, considered to be one of the best military organizations in the world.
Sagger	Russian anti-tank guided missile.
Salient	An area projecting into enemy territory beyond what is regarded to be an army's frontline.
Sapper	A soldier with an engineer regiment, often responsible for the removal of mines. In Croatia the Canadian Combat Engineer Regiment was only responsible for overseeing the removal of mines by the people who laid them, not for doing the job itself. But as Russ Beaton indicates, it didn't always work out that way.

SHARP training	Standard for Harassment and Racism Prevention training.
SK	Guns used by the Croatian forces.
TDF	Bosnian Territorial Defence Forces.
TOW	Tube-launched, optically-tracked, wire-guided missile. An anti-tank missile system which can be mounted on a number of different vehicles.
Track	Generic name for a tracked (non-wheeled) armoured personnel carrier.
UN CivPol	United Nations Civil Police. Present on peace-keeping missions, personnel are drawn from the police services of participating countries, including the RCMP from Canada.
Unification	Under Paul Hellyer's tenure as minister of national defence in the mid-1960s the three Canadian armed forces were united into one service for economic and administrative reasons, and the traditional uniforms of the army, air force and navy were replaced by dark green costumes for everyone. Service-specific uniforms were reintroduced in the 1980s.
UNPAs	United Nations Protected Areas.
UNTSO	United Nations Truce Supervision Operation in the Middle East.
Van Doos	Common name for the Royal 22nd Regiment from the French words for twenty-second, *vingt-deuxième*.
VBL	Fast accelerating, French light-armoured scout car made by Panhard.

Warsaw Pact weapons Weapons from countries in the Warsaw Pact (Albania, Bulgaria, Hungary, East Germany, Poland, Czechoslovakia, Romania and USSR), especially AK-47s, from the Soviet Union.

APPENDIX

Chapters VI and VII of the Charter of the United Nations

CHAPTER VI

PACIFIC SETTLEMENT OF DISPUTES

Article 33
1. The parties to any dispute, the continuance of which is likely to endanger the maintenance of international peace and security, shall, first of all, seek a solution by negotiation, inquiry, mediation, conciliation, arbitration, judicial settlement, resort to regional agencies or arrangements or other peaceful means of their own choice.
2. The Security Council shall, when it deems necessary, call upon the parties to settle their dispute by such means.

Article 34
   The Security Council may investigate any dispute, or any situation which might lead to international friction or give rise to a dispute, in order to determine whether the continuance of the dispute or

situation is likely to endanger the maintenance of international peace and security.

Article 35

1. Any member of the United Nations may bring any dispute, or any situation of the nature referred to in Article 34, to the attention of the Security Council or of the General Assembly.
2. A state which is not a member of the United Nations may bring to the attention of the Security Council or of the General Assembly any dispute to which it is a party if it accepts in advance, for the purposes of the dispute, the obligations of pacific settlement provided in the present Charter.
3. The proceedings of the General Assembly in respect of matters brought to its attention under this Article will be subject to the provisions of Articles 11 and 12.

Article 36

1. The Security Council may, at any stage of a dispute of the nature referred to in Article 33 or of a situation of like nature, recommend appropriate procedures or methods of adjustment.
2. The Security Council should take into consideration any procedures for the settlement of the dispute which have already been adopted by the parties.
3. In making recommendations under this Article the Security Council should also take into consideration that legal disputes should as a general rule be referred by the parties to the International Court of Justice in accordance with the provisions of the Statute of the Court.

Article 37

1. Should the parties to a dispute of the nature referred to in Article 33 fail to settle it by the means indicated in that Article, they shall refer it to the Security Council.
2. If the Security Council deems that the continuance of the dispute is in fact likely to endanger the maintenance of international peace and security, it shall decide whether to take action under Article 36 or to recommend such terms of settlement as it may consider appropriate.

Article 38

Without prejudice to the provisions of Articles 33 to 37, the Security Council may, if all the parties to any dispute so request, make recommendations to the parties with a view to a pacific settlement of the dispute.

CHAPTER VII

ACTION WITH RESPECT TO THREATS TO THE PEACE, BREACHES OF THE PEACE AND ACTS OF AGGRESSION

Article 39

The Security Council shall determine the existence of any threat to the peace, breach of the peace or act of aggression and shall make recommendations, or decide what measures shall be taken in accordance with Articles 41 and 42, to maintain or restore international peace and security.

Article 40

In order to prevent an aggravation of the situation, the Security Council may, before making the recommendations or deciding upon the measures provided for in Article 39, call upon the parties concerned to comply with such provisional measures as it deems necessary or desirable. Such provisional measures shall be without prejudice to the rights, claims or position of the parties concerned. The Security Council shall duly take account of failure to comply with such provisional measures.

Article 41

The Security Council may decide what measures not involving the use of armed force are to be employed to give effect to its decisions, and it may call upon the members of the United Nations to apply such measures. These may include complete or partial interruption of economic relations and of rail, sea, air, postal, telegraphic, radio and other means of communication, and the severance of diplomatic relations.

Article 42

Should the Security Council consider that measures provided for in Article 41 would be inadequate or have proved to be inadequate, it may take such action by air, sea or land forces as may be necessary to maintain or restore international peace and security. Such action may include demonstrations, blockade and other operations by air, sea or land forces of members of the United Nations.

Article 43

1. All members of the United Nations, in order to contribute to the maintenance of international peace and security, undertake to make available to the Security Council, on its call and in accordance with a special agreement or agreements, armed forces, assistance and facilities, including rights of passage, necessary for the purpose of maintaining international peace and security.

2. Such agreement or agreements shall govern the numbers and types of forces, their degree of readiness and general location and the nature of the facilities and assistance to be provided.

3. The agreement or agreements shall be negotiated as soon as possible on the initiative of the Security Council. They shall be concluded between the Security Council and members or between the Security Council and groups of members and shall be subject to ratification by the signatory states in accordance with their respective constitutional processes.

Article 44

When the Security Council has decided to use force it shall, before calling upon a member not represented on it to provide armed forces in fulfillment of the obligations assumed under Article 43, invite that member, if the member so desires, to participate in the decisions of the Security Council concerning the employment of contingents of that member's armed forces.

Article 45

In order to enable the United Nations to take urgent military measures, members shall hold immediately available national air-force contingents for combined international enforcement action. The strength and degree of readiness of these contingents and plans for their combined action shall be determined within the limits laid down in the special agreement or agreements referred to in Article 43, by the Security Council with the assistance of the Military Staff Committee.

Article 46

Plans for the application of armed force shall be made by the Security Council with the assistance of the Military Staff Committee.

Article 47

1. There shall be established a Military Staff Committee to advise and assist the Security Council on all questions relating to the Security Council's military requirements for the maintenance of international peace and security, the employment and command of forces placed at its disposal, the regulation of armaments and possible disarmament.

2. The Military Staff Committee shall consist of the chiefs of staff of the permanent members of the Security Council or their representatives. Any member of the United Nations not permanently represented on the committee shall be invited by the committee to be associated with it when the efficient discharge of the committee's responsibilities requires the participation of that member in its work.

3. The Military Staff Committee shall be responsible under the Security Council for the strategic direction of any armed forces placed at the disposal of the Security Council. Questions relating to the command of such forces shall be worked out subsequently.

4. The Military Staff Committee, with the authorization of the Security Council and after consultation with appropriate regional agencies, may establish regional subcommittees.

Article 48

1. The action required to carry out the decisions of the Security Council for the maintenance of international peace and security shall be taken by all the members of the United Nations or by some of them, as the Security Council may determine.

2. Such decisions shall be carried out by the members of the United Nations directly and through their action in the appropriate international agencies of which they are members.

Article 49

The members of the United Nations shall join in affording mutual assistance in carrying out the measures decided upon by the Security Council.

Article 50

> If preventive or enforcement measures against any state are taken by the Security Council, any other state, whether a member of the United Nations or not, which finds itself confronted with special economic problems arising from the carrying out of those measures shall have the right to consult the Security Council with regard to a solution of those problems.

Article 51

> Nothing in the present Charter shall impair the inherent right of individual or collective self-defence if an armed attack occurs against a member of the United Nations, until the Security Council has taken measures necessary to maintain international peace and security. Measures taken by members in the exercise of this right of self-defence shall be immediately reported to the Security Council and shall not in any way affect the authority and responsibility of the Security Council under the present Charter to take at any time such action as it deems necessary in order to maintain or restore international peace and security.

INDEX